MW01506243

SEARCHING FOR JIMMIE STROTHER

SEARCHING FOR JIMMIE STROTHER

A TALE OF MUSIC, MURDER, AND MEMORY

GREGG D. KIMBALL

RIVANNA BOOKS

University of Virginia Press
Charlottesville and London

The University of Virginia Press is situated on the traditional lands of the Monacan Nation, and the Commonwealth of Virginia was and is home to many other Indigenous people. We pay our respect to all of them, past and present. We also honor the enslaved African and African American people who built the University of Virginia, and we recognize their descendants. We commit to fostering voices from these communities through our publications and to deepening our collective understanding of their histories and contributions.

RIVANNA BOOKS
An imprint of the University of Virginia Press

© 2025 Gregg D. Kimball
All rights reserved
Printed in the United States of America on acid-free paper

First published 2025

9 8 7 6 5 4 3 2 1

LIBRARY OF CONGRESS CATALOGING-IN-PUBLICATION DATA

Names: Kimball, Gregg D., author.
Title: Searching for Jimmy Strother : a tale of music, murder, and memory / Gregg D. Kimball.
Description: Charlottesville : Rivanna Books, University of Virginia Press, 2025. | Includes bibliographical references and index.
Identifiers: LCCN 2024041085 (print) | LCCN 2024041086 (ebook) | ISBN 9780813952307 (hardcover) | ISBN 9780813952314 (paperback) | ISBN 9780813952321 (ebook)
Subjects: LCSH: Strothers, Jimmie. | Folk singers—United States—Biography. | Banjoists—United States—Biography. | Blind musicians—United States—Biography. | African American musicians—Biography.
Classification: LCC ML420.S9179 K56 2025 (print) | LCC ML420.S9179 (ebook) | DDC 782.42162130092 [B]—dc23/eng/20240904
LC record available at https://lccn.loc.gov/2024041085
LC ebook record available at https://lccn.loc.gov/2024041086

Cover photo: Jimmie Strothers on left with guitar, Joe Lynn Lee on right singing "Do Lord, remember me," June 14, 1936. (LOT 7414, Library of Congress Prints and Photographs Division, Washington, DC)
Cover design: TG Design

CONTENTS

LEGACIES

FOREWORD

Within the halls of the Library of Congress in Washington, DC, is a vast repository of items that symbolize the depth and complexity of our country. At the top of the main stairs of the Jefferson building stands the American Folklife Center, which contains the Archive of Folk Culture, the home of one of America's greatest exports: songs. With a catalog of over 150,000 sound recordings, this archive contains the deepest expression of American folklife and cultural memory. Collected by a variety of folklorists over the past century, these recordings are important artifacts that preserve the sounds, words and melodies of the songs that best define American life.

The story you are about to read in Gregg Kimball's *Searching for Jimmie Strother* pertains to a single folkloric expedition set out by folklorist John Avery Lomax for the benefit of the Library of Congress's folk song archive. Over the weekend of June 13–14, 1936, Lomax, along with recordist Harold Spivacke, traveled to the Virginia State Prison Farm searching for old folk songs sung by the inmates. While there were several performers who sang into Lomax's microphone, it was James Lee Strother, a blind singer, guitarist and banjoist, who left the deepest impression on him. Strother's thirteen songs would go on to have a much larger influence on American popular music than either the folklorist or the subject could have ever imagined. Yet before this book was written, little to nothing has been known about Jim Strother and his life before and after his time in the penitentiary.

Who was this black banjoist and guitarist with the powerful voice who is now forever preserved on wax acetates in the nation's capital? Where did he come from and where did he learn these beautiful songs, both secular and sacred, that are now a part of our national identity housed in the Library of Congress? Also, he was recorded in the Virginia State Prison Farm. How did he get there? What was his life like before and after he served his time there?

The photograph on the cover of the book is only one of two pictures that survive of Strother. The other photo is his mug shot when he entered the prison farm. The cover photo shows a side profile of Strother, holding a guitar, alongside his fellow inmate Joe Lee. Strother looks calm and relaxed in the picture. This is in stark contrast to his mug shot taken straight on, showing his eyes, robbed of sight, emoting an intensity that betrays the beauty of the music he recorded for the Library of Congress on that hot summer day in 1936.

While a sound recording can document a singular moment in time with great clarity and permanency, as you read more details of the overall life of Strother, it is obvious that thirteen songs cannot fully convey the full extent of this singer's troubled life.

My first experience with Strother's music came from hearing the Library of Congress LP *Negro Religious Songs and Services,* which features several of Strother's religious songs, including "Do Lord Remember Me" and "We Are Almost Down to the Shore," which I later added to my repertoire and recorded on my own album *Traveling Wildfire.*

Being an avid listener of folk music, I would make my own compilations of musicians' recordings in the hope of collecting all of the known songs by a given performer. This would be followed by looking up all information available to me to learn more about the performer's life. When it came to Strother, however, I only found a track here and there, grasping for another piece of the puzzle. There were a couple of tracks on the Blue Ridge Institute's album *Non-Blues Secular Black Music.* A few more I found on the Deep River of Song collection from Rounder Records and the reissue company Document Records. Finally, I beheld the infamous mug shot photo, first in Stephen Wade's book *The Beautiful Music All Around Us: Field Recordings* and then *The American Experience.* As far as I could glean the excerpts written by others, Strother was not only serving in the Virginia State Prison Farm but had apparently killed his wife with an ax. I was shocked to read such a horrific account of someone who sang such beautiful music. Yet Strother's repertoire of songs, as recorded by Lomax, provide a microcosm of black music as it was played in the late nineteenth century moving into the twentieth. Songs like "Tennessee Dog" displayed the unique banjo picking of the medicine show, while his version of "Cripple Creek" provides a small window into the dangerous world of the Jim Crow South.

Each song sung by Strother during his one field recording session tells an elaborate story of not only the singer himself but the musical tradition that he represents. Gregg Kimball has taken a deep dive into the paper trail Strother left behind, and he proves that everyone, including myself, and including John Lomax and the Library of Congress, have been telling Strother's story wrong the whole time. While there may be large swaths of his story lost in time forever, there are prison records, newspaper accounts and the songs themselves that give us a whole new perspective on his extraordinary life. *Searching For Jimmie Strother* brings back to life for us the world of a black man born in the rural South who migrated to the city and was blinded, literally and figuratively, by the adversity and racism he met all along the way. When Strother's story seemed like it would only end in hopelessness, betrayal, and shame with no chance of redemption, he used the one tool that had always guided him through it all: music. All of the songs he recorded for John Lomax make a grand statement that would prove to be his most poignant legacy. Jim Strother, a banjoist lost in time, became a national treasure without ever knowing it. Gregg Kimball's moving book shows that Strother's story is another powerful reckoning and acknowledgment of the power of song and its undeniable ability to loosen the dark shackles of oppression, if even for a moment.

Dom Flemons

ACKNOWLEDGMENTS

This book is the result of the cumulative wisdom of many scholars, musicians, and everyday people. I apologize to any and all that I have inadvertently left out of the following tribute. I must begin with Zann Nelson, local historian and activist extraordinaire. Her passion for telling hard stories about race, her encyclopedic knowledge of Culpeper County, and her willingness to dig into courthouse records immediately impressed me. Traveling the backroads and towns of Madison and Culpeper County with her was a revelation. Seemingly every farmstead, crossroads, and cemetery had a story that linked past and present. People I only knew from the canvasses of census enumerators and the pinched scribblings of county clerks in birth, marriage, and death registers came to life in the landscape. Later, Zann introduced me to James C. and Shirley Greene, who allowed me to enter the world of James's mother, Blanche Greene, Strother's second wife. What it meant to be Black in Culpeper County came alive as Jim Greene described his summers in segregated Culpeper County and his family's experience. Zann also facilitated my conversations with Jennie Strother Woolen, a Culpeper native who recounted her own experiences and family stories. These generous guides gave shape and meaning to the mass of paper that I accumulated from libraries and archives.

I returned to Culpeper County, the Virginia State Prison Farm, and to Baltimore once more with a mind to capture images for use in the book. I knew just the person to visually record these places—my sister, Corlis Kimball Chamberlain. Not only is she a skilled photographer with an eye for landscapes, but she is more than willing to tramp through forgotten neighborhoods and overgrown cemeteries. I am delighted that we could collaborate on this project.

My fellow archivists and librarians supported this work in sometimes extraordinary ways. My colleagues at the Library of Virginia helped me make sense of the Virginia State Penitentiary records, Virginia's Executive Papers and many other collections. Special thanks go to Roger Christman, who discovered and blogged about James Lee Strother's pardon file, which was key to understanding his background and family connections. The Maryland State Archives staff, most notably Kevin Swanson, Jennifer Abbott, and Owen Lourie, assisted me with Maryland's police records and vital statistics. Other repositories who shared records and insights were the Dolph Briscoe Center for American History at the University of Texas at Austin, the Oral History Archive at Columbia University, the Oberlin College Archives, the Maryland Center for History and Culture, and the Maryland Department at the Enoch Pratt Free Library. The staff at the Culpeper County Courthouse put up with constant questioning about the county and its records.

I spent hours in the American Folklife Center's reading room at the Library of Congress. My last visit was a fine day in March 2020. Upon returning to Richmond, I began to hear the news of shutdowns due to a strange new virus sweeping the world. In the midst of the COVID lockdown, the AFC staff went above and beyond to provide access to materials through the wonders of digitization. As a staff person at a major archival repository myself, I know what it was like to work through those uncertain times, and I salute their professionalism and steadfastness—Todd Harvey and John Fenn, especially.

Many individuals assisted in varied ways. Fellow record collector David Lennick gave me access to a rare recording on the Thesaurus label; Larry Hanks and Deborah Robins recounted the folk origins of Jefferson Airplane's version of a Strother song and sent me a video of the version played by Hanks and his musical partner Roger Perkins. Musicologists Sandra Graham and Kip Lornell gave me sound advice that helped me conceptualize the work. Kip and Kristina R. Gaddy read the book for the press and made many useful suggestions and corrections that greatly improved the narrative. Brent Tarter and Edward L. Ayers commented on the first version of the manuscript. Dom Flemons not only read that version, but also agreed to sit for an interview about my subject. You can't beat the American

Songster commenting on an original American songster! I was delighted when he enthusiastically agreed to write a foreword to the book.

Finally, I learned many things that you can't find in books, archives, and courthouses from the traditional musicians whom I've interviewed, played with, and sometimes presented to audiences through the years. John Cephas, Jeffrey Scott, Phil Wiggins, John Jackson, and Warner Williams are just a few of the songsters and bluesmen who've shaped my understanding of the music. This book is dedicated to them and the many young musicians who now carry on the tradition.

SEARCHING FOR JIMMIE STROTHER

Introduction

"Go ahead, Jim. Sing."

James Lee Strother obliged. A comedic ditty poured forth into the Library of Congress's microphone and hulking recording machine. The blind musician's lively banjo rang out against the stark brick walls of the Virginia State Prison Farm's cellblock. He sang of lame mules, unfaithful women, frolicking bullfrogs, gun-shot devils, and Moses in the wilderness. Strother next picked up his guitar, its insistent rhythms driving a spiritual while fellow prisoner Joe Lynn Lee's keening vocals doubled Strother's baritone voice. Blues, work songs, medicine-show numbers, and risqué rags filled the air. By the end of the day—June 14, 1936—the recording machine had inscribed, however imperfectly, a lifetime of music-making on aluminum discs.

That evening, recordist Harold Spivacke and folklorist John Lomax drove northward toward the nation's capital, well pleased with their song catching. Lomax was a highly experienced and nationally known folklorist. He had been traveling the country under the auspices of the Library of Congress since 1933, making visits to a number of prisons where he hoped to capture Black folksong "uncorrupted" by modern media. Lomax had spied Strother playing a battered banjo on the steps of the prison superintendent's house at the Virginia State Prison Farm. His interrogation of the blind musician convinced Lomax that here was an authentic folk artist worthy of their limited time and the precious metal discs. He wasn't disappointed. Back in Washington, the two men listened with satisfaction to the musical bounty from the prison farm.

While Lomax and Spivacke casually listened to the disembodied voices they had captured, Jim Strother remained incarcerated at the Virginia State

Prison Farm. He was a little more than a year into a twenty-year stretch for murdering his second wife, Blanche Greene, in Culpeper, Virginia, the place of his youth. His recordings for the men from Washington evoked his long experience as a city busker, medicine-show man, and dance-hall performer in Virginia and Maryland. Perhaps the recording session brought back memories of his life on the streets of Baltimore, where he skillfully gauged the musical tastes of passersby—just as he likely shaped his repertoire for John Lomax. Yet the songs he sang for Lomax and Spivacke still showed his remarkable range and echoed his lived experience—the dangers of the road, spiritual struggles, and forced, heavy labor.

A few years later, Strother began to dictate letters to James H. Price, the governor of Virginia, seeking his freedom and his release to relatives in Baltimore. In the meantime, folklorists Alan Lomax—John's son—and Benjamin Botkin began their own letter-writing campaign in the early 1940s. Both sought to provide some small compensation to Strother for the use of his songs on some of the earliest 78-rpm album sets produced by the Library of Congress. Letters to family members, postmasters, sheriffs, and prison officials regarding Strother's whereabouts only brought back letters in the negative or envelopes marked "return to writer." Jim Strother had gone, but his music lived on.

The Lomaxes and Botkin ensured that Strother's songs would be well known to folk enthusiasts and the public, publishing them in books, on 78-rpm records and LPs, and even on radio broadcasts. Today, his entire recorded work for the Library of Congress—save one take of his most salacious song—can be found on YouTube, Spotify, and Apple Music. Artists as diverse as the rock band Jefferson Airplane, folk musicians Pete and Mike Seeger, gospel stars The Golden Gate Quartet, and most recently African American songster Dom Flemons have covered his songs. These musicians and folklorists believed in Strother's continued importance and relevance. And so should we.

I first encountered James Lee Strother at the Valentine, Richmond's city museum, while searching for music for a 1988 exhibition on antebellum Black life in the city. A colleague suggested tracks from Virginia musicians found on the Library of Congress compilations; Strother and Joe Lee both featured. Despite being recorded in the 1930s, "Do Lord, Remember Me" seemed entirely appropriate for the exhibition, harking back to origins deep in slavery. Later, as I became reengaged with performing and researching folk music in the 1990s, the Virginia penitentiary and prison farm recordings intrigued me. As a musician, I found them compelling; as a historian, I wanted to know who these people were. What was their lived experience?[1]

The more I learned about Strother, the better I understood why his music captured the imagination of so many musicians. His music is part of a poorly understood and largely unexplored period between the songs of slavery and the rise of other Black musical styles, such as jazz and blues. Strother was at least a generation older than most of the Black artists who came to the attention of the commercial studios in the late 1920s. He and his close contemporaries epitomized the early East Coast songsters: skilled multi-instrumentalists adapting their material and musical approach to the demands of street performance, house parties, frolics, and a variety of audiences. Strother himself referred to his genre as "string music," a pliable catchall for his wide-ranging repertoire that also typically spoke to a musician's abilities on numerous instruments. Strother and his repertoire provide a window onto a musical world that easily crossed genre boundaries—the province of the late nineteenth-century songster and "musicianer."[2]

The term "musicianer" has a long history in African American culture. Among the enslaved, it typically referred to skilled fiddlers and other musicians who performed for local fish fries, dances, and frolics. Enslaved people not only honored the skill of such players but also recognized their importance to and status within the community. The musicianers presided over the few joyful social events available to the enslaved and also served as bearers of the community's culture. In this role, the musicianer was as essential to the spiritual life and psychic survival of bondspeople as the enslaved preacher or exhorter.[3]

The term persisted well into the twentieth century in the rural South. University of North Carolina sociologist Howard Odum first noted the common usage of "musicianer" among Black performers and audiences as well as the appellation "songster" in his landmark 1911 article on Black secular song. Eubie Blake's mother, who had been born enslaved in Mathews County, Virginia, scolded a Baltimore salesman who tried to sell her a pump organ for her young son, exclaiming, "I don't want my son to be no musicianer." Blake wryly remarked to his interviewer, "Yeah, 'musicianer,' that's the way my mother talked," suggesting that the term was by that time somewhat "country"—unsophisticated and out-of-date. Yet jazz musician Sidney Bechet referred to himself as a musicianer, self-consciously connecting his music to his enslaved grandfather who performed on Congo Square in New Orleans. No matter where he plays his song, Bechet related, the true musicianer hears the music "starting way behind you. There's the drum beating from Congo Square and there's the song starting in a field just over the trees. The good musicianer, he's playing with it, and he's playing after it. He's finishing something. No matter what he's playing, it's the long song that started back there in the South. It's the remembering song." This is a beautiful invocation of the musicianer's rootedness in a musical and spiritual world shaped by the past but always in a state of becoming.[4]

Undoubtedly, Strother's career as a street singer partially explains his eclectic, chameleonlike ability to play many styles. The recent literature on blues has emphasized the importance of such versatility, arguing that players such as Robert Johnson and Charley Patton could perform a strikingly wide range of tunes. Strother, too, demonstrated his mastery of an eclectic repertoire in his Library of Congress recordings. Dom Flemons, one of today's foremost practitioners of the Black songster tradition, extolled Strother's stylistic versatility. As befitted a professional songster, Strother was "adept at a lot of different types of music," Flemons mused, "and especially in the settings of field recordings, most times a musician is playing one or two styles."[5]

Strother's story echoes that of the thousands of other itinerant Black musicians who plied their trade wherever they could—on the medicine-show stage, in small dance halls, at house parties, and on the streets. I discovered many illuminating accounts of Strother's contemporaries in my research— far more than I thought possible. Most of these men and women had no John Lomax or record label to immortalize them. Despite that fact, I believe that by weaving their narratives into Strother's story, we can hear their voices—voices that will fill in some of the silences in Strother's own life.

Strother's music is compelling and important; his songs and life story illuminate not only the musical world of the Virginia songster but also his community's experiences. Like Bechet, Strother sang the "long song," a song simultaneously of the past and the present. Early on in my search, I realized that the marriage registers, census entries, and official documents could only give me fleeting glimpses of Strother. I would need to decode the messages buried deep in the grooves of the thirteen remarkable songs memorialized on metal discs at the Virginia State Prison Farm in 1936. Strother's performances described the world that he, his family, and thousands of other African Americans experienced in the transition from a tenuous freedom during Reconstruction to Jim Crow segregation. Many of his songs, such as "Corn Shucking Time," also contain echoes of the experience of slavery. As an agricultural and industrial worker, a Southern migrant to the urban mid-Atlantic, and a Black, blind itinerant musician in a world of vagrancy laws, sundown towns, and white supremacy, Strother's experiences tell us much about the struggles of America's marginalized people. Poverty, disability, and even the politics of Progressivism all shaped Strother's world and came to be expressed in his music.[6]

Strother's music is inseparable from the everyday realities of Black life. As Hampton Institute's Robert Russa Moton said of the spirituals, "They are not merely poetry, they are more than poetry, they are life itself." Likewise, theologian James H. Cone emphasized what he called the "functional character" of African and African American music, deeming it "not an artistic creation for its own sake; it was directly related to daily life, work and play." Cone further proclaimed the blues to be "secular spirituals," asserting a unity of Black music: "If the blues are viewed in the proper perspective, it is clear that their mood is very similar to the ethos of the spirituals. Indeed, I contend that the blues and the spirituals flow from the same bedrock of experience, and neither is an adequate interpretation of black life without the commentary of the other." Strother did not view the world or his music through dichotomies of secular and sacred, good and evil, commercial or folk. He *was* his music and the music *was* his experience, just as many a bluesman proclaimed, "I *am* the blues."[7]

While Strother's songs constitute part of a collective oral history of the broader African American community, they also reflect his personal thoughts, problems, and prejudices. Strother was not just an archetype—he was a real person living day-to-day in difficult and sometimes dangerous circumstances. Strother's music certainly uses tropes and formulas found in many other folk and popular compositions, but his songs often expressed a collective sense of injustice in strikingly original and personal ways. When Strother sang "Don't let sundown catch you here," he recounted his own fear and loathing as an itinerant songster on the streets of America as well as the situation of all Black people traveling the lonesome roads of the Jim Crow South. Likewise, his lament that a young Alexandria woman had a "handful of gimme and a mouthful of much obliged" was not only a common folk expression found in many blues songs (for example, Charley Patton's "Going to Move to Alabama" and Bessie Smith's "Gulf Coast Blues") but also a very explicit commentary on his second wife, Blanche Greene.[8]

In sum, Strother is a remarkable example of the musicianer and songster traditions; an American griot, recounting stories of Black life and times from Reconstruction to Jim Crow; and a compelling and original artist.

My search for James Lee Strother has been much more than a scholarly exercise. My ideas about Strother and his contemporaries are also rooted in my personal experience as a musician and presenter within the world of blues and roots music. Early on I sensed that much of what we term "blues" in Virginia music is in fact the legacy of pre-blues music that survived long into the twentieth century. The echoes of this music still enrich us today. Finding this music and its meaning also meant a journey that sprawled across many years and miles, from the back roads of Virginia to the streets of Baltimore to the Virginia State Prison Farm. Along the way I met people—community tradition-keepers, local historians, musicians, and even descendants of Strother and his contemporaries—with deep connections to these places who opened my eyes to things hidden from even the most observant outsider.

I have traveled the landscape of Jim Strother's early life many times. Routes 15 and 29 traverse the spine of the central Virginia Piedmont, plotting a virtual road map to his and his kinfolk's places of birth, life, and death: Locust Dale, Clarkson, The Forest, and of course the town of Culpeper. If you keep on rolling north, you'll hit Warrenton, the last residence and burial place of songster William "Barber Bill" Moore. If you hang a left in Culpeper onto the Sperryville Pike, you'll pass a spot on the road that's the birthplace of yet another legendary Virginia songster. That's where I was heading on a fine spring day in 2005.

Ask just about anyone who knew John Jackson and they'll mention his sweet disposition, fine guitar playing, and unusual accent. I first met him in the mid-1990s after rekindling my interest in traditional music. I had played a few festival venues on the same bill with John. I also recall a guitar workshop in Richmond where I ended up translating John's instructions and chord shapes to the puzzled students. I wish I had known him longer and better. On that day in 2005, I drove with a specific purpose: to attend a historic marker dedication for the legendary Virginia songster. Navigating a bend in the road, I finally caught a glimpse of the draped marker awaiting its unveiling. Friends, family, musicians, and longtime fans of John's anxiously milled around the base, anticipating its dedication.

I had traveled with my bandmates, hoping that a musical session would break out; we came armed with stringed instruments. We weren't disappointed. After the speechifying and marker unveiling, John's son James, musicians from the DC area, and his nephew, Jeffrey Scott, formed a circle near the marker under a fine shade tree and launched into the quintessential Virginia Piedmont repertoire. Sacred songs, early blues, classics, bad man ballads, and even early country compositions poured forth. I felt honored to take part in this celebration of John and to share in a unique musical moment within this community. That day in Woodville, Virginia, and many other similar experiences taught me a great deal about how to approach the story of James Lee Strother.

The marker dedication was one of several I helped organize as part of a program I launched with Jan Ramsey of the James River Blues Society using funding from Virginia Humanities. We traveled deep into coal country to pay tribute to Carl Martin in Big Stone Gap, celebrated William Moore along the Rappahannock River (to which Moore paid tribute in song), and commemorated the 1936 recording sessions at the Virginia State Prison Farm where Jim Strother stole the show. Each event was part of the musical and personal journey that eventually led to this book. These moments satisfied my mind more than any others I have experienced personally or in my career. These acts of public storytelling, musical exchange, and community building brought together everything that has given meaning to my work.

These moments also crystallized the central question of this book. The jam in Woodville channeled the music of men like Strother who came from a generation before the advent of blues and jazz but who later integrated these musical forms into their arsenal. How do we make sense of the world of the early Black songsters and "musicianers" who entertained at frolics, busked on town and city streets, hit the road with the medicine shows, and played the alley dives and bars? It seemed to me that Strother epitomized this musical world. The "string music" of James Lee Strother reveals an experienced musicianer rooted in Virginia traditions of folksong and performance but readily adapting to and embracing the repertoire and instrumental techniques of emerging musical styles, such as ragtime and blues. It is that music and that world that I hope to illuminate in this book.

A state historical marker memorializes the recording session where James Lee Strother made his mark. The author wrote this signage as part of a project by the James River Blues Society to commemorate Black musicians around the state. State historical marker SA-70, Virginia Department of Historic Resources, 2005. (Photograph by Corlis Kimball Chamberlain)

Editorial Note

Inconsistencies in documentation prompted me to make several editorial decisions regarding personal names, song titles, and citations. The most important one was how to name my protagonist. James Lee Strother was identified by the Lomaxes as "Blind Jimmie Strothers" or simply "Jimmie Strothers," a convention followed by many later folklorists and discographers. The most basic error here is the spelling of his surname with an "s" at the end. Neither the preponderance of period sources nor current usage among the family supports this spelling.

Likewise, I have followed current family convention and used the surname "Greene" when discussing the family of Blanche Greene, Strother's second wife. Not surprisingly, the name is also recorded as "Green" in some archival sources. Hopefully this will also assist the reader in distinguishing among the various Green/Greene families discussed in the book.

The diminutive "Jimmie" also seems strange given that Strother was a robust man, a steelworker, and around six feet tall. In fact, he is called "James" or "Jim" in most contemporary newspaper accounts, manuscript sources, and in spoken asides captured in the Library of Congress recordings. The addition of the term "blind" also grates; it is a calculated appendage to his name, probably as part of his performing persona. I suspect that James "Jim" Strother became "Blind Jimmie Strother" as he hustled on the street and performed on the medicine-show stage. Accordingly, I will generally use the name that he most likely went by in everyday life—Jim Strother— while, when appropriate, using his full given name. Only in the context of performance for a white or mixed audience will "Blind Jimmie Strother" appear—with one major exception. I have titled the book "Searching for Jimmie Strother" quite intentionally. This was indeed the person I began searching for many years ago, only to discover a very different James Lee Strother.

I have also standardized the titles of Strother's songs, which vary significantly in archival and printed sources. Generally speaking, I have used the titles given on the Library of Congress index cards, which are digitized and available on the internet, except when my own ears disagree. These were prepared under the Works Progress Administration and certain obvious errors have crept in. I have silently corrected some of the dialect affectations in the index card titles and in my lyric transcriptions in Appendix A. Strother usually enunciated his words quite well; for example, I hear him clearly singing "going"—not "goin'"—in "Going to Richmond." I have also consolidated citations for Strother's recordings in Appendix B and summarized their availability on currently available CD releases. Unless I am quoting from the liner notes of a release, these will not appear in the endnotes.

I have heavily mined archival records to reconstruct Strother's family and that of his second wife, Blanche Greene. Accordingly, Appendix A summarizes public records related to his kin in order to avoid burdening the endnotes with repetitive citations.

THE WORLD OF CULPEPER

1

Family

Oh, a train ran north and killed a man,
A mile and a half from town,
Yes, his head was found in a driving wheel,
And his body's never been found.
—JAMES LEE STROTHER, "Daddy, Where You Been So Long," recorded
1936

James Lee Strother's lament about an anonymous man decapitated by a steam locomotive—a verse found in several venerable folk tunes—could easily serve as a metaphor for his own life and legacy. While his "head"—the music he produced—has been "found" and enjoyed by musicians and roots music fans worldwide long after his death more than seventy-five years ago, his "body"—the living, breathing Jim Strother—has remained mysterious. The folklorists who recorded his music and later brought it to the attention of the larger world left tantalizing but scant biographical clues to James Lee Strother's story. Folklorist Kip Lornell, who included a number of Strother's songs on the pathbreaking compilations of Virginia folk music issued by Ferrum College's Blue Ridge Institute in 1978, reported that "virtually nothing" was known about Strother. I, too, must confess that even after decades of research he remains something of an enigma to me. This is especially true of his upbringing and youth. The following is all that I can say about his family and the first twenty years of his life.[1]

Strother was a common name in Piedmont Virginia among both Black and white families in the late nineteenth century—no doubt a legacy of slavery—especially in the counties of Greene, Orange, Madison, Culpeper, and Rappahannock. A patchwork of archival records, the federal census, military registration cards, and various state records slowly revealed hints to Jim Strother's kinfolk, including his second wife's people, the Greenes. Maddeningly, a disastrous 1921 fire in the Commerce Building in Washington, DC, badly damaged the records of the 1890 federal population census, robbing us of one crucial window onto his early family life. These census materials were subsequently destroyed in the 1930s.[2]

Only one surviving document—at least the only one that I could find—records both of his parents' names: a marriage register containing an entry for his nuptials to Blanche Greene in 1923. His father, James, and mother, Susan, are listed therein as the parents of the blind musician. One column of the marriage register confounded me for years. Under "place of birth," the Alexandria, Virginia, clerk wrote "James City, Virginia." I wondered why someone whose life was clearly rooted in the central Piedmont of Virginia would be born in a county in the Tidewater region more than one hundred miles away. Digging in James City County records yielded nothing. It was only years later, while poring over a Civil War–era map of Culpeper, that I noticed a community called James City just across the county line in Madison County. A thriving settlement existed there in the nineteenth century, and a Civil War battle occurred nearby. It is now deserted and overgrown but honored as the James City Historic District on the National Register of Historic Places because of its significant architecture. Local knowledge is often the most important knowledge in solving a historical puzzle.[3]

What else can we know of James Strother's birth and family? After many hours of scouring birth indexes and vital records, the most compelling entry that fits the preponderance of evidence is the June 4, 1881, birth of a boy named James to Susan Strother of Cedar Mountain Township, Culpeper County, Virginia. No father is identified. Although other researchers have found birth records for other James Strothers in surrounding counties, records point to Culpeper as his mother's residence at the time of his birth.[4]

Now I faced the challenge of finding out which of the several Susan Strothers living in Culpeper and the surrounding counties gave birth to our protagonist. As most experienced family historians will tell you, it pays to work backward. A Culpeper death certificate from 1931 became a key for settling the issue (as far as it will ever be settled). That year, Susan Stanton passed away from sarcoma of the jaw; her parents were listed as Thornton and Elsie Strother. The person reporting her death was her son, James

Strother. The fact that Susan Strother Stanton and her husband lived just two houses away from Jim and Blanche Strother in 1930 gave me added confidence that this was his mother. I also discovered that Robert Stanton and Susan Strother had married late in life. Susan had married Robert, a man twelve years younger than herself, at the age of sixty-eight in 1922, placing her birth around 1854.

Now that I had an approximate date of birth, I could sort out which of the several Susan Strothers in earlier censuses fit the bill. A twenty-seven-year-old head of household in the Cedar Mountain District in 1880 matched the age and area of residence. Susan Strother was listed as single with three young daughters under the age of ten. Sally, Mary Jane, and Virginia are all recorded as already working "with cook." In 1900, the forty-seven-year-old Susan lived in the town of Culpeper, a washerwoman with two additional children, Walter and Susie. James Strother is not listed, presumably because by this time he had left the household and labored in the steel furnaces of Sparrows Point southeast of Baltimore. Susan Strother reported to the census taker that she had borne eight children but only four still lived. Unfortunately, she is always listed as unable to read or write.

What became of Susan Strother between 1900 and 1922? There is no definitive answer, but my research suggests that she migrated to Washington, DC, along with some of her remaining children. Just as Jim Strother and other male Culpeper relatives sought industrial and blue-collar work in the urban mid-Atlantic, Black women from his extended family came to the US capital to find domestic work, along with tens of thousands of other rural migrants. A federal census taker knocked on the door of a Susan Strother born in Virginia living with her married daughter Mary Davis at 2519 Tea Alley in Washington in 1910. Young Susie Catherine Strother also lived with them.

Susan Strother's death certificate, coupled with a one-page document in Strother's pardon file, opened up another pathway to identify his family members. This document listed the few relatives he still had in 1939—or at least the ones he thought he could rely on. By linking these relatives to the newly discovered names of Strother's grandparents, Thornton and Elsie, I hoped to identify them conclusively. Strother's first cousin Lizzie Green seemed like a logical place to start. One of her parents would have to be either a brother or sister of Strother's mother, Susan. Thornton and Elsie Strother had only one other child whom I could find in the records other than Susan: daughter Caroline Strother, thus Jim's aunt. Sure enough,

Caroline had a daughter with her husband, Lewis Green, named Elizabeth Virginia Green. Elizabeth married in 1912 but the union didn't last. By 1920 she was back living with her parents and two children. For a time, she took her husband's surname—Gaines—but by 1940, just as Jim Strother became a free man, she was again Lizzie Green. Reflecting the differing fates of the family, Lizzie was not only literate but also worked as a teacher in the segregated Culpeper schools. (She later sent a daughter to Virginia Normal and Industrial Institute, now Virginia State University.) Further cementing the identification of this Lizzie Green as Strother's first cousin is an entry in Strother's pardon file. Strother reported her residence as "Forest, Virginia"—not the town in Bedford, Virginia, as I first thought, but a small Black enclave near the Cedar Mountain battlefield known locally as "The Forest." She taught for a time in the one-room schoolhouse there, which stood next to the Crooked Run Baptist Church.[5]

Strother's pardon file also identified his second cousins Susan Taylor and William Taylor and cousin by marriage Sarah Truman as people who might assist him. (At this point, he either had no connection to his siblings or none were living.) Again, a single document provided a possible connection. When Susan Taylor's husband, Charles William Taylor, died, his death certificate listed his mother as Mary Strother. The full story of the Taylors and their intertwined lives with Jim Strother will unfold later in our story.

Like the many genealogists with whom I've collaborated in my long public history career, I celebrated these hard-won discoveries but also rued the silences and brick walls in the records. Who was the Lizzie Strother living in Washington, DC, whom Strother reported as his closest family contact to the World War I draft board in Culpeper? Perhaps another researcher will unravel that mystery. Suffice it to say for now that the Taylors, Greenes, and Strothers formed a deeply intertwined kinship network within Culpeper County, the northern Virginia Piedmont, and beyond, in the urban mid-Atlantic.

What else can we learn from these entries in dusty ledgers and archival files (and now mostly on the internet at FamilySearch and Ancestry.com)? One thing that struck me was the differing fates of family members as they transitioned from slavery to freedom. Sisters Caroline and Susan Strother endured about a decade of their lives under enslavement. Neither they nor their parents had the advantage of a formal education or a skilled trade. The first census that listed them as free people also noted that neither could read or write—but their paths would thereafter diverge.

The census taker who visited the family in 1880 recorded that Caroline could now read but not write—two different skills in the nineteenth century—but by 1900 she was fully literate. Two factors seem to be at play. Her husband, Lewis, progressed from a farmhand to an independent farmer in the late nineteenth century, giving the family some economic stability. Caroline may have also been assisted and inspired by her daughter Lizzie, who became a teacher for at least thirty years in Culpeper's Black school system. Susan, Jim Strother's mother, never seemed to have enjoyed a similar stability. She may have been hired out as a domestic servant at an early age to support her parents. At some point she was widowed and continued to be the breadwinner for her family. She never gained literacy, nor did her musician son James Lee Strother.

2

String Music

I can earn some money from the playing of string music in which I am considered to be proficient & accomplished.

—JAMES LEE STROTHER to Governor James H. Price, June 12, 1939

Jim Strother desperately wanted out of the Virginia State Prison Farm. His pleading letters to Governor James H. Price ran the gamut of circumstances and excuses: his wife had abused him; as a blind man he was useless to the state; he would immediately leave the commonwealth if freed. One rationale particularly intrigued me. Strother asserted that his "string music" could support him upon his release—as it had for most of his adult life—and that audiences considered him "proficient & accomplished." Folklorist John Lomax obviously concurred, having recorded thirteen of Strother's songs. Modern-day musicians and songsters also agree on his remarkable range and skill.

Where and how did Strother build his broad repertoire and performing abilities? The where seemed obvious to me. Blinded sometime in his early twenties, Strother turned to a grab bag of musical knowledge and skill developed during his youth in the central Piedmont region of Virginia. To understand the "how," we must imagine the rich musical world of Culpeper County and its environs. The everyday soundscape that Jim Strother experienced and absorbed in his early years borrowed heavily from the past but also reflected the evolving musical landscape of the late nineteenth century. These early influences included the Black string band tradition, minstrelsy, sacred tunes, and work songs. His songs themselves must be our primary guide in unlocking his early musical and cultural world as well as the experiences of other Virginia songsters.

"String music" is a capacious term that could encompass the full range of Strother's classic songster repertoire. Folklorist Kip Lornell recounts that after gaining some experience as a field researcher seeking Black folksong in North Carolina and Virginia, he realized that he needed to be more expansive in how he approached locals about possible candidates for recording. Pulling up to a country store or a street-corner congregation of Black people, he would ask "who played string music or who picked a banjo, guitar, or fiddle." He had come to realize that using genre terms like "blues" would greatly limit the response to his query, "[b]ut almost anyone middle-aged or older had a much clearer and expansive version of what *string music* might encompass."[1]

One strand of "string music" points back into enslavement, when the melding of the fiddle and banjo in the antebellum American South produced one of the tangled roots of country music. Strother's performance of "Thought I Heard My Banjo Say," a song commonly known today as "Cripple Creek," represents a prime example of the continuation of the banjo and fiddle repertoire among late nineteenth-century songsters in the South. On this traditional dance tune, he employs an early banjo style often called clawhammer or stroke style, maintaining a strong rhythmic pulse as he strikes downward across his strings. The Library of Congress's notes indicate that he is playing a four-string banjo; some listeners hear Strother bringing the five-string banjo's short drone string into play. Whatever the case, Strother expertly delivers this hoary standard in all its rhythmic urgency and complexity.[2]

Another aspect of "Thought I Heard My Banjo Say" that displays a distinctive African American sensibility and sets it apart from recordings by white string musicians is the call and response of the banjo and voice. Versions of the song by mountain songsters typically break the lyrics and the banjo repetition of the melody into distinct stanzas. Strother, echoing African American practice in early sacred singing, work songs, and blues, lets his vocal line "call" and his banjo "respond." The repeated verse that Strother intones throughout the song—"thought I heard my banjo say"—insists that the instrument has its own distinct voice. Strother sings, "Thought I heard my . . ." and then lets his banjo ring out to conclude the line. This technique of letting the instrument complete the vocal line can be found in the recordings of many later twentieth-century Black artists as varied as Delta bluesman Charley Patton and Texas gospel singer Blind Willie Johnson.

Alan Lomax understood that Strother's "Thought I Heard My Banjo Say" stood out as a rare example of early Black string music in his father's recorded fieldwork. Accordingly, he gave it pride of place as the first recording on the compilation *Black Appalachia*, belatedly issued in 1999 by Rounder Records. Lomax noted that "the earliest records of slavery in Virginia show the importance of black fiddlers, dance callers, and banjo players in the musical life of the South," and he emphasized that this was "the black music that preceded ragtime, jazz, and blues." When finally issued as part of the Deep River of Song series, *Black Appalachia* featured two of Strother's songs, including "Thought I Heard My Banjo Say." Stephen Wade's liner notes contextualized the song by pointedly noting how urbanization and the banjo's minstrel associations had helped bring about the demise of such songs among Black musicians. "But," Wade added, "those who remained within the ambit of rural social life, old-time musicians— black and white—continued to draw upon a shared body of tunes." As we will see, Strother's "ambit" extended well beyond rural Virginia, and like any good string musician he drew both from the deep past and the most contemporary styles.[3]

Jim Strother's elders and contemporaries knew the old tunes, as did Black people throughout the South. In the 1930s, formerly enslaved people told Works Project Administration (WPA) interviewers about the songs they recalled at frolics and other social gatherings. Many recalled "Turkey in the Straw" as a favorite—rather ironic, as some modern interpreters of "old-time" music have cast it aside as racist, given its later minstrel lyrics. The song is thought to have derived from "Natchez Under the Hill," itself a recasting of tunes of British origin. "Natchez" is also speculated to be the inspiration for George Washington Dixon's commercially successful minstrel composition "Zip Coon." Dixon's racist song appeared in print in 1834, while a Farmville, Virginia, music store owner and teacher, George P. Knauff, published an instrumental version of "Natchez Under the Hill" in 1839. We can assume that the tune and its variations were widely known well before that time. Other tunes mentioned by formerly enslaved men and women that are still staples of the current revivalist repertoire include "Arkansas Traveler," "Molly Put the Kettle On," "Hop Light Ladies," and, not surprisingly, "Cripple Creek," which Strother recast as "Thought I Heard My Banjo Say."[4]

We do not have to look far to document this tradition in the central Piedmont during Strother's youth. John Haney, who was born in 1891 and therefore about ten years younger than Strother, described the music he experienced growing up in rural Rappahannock County. Most people made their own music in their homes and churches, but patrons of house parties and dances called on experienced musicianers. Haney identified fiddlers and musicians from Madison County as the area's chief exponents: Charlie Weaver, Morris Kaufman, and the Grigsby Family.[5]

Intrigued by Haney's invocation of these musicianers, I dug into the census and other records to see if I could catch a glimpse of them. The Grigsbys immediately appeared. They lived in eastern Madison County near the Culpeper County line—Jim Strother's stomping grounds. John Haney specifically mentioned Will and Jesse, two of the seven sons of Lewis and Elicia Francis Grigsby. William was born around 1866 and Jesse in the early 1880s. Most of the Grigsby sons had moved to Scottdale, Pennsylvania, to find work by at least 1920, so Haney would have seen them at house parties and rural frolics sometime between 1895 and 1915. (Will remained in Virginia in neighboring Page County.) Haney clearly remembered the string bands performing two-steps and waltzes and accompanying buck dancers on the banjo, guitar, fiddle, and sometimes harmonica. Blues had not made its way into the repertoire. The setting for these songs included barn dances, house parties, and just about any outdoor entertainment.[6]

Strother's connection to this older style of music is only represented by "Thought I Heard My Banjo Say" in his prison recordings. This is unfortunate, because one source hints at the tantalizing possibility that Strother's "string music" extended beyond the banjo and guitar. A newspaper reporter declared that a family benefactor "appealed to the police department for a permit for [Strother] to play a fiddle on the street as a means of livelihood." If Jim Strother did entertain passersby on the fiddle as well as the banjo and guitar, it would be unsurprising. The fiddle still held sway at rural dances in Strother's youth in Culpeper, and it remained a key instrument for the musicianer, along with the guitar and mandolin.[7]

The banjo has received much recent attention as a cultural descendant of African instruments transformed on their way to North America by way of the Caribbean, but fiddlers of African heritage also played a major role in the early American colonies. When enslavers placed advertisements for the capture of men and women who had claimed their own bodies by "running away," these so-called masters thoroughly cataloged identifying features of clothing, physical features such as scars, and even the freedom-seekers' disposition and personality. Importantly, enslavers filled the columns of the *Virginia Gazette* with calls to apprehend musicians of all stripes but especially fiddlers, some of whom had absconded with their instruments. Likewise, aged former bondspeople interviewed during the Great Depression by WPA field workers mentioned the fiddle more often than any other instrument, although the banjo had clearly become more prevalent in the years leading up to the Civil War.[8]

If Strother did play the fiddle, it is a shame that he was not recorded on the instrument. Few of his generation were. We know about them mostly through the memories and family stories of later musicianers, songsters, and bluesmen. A family string band provided one of the first musical memories for bluesman Henry Harris, a native of nearby Albemarle County. His uncles William and Charlie Harris performed for dances on fiddle and banjo, respectively, and were joined by Harris's older brother Nathan on guitar. Musician Carl Martin also came from a musical family that performed in the string band tradition. His father, known as "Fiddlin' Martin," had been sold twice during his bondage. Carl Martin, born in Big Stone Gap in Wise County, Virginia, recorded in 1930 with a Black string band labeled as the Tennessee Chocolate Drops for Vocalion Records's Race Record series. In an unusual move, the label also issued the recording in the hillbilly series under the moniker "The Tennessee Trio." Such instances were rare. The segregation of musical markets by record companies dominated the American music scene at the time, reflecting ingrained assumptions about genres of music, who played them, and for whom they were played. Martin later made numerous solo guitar-based blues records and reprised his earlier repertoire with the Black string band Martin, Bogan, and Armstrong during the 1960s folk revival.[9]

Black rural string band traditions remained strong across the rural South, but few recording executives or A&R men recorded them. Only two other Black musicians recorded versions of "Cripple Creek" on commercially issued 78-rpm records: Sam Jones, a Cincinnati street musician, and John Booker, a member of the Booker Orchestra, an influential Kentucky family band. John Booker plays the guitar accompaniment for white fiddler Doc Roberts on the tune. John and his brothers Joe and Jim learned from their fiddling father and became seasoned multi-instrumentalists. Jim Booker's few issued sides with Taylor's Kentucky Boys are exciting and rare examples of Black old-time fiddling and include the venerable "Grey Eagle" and "Forked Deer." They also represent an uncommon white-Black collaboration in the recording studio during the era of segregation. The Bookers, like Strother, were born in the first generation after Emancipation. The Booker Orchestra's only issued recording on the Gennett label, "Camp Nelson Blues," gives us a hint of the remarkable variety of "string music" performed by Black musicians of the era.[10]

The recordings of Sam Jones, identified on Columbia Records as "Daddy Stovepipe No. 1," provide an especially good comparison to Strother's work. Jones and Strother had similar repertoires—sacred songs, minstrel and tent show material, and old-time breakdowns—and both made their living as street musicians in regional cities with large populations of white and Black Southern migrants. Like many central Kentuckians, Jones had made his way across the Ohio River to Cincinnati, where he worked primarily as a street musician. He recorded for Gennett, Columbia, and OKeh Records in the 1920s, and his grab bag of tunes is similar to Strother's, although his approach is stylistically different. Jones, advertised as a "one man band," camped it up with his stovepipe kazoo and harmonica playing. Of particular note are Jones's dance tunes with calls and singing. He recorded a medley of the breakdowns "Cripple Creek" and "Sourwood Mountain" backed with "Turkey in the Straw." He also waxed "Arkansas Traveler" and "Fischer's Hornpipe."[11]

The examples of the Grigsby, Harris, and Booker families, as well as musicians such as Carl Martin and Sam Jones, tell us two important facts. First, the old songs of the antebellum era were still being performed and heard well into the early twentieth century, and second, by the dawn of the new century, the banjo, guitar, and fiddle had evolved into prominence as part of what Strother called "string music." It is especially important to note that Strother's primary instrument on the 1936 recordings—the banjo—had not fallen into disuse but had simply become another instrument in the songster's arsenal.

Interviews with thirteen Black banjo players in Virginia and West Virginia in the late 1970s underscore this point. Almost all of these men described rich and long-standing local networks of Black fiddle and banjo playing across a wide swath of Virginia. Some recalled musical genealogies of teachers and students stretching back, in some cases, to the 1850s.

Many of these musical lineages came down through families, of course, with uncles, mothers, fathers, and cousins imparting traditional musical folkways. Other musicians learned from neighbors and even traveling musicians. These interviews, along with historical documentation, prove without a doubt that the banjo was still a vital musical instrument in Black communities in the twentieth century. In other words, despite its association with minstrelsy and a romanticized aural and visual culture that promoted a racist image of Black people and bucolic images of plantation life, the banjo remained.[12]

Strother also played the guitar on his recordings. Being "proficient & accomplished" at "string music" suggests not only the ability to play a wide-ranging repertoire but also mastery of several instruments. Many Virginia musicians easily picked up and played the mandolin and fiddle as well as the guitar and banjo. Virginia songsters demonstrated their versatility as "string musicians" even when the recording companies largely consigned them to guitar-based blues. The only published photograph of Stephen Tarter, a native of Scott County, Virginia, shows him playing the mandolin with a tenor banjo sitting in front of him, while his cousin Carson Anderson holds a guitar. Tarter's only released recordings, two songs on a single 78-rpm record waxed at the second iteration of the famed Victor Bristol Sessions in 1928, demonstrate his considerable guitar skills on two ragtime blues numbers with his musical partner and guitarist Harry Gay. Yet this remarkable photograph documents his ability to play a range of stringed instruments. Indeed, bluesman Brownie McGhee recalled his father playing with "Master Musician" Tarter, who, McGhee recalled, played "all string instruments. . . . That three-stringed thing we called the zither then; and he also played mandolin, ukulele, violin, bass, guitar, and piano."[13]

The ubiquity of multi-instrumental performers is evident in Strother's native region. John Jackson of neighboring Rappahannock County played the banjo on some of his earliest recordings after his "discovery" by University of Virginia folklorist Chuck Perdue. Later in his career, he played guitar almost exclusively as he became identified as a bluesman. Many of his later fans probably would have been surprised and confused by his recordings of songs by white country stars Ernest Tubb and Jimmie Rodgers on his early albums on the Arhoolie label. Not surprisingly, he also knew some of the common string-music numbers performed in the enslaved community, including "Get Along, Cindy," which his great-nephew Jeffrey Scott still performs on banjo.

Yet another performer demonstrated such versatility across the East Coast scene. Barber William "Bill" Moore, best known for his 1928 Paramount recordings of ragtime guitar showpieces such as "Barber Shop Rag" and "Old Country Rock," migrated north from Georgia. He first made the trek to New Jersey, where he met his wife (a native of Warsaw, Virginia, on the Northern Neck). The couple settled in Tappahannock, Virginia, just across the Rappahannock River from his wife's hometown—the same river that Moore referenced in his "Old Country Rock." About twenty years ago, I had the pleasure of interviewing Moore's son Edsel, and later I met a number of his relatives at a historic marker dedication organized by Essex County native Bessida Cauthorne White. His son and several other relatives reported that Moore played numerous instruments, including the violin, in church—a minor breach of typical Baptist protocol that precluded instruments other than a piano. Moore later resettled in Warrenton, Virginia, and thus lived only a few counties away from Strother after his return to Culpeper with his second wife, Blanche Greene.[14]

Moore, Strother, and their contemporaries absorbed the sounds of the banjo, fiddle, and guitar, but they also heard the voices of their elders and neighbors praising God. That music would form another pillar of Strother's musical education.

3

Spiritual Songs

His commandments in Moses's mind,
Said "Moses, don't leave my children behind,"
We are almost down to the shore.
—JAMES LEE STROTHER, "We Are Almost Down to the Shore," recorded 1936

Musicians at the barn dances, frolics, and house parties provided young Jim Strother with plenty of musical material. Likewise, he drank deeply at the well of religious expression in Piedmont Virginia. His renderings of sacred songs transformed the sounds of the enslaved past into the pleas of the roadside songster or even the rough traveling-show stage. Strother took the collective, community expressions of his childhood experience and molded them into individual performances— frequently for an audience of strangers, white and Black. Unlike the hymnody of the Baptist church meeting, Strother's songs blended traditional lyrics and melodies with the sounds of the banjo and the guitar.[1]

Strother's "We Are Almost Down to the Shore" is an excellent example of his recasting of spiritual material as he recounts God's call to Moses to deliver his commandments to his people:

God called Moses on the mountain top,
Placed his laws in Moses's heart,
We are almost down to the shore.

His lyrics are a classic example of the poetry of the spirituals. Strother moves easily between the Old Testament times of Moses and his own people's present reality, standing at the edge of the "shore" to eternal life. The simple, concluding line both evokes the memory of Exodus and declares the here-and-now reality that we are all "born to die." This transcendence of time and space, as well as the movement between the sacred and secular realm, is characteristic of the best versification found in the spirituals. Hampton Institute's student songbook notates a fine version titled "Fighting On," but Strother's banjo gives the old song a different gait; his vocals are somewhat resigned and melancholy. Yet the song still harks back to an earlier era.[2]

Jim Strother would have heard a variety of religious songs from older members of his community: the boisterous camp meeting anthems with their powerful rhythmic pulse and simple but stirring choruses; the "Doctor Watts" songs lyrically based in early Anglo-British hymnody; and the plaintive spirituals so well known to the modern listener in their concertized form. Such songs were not exclusive to church services but could be heard in the fields, in the schoolhouse, and even at play. Laid on this rich base were the commercial spirituals written in the post–Civil War era by Black and white composers. In the hands of the best Black songsmiths, these mirrored some of the defining features of the antebellum songs— gapped melodies, internal refrains, and the use of vocal melisma (rapidly singing a series of notes on one syllable). In the worst case, they were pale imitations or parodies full of stereotypical content. Jim Strother would have had access to all of these forms as he matured musically in the last decade of the nineteenth century in Culpeper County.[3]

The old songs that Strother absorbed had been forged in the fire of enslavement and repression. Ironically, most of Virginia's antebellum churches served Black and white congregants in the same buildings, although segregation within them was maintained. Many of the enslaved described going to services at white churches, typically sitting in a segregated gallery. Other enslavers provided separate worship services for their bound laborers. They remembered these experiences, but frequently not in a positive way. Several sarcastically mentioned white ministers preaching obedience to "masters." They understood that these were white-dominated spaces and that they were in, but not of, the church. "Dat old white preachin' wasn't nothin'," Nancy Williams ruefully remembered, adding, "Ole white preachers used to talk wid de tongues widdout sayin' nothin' but Jesus told us slaves to talk wid our hearts."[4]

Enslaved people organized secret meetings to practice religion on their own terms, away from the prying eyes of enslavers, overseers, and patrol-lers. These spaces included their homes, remote workspaces, and "brush arbors." Arthur Greene described the construction of a brush arbor deep in the woods: it involved "cuttin' bushes dat was full of green leaves an' puttin' 'em on top of four poles reachin' from pole to pole. Den sometimes we'd have dem bushes put roun' to kiver de sides an' back from der bottom to der top." Charles Grandy recalled, "Whites in our section used to have ser-vice fo' us slaves ev'y fo'th Sunday, but da twasn't 'nuf fo' dem who wanted to talk wid Jesus. Used to go 'cross de fields nights to a old tobacco barn on de side of a hill."[5]

Enslavers viewed such meetings as breeding grounds for resistance and insurrection and forbade them. White people's disquiet was amplified be-cause of the fact that they were outnumbered. Culpeper's enslaved popula-tion of 6,675 represented more than half of the county's residents in 1860. The enslaved described the movements of the hated "paddy rollers"—slave patrols on the lookout for runaways and banned activities—who would break up religious meetings. Some described countermeasures taken to fool or literally trip up the patrols. Many Black people described the placing of a pot or tub outside a meeting to catch the sound, a practice apparently de-rived from West Africa.[6]

Virginia's political leadership had discussed gradual emancipation schemes in the wake of the American Revolution, but no real action was taken. Instead, the legislature passed increasingly repressive laws constrict-ing the lives of free people of color and the enslaved alike. A new and virulent pro-slavery ideology permeated the political stump, the pulpit, and society in general. The state launched programs designed to rid Virginia of free people of color, providing funds to transport them to the state of Liberia on the west coast of Africa. Culpeper's most prominent white clergymen supported these efforts. The Reverend Thornton Stringfellow became one of Virginia's foremost proponents of pro-slavery Christianity, advancing the ideology that the Bible sanctioned slavery and was beneficial to the enslaved. The Rever-end Philip Slaughter also believed in the civilizing effect of slavery on people of African descent. He campaigned to send those who enjoyed a modicum of freedom in America back to Africa to evangelize the continent.[7]

Even before the Civil War, a group of Black worshippers had organized their own congregation—the African Church—within Mount Pony Bap-tist at Culpeper Courthouse (then known as Fairfax). There they operated within the strictures of antebellum law that required white ministers and strict control of the movement and gatherings of the enslaved. White Virginians had criminalized Black preaching for fear of insurrection after Nat Turner's rebellion in Southampton County in 1831, but many rural exhorters continued to serve the Black community. After Emancipation, the congregants constructed their own building and renamed the church Antioch. With freedom came an outpouring of faith and the rapid establishment of new congregations across the Virginia and the South, including Culpeper County. A few older Black congregants remained in the majority-white churches, but most Black men and women sought to take control of their religious affairs and to fully worship in their own way.[8]

Jim Strother and his contemporaries still heard and learned the old songs, but the settings for religious expression now became more numerous and public. By the time of Strother's birth, Culpeper County had at least nine Baptist churches—the dominant denomination of Black Virginians. Strother and his extended kinship network of Strothers, Greenes, and Taylors worshipped close to home in the Cedar Mountain and Salem Districts and the town of Culpeper. Members of Strother's Taylor kin lived in the southern section of Culpeper's Salem District in the Clarkson area, west of White Shop near the Madison County line. Mount Olive Baptist Church, founded around the time of Strother's birth, served the area's worshippers and many generations of Taylors, including Susan Taylor, Strother's second cousin by marriage, whom he had listed as a relative on his pardon documents. The church still serves the Black community today.[9]

Similarly, Free Union Baptist Church continues to thrive as an active congregation in Culpeper County. This is the church that Strother's second wife, Blanche Greene, attended. Her father, Lee Greene, married his wife Alice Deane in the church in 1879 and later served as a deacon. The church is located in the Poplar Ridge area, about four miles southeast of the town of Culpeper. Blanche's mother's people had lived in the area for several generations, while her grandfather Noah Greene migrated to the area from Locust Dale in Madison County in search of cheap (but challenging) land. Blanche was almost certainly laid to rest beside her mother and other kinfolk in the churchyard, although no marker memorializes her passing. The one-room clapboard Eckington School still stands next to the church. The other major pillar of postwar Black society, schools were often associated with religious congregations. Although the school is unused today, a state historical marker bears witness to its importance to Culpeper's Black citizens.[10]

Both Black and white ministers held major revivals in Culpeper and the surrounding counties, drawing thousands of participants during Jim Strother's youth. The Reverend Harrison Blair of Antioch Baptist Church held a revival in the town of Culpeper with several other local African American preachers, culminating with an address from Dr. W. B. Johnson of the Home Mission Society in Baltimore. Born in 1820, Blair drew from a deep well of experience as an enslaved preacher. William Yager recalled that Blair had surreptitiously preached widely before the Civil War and baptized Yager in 1859.[11]

Whites sometimes attended Black revivals, although it is unclear whether they truly participated or simply looked on out of curiosity or nostalgia. Two "distinguished divines"—respected Black ministers of standing in the community—held an extended revival near Swift Ford in Madison County in 1897, impressing white observers who attended the night sessions with their "splendid" preaching. The press reported "amusing scenes and incidents, such as the old-time going around, shaking hands and keeping time with their bodies, and occasionally calling out 'Say that again,' 'talk it out,' 'Hallelujah.'" These characteristic expressions of ecstatic Black religion and styles of worship no doubt made an impression on Strother.[12]

Another possible influence on Strother came from a poorly documented Holiness movement that sprang up in the rural South in the late nineteenth century. In 1899 the Culpeper newspaper cryptically noted a Holiness meeting in nearby Amissville in Rappahannock County, and scattered news of other meetings in Culpeper and Orange Counties suggest the growth of the movement in the north-central Piedmont. Based in Methodist ideas of grace and sanctification, Holiness worshippers typically were less restrained in physically expressing the Holy Spirit and, unlike most Baptists, employed a range of instruments in their praise of God.[13]

Out of this dynamic religious environment came versions of pre–Civil War songs such as Strother's "Run Down, Eli." The song would have been familiar to most Black Virginians. Strother intones that in the world of his ancestors, "All got right to the Heaven's door," privileging neither the rich over the poor nor Black over white. Ultimately, "Run Down, Eli," is a longing for the afterlife where a mother has gone before and the vicissitudes of life will be over:

> Look way in the East, way in the West
> My Lord burned out the wilderness,
> Don't want to stay here no longer.

Chorus: Won't you run down, Eli,
Run down, send down the road,
Don't want to stay here no longer.
(repeated after each verse)

Lord, I'm sometimes up, sometimes down,
Sometimes level with the ground,
Don't want to stay here no longer.

This is the way my mother have gone,
Left me here to follow on,
Don't want to stay here no longer.

Folklorists have noted many examples of such songs that either express aspirations to heaven or voice concern at being left behind in the world, for instance, "My mother an' my father both are dead / Good Lord, I cannot stay here by merself." Howard Odum catalogued the various iterations of the "don't want to stay here no longer" chorus, declaring them "common and classic verses of negro song."[14]

The earliest version that I have located comes from a freedman identified only as "Meredith L.," who was interviewed by freedmen's school teacher Jane Boswell Moore in Winchester, Virginia, in 1865. Meredith conveyed two songs to Moore that conclude with "don't want to stay here no longer." Moore asked Meredith about this sentiment: "I suppose you often felt so, Meredith, for I have noticed that that is a favorite chorus." His reply was succinct: "Indeed we did." The verses of the second song that Meredith sang for Moore relate in interesting ways to Jim Strother's composition. Strother invoked his mother; Meredith declared that he would "take my sister by the hand." Most notably, both songs include this verse:

If religion was a thing money could buy,
The rich would live and the poor would die,
Swing low, sweet chariot
Pray let me in,
I don't want to stay here no longer.

While Strother did not invoke the chariot, Moore speculated that the "simile in this, which is certainly poetic, may have been borrowed from the chariot of fire in which Elijah went home." One has to wonder if "Eli" is short for Elijah, who did indeed "run down the road" in several episodes in the Bible.[15]

The song became codified as the "Danville Chariot," no doubt through popular renditions by singing groups and later composers. Edward King, an English traveler who surveyed the American South in the Reconstruction era, remarked that "Danville Chariot" was "very popular with the Negroes in Virginia," citing a verse about the Devil that also appears in the 1874 Hampton songbook:

> Oh shout, shout, the deb'l is about,
> Oh shut yo' do' and keep him out
> I don't want to stay no longer
> For he is so much-a like-a snaky in de grass
> Ef yo' don't mind he will get yo' at las',
> I don't want to stay no longer.[16]

The popularity of the song would not end with the passing of the generations that sang it in brush arbors and small country churches. The song appears in the repertoire of Hampton Institute (now Hampton University), founded in 1868. Hampton and other Black educational institutions that sprang up after Emancipation employed their students' musical talents to raise funds for their fledgling schools. The Hampton Institute Singers and Quartette followed in this tradition.

In the early twentieth century, Black composers recast folk tradition into art song for a new generation of listeners, and, again, Hampton played a key role. Afro-Canadian composer and musician R. Nathaniel Dett used "Danville Chariot" and other early spirituals in his work. His most widely performed composition, "Listen to the Lambs," is based on the spiritual of the same name. Dett received classical training and graduated from the Oberlin Conservatory of Music in Ohio. Director of Hampton University's music department for many years, he included "Danville Chariot" in his 1927 compilation *Religious Folk-Songs of the Negro: As Sung at Hampton Institute*. Later, Harry Burleigh, perhaps the greatest of the African American composers to recast the spirituals for the concert stage in the early twentieth century, "concertized" and published the song.[17]

The 1874 Hampton songbook version is significantly different melodically from Strother's performance. Transcribed by white choral director

Thomas Fenner, it features a main melody that is stately, hymnlike, and much more elaborate than Strother's "Run Down, Eli." In contrast, Strother creates a darker, more contemplative atmosphere, hewing to the pentatonic scale—a scale of five tones—more typical of African American folksong. The written and performed versions of nineteenth-century religious songs often varied greatly. Some singers eschewed written music altogether, such as the white and Black common folk who still lined their hymns in a call-and-response style; some denominations, most notably the Old Regular Baptists of eastern Kentucky and southwest Virginia, still do today. (While discussing sacred music, I often play a recording of "Amazing Grace" that I captured while deep in Virginia coal country. It illustrates better than any words how differently a familiar song can be sung.)

Actual performances of Black spirituals undoubtedly sounded far different from the printed arrangements, even when sung directly from a particular songbook. Robert Russa Moton, a Hampton graduate, educator, and later principal of the Tuskegee Institute, said as much in his introduction to the 1909 edition of the Hampton compilation. "For nearly a score of years I have led the Plantation Songs at Hampton Institute," he reminisced, "and while in a general way we adhere to the music as notated in this book, we find that the best results are usually obtained by allowing the students, after they have once caught the air, to sing as seems to them most easy and natural." Fenner himself had addressed the difficulties of capturing the songs of the formerly enslaved—not only the bare melody but the various ornamentations, slides, and rhythmic effects that seemed to contravene Western conventions. More so than many of his contemporaries, Fenner tried to at least suggest some of these novel features in his arrangements.[18]

Jim Strother and other religious singers combined a common stock of ideas, expressions, and imagery into their compositions. Eileen Southern, a foundational Black musicologist, observed that "the black folk composers culled lines and phrases from their favorite hymns and Scriptural passages, and adapted motifs, images, and themes from such sources to compose the texts of their spirituals, to which they then added verses of their own invention." She reported one white church father's chagrin at this method. He groused that "the coloured people get together, and sing for hours together, short scraps of disjointed affirmations, pledges, or prayers, lengthened with long repetition choruses." These improvisational and free-flowing singings violated Western conventions but produced folk poetry of often striking power.[19]

Eileen Southern's account accurately describes the nature of the recordings of sacred songs and even the proto-blues and minstrel tunes sung by Strother in 1936. Strother, like other musicianers and songsters who traveled the postbellum South, easily combined elements of verse into evocative song-stories that became the so-called blues ballads and other pre-blues Black secular music. Unlike the chronologically linear stories of balladry brought by British settlers, the lyrics of African American folk songs combined impressionistic elements into a powerful whole. Several of Strother's recorded songs also display his remarkable ability to create original and sometimes disturbing visions in his music.

Strother absorbed many aspects of the folk hymns and spirituals commonly sung across Virginia, but one of his most famous songs evokes both traditional themes and strikingly original elements. There has been considerable confusion about the title of the song. Early transcriptionists heard Strother intoning "Blood-Strained Banders." This hearing seems improbable and is more likely a function of Strother's diction and the inferior recording. A far more plausible interpretation is "Blood-Stained Banners," and certainly this expression had currency in Christian religious writing and in African American hymnody, but the dominant usage of the phrase contradicts its meaning in Strother's song. Christians typically held up the blood-stained banner of Christ as part of his army—not something from which a follower of Jesus would "keep away." For example, Black minister C. H. Lyon offered this testimony during a banner presentation in 1888: "This banner, love, is Christ the Lord's / And in his name we hoist / Aloud the battle cry against / All hostile to our host." One of my colleagues suggested that perhaps Strother was referring to the "Bloody Benders," a family of serial killers on the western frontier who made national news in the early 1870s. Indeed, accounts did appear in Virginia newspapers—intriguing, but impossible to prove. Folklorist Alan Lomax offered a more conventional interpretation: the title was a "folkism" for "the blood stained bandits."[20]

Whatever the words, the overall imagery of the song is compelling and intriguing. For clarity's sake, I will use "Blood-Stained Banders" throughout this book because that's what I hear on the recording. Jim Strother sang in his baritone voice:

> If you want to go to heaven, over on the other shore
> Keep out the way of the blood-stained banders,
> Lord, good shepherd, feed my sheep.

Chorus: Some for Paul, some for Silas
Some for to make a-my heart rejoice;
Don't you hear lambs a cryin',
Lord, good shepherd, feed my sheep.[21]

Strother then warns his listeners to "keep out the way of the gun-shot devils" and the "long-tongued liars," invoking the dangers of earthly evils.

The song's chorus is similar to that of the gospel song "Let Thy Kingdom, Blessed Savior," credited to Methodist circuit-rider John Adam Granade and composed at the dawn of the nineteenth century. The song soon appeared in hymn and spiritual song collections, including African American minister Marshall W. Taylor's important 1882 compilation *A Collection of Revival Hymns and Plantation Melodies.* Sometimes called "The Good Shepherd" or "Good Shepherd, Feed My Sheep," the song entered the world at the time of the Second Great Awakening, when New Light Presbyterians, Methodists, and Baptists endeavored to convert enslaved people to Christianity. Granade was one of the most colorful and dynamic figures of the tent revivals, and his hymn gained immediate currency. The singing of such hymns and gospel songs in ecstatic performance would have appealed to unlettered white congregants as well as enslaved people. Strother, unable to read or write, received the musical elements that flowed into "Blood-Stained Banders" as part of the oral tradition, as most music has been learned for all of recorded history—including today.[22]

The theology, tone, and delivery of Strother's chorus is radically different. Granade urged his listeners to "come, and bid our jarring cease," bemoaning the divisions in Christ's church. His chorus's exhortation, "Some for Paul, some for Apollos / Some for Cephas; none agree," mirrored St. Paul the Apostle's plea to Jesus's followers in Corinthians to "speak the same thing, and that there be no divisions among you." This was an important message for the early Protestant churches in America, as rival congregations divided along various doctrinal and theological lines.

Strother's chorus invokes a very different and much more common story-theme in African American hymnody and spirituals—the persecution of the early church fathers Paul and Silas while they were evangelizing. Testifying on the streets of Philippi, they are arrested. Cast into jail, they pray fervently to God for their release. A "great earthquake" shakes loose the prison's foundations, releasing their bonds and throwing open the door of their cell. One can imagine "the lambs a-crying" as a reference to Paul and Silas's prayers to God as they sat bound in their cell. The moment of Strother's recording of the song must have been poignant; the blind singer sat at the Virginia State Prison Farm just outside the cellblock where he was imprisoned. The parallels to Strother's life are stark—life as an unwanted "testifier" on the streets and being cast into jail.[23]

It is not difficult to understand how this Bible story would resonate with enslaved Americans and their descendants living under Jim Crow. During the Civil War era, recently liberated Black people on Port Royal Island, South Carolina, sang: "Paul and Silas bound in jail, / Sing God's praise both night and day / And I hope dat trump may blow me home / To de new Jerusalem." The compilers of Slave Songs of the United States who transcribed the song suggested that it was well known on the eastern seaboard and speculated that the song originated in the Old Dominion.[24]

Perhaps the most striking elements of Strother's song are his invocation of the evil in the world. Instead of God's judgment and wrath, a theme not uncommon in the chiliastic eschatology of some early Black spirituals, Strother describes the evils of the earthly realm. Here Strother speaks as a marginalized, blind musician living in a dangerous and exploitative post-Emancipation world while reflecting the dark experience that his elders had faced under slavery. The song is rightly considered his most powerful work and is certainly the most imitated.[25]

4

Land and Labor

Used to work [for] a 'tractor,
Mike Hardy was his name;
Wanted me to make four loads a day,
Doggone mule was lame.
—JAMES LEE STROTHER, "I Used to Work on a 'Tractor," recorded 1936

Strother's ancestors and elders grew up in a culture rooted in the system of slavery and the rhythms of agricultural life. Unlike the "Cotton South" or even the "Tobacco Kingdom" of Southside Virginia and North Carolina, the northern Piedmont counties had been transformed into a land of wheat, corn, and animal husbandry that looked very different from the monoculture found elsewhere. White enslavers employed Black laborers in new ways and also reaped the rewards of a growing trade in human beings. Most laborers lived on small holdings in close proximity to their enslavers. A prosperous farmer might enslave thirty to forty people on his holdings, but the typical farmstead was much smaller. And as Alexandria and Richmond expanded as the centers of the Upper South slave trade to the Cotton South, towns like Culpeper became regional hubs feeding the maw of the brutal slave system. Traders cannily appraised the "merchandise" at the county seat on court days and lured sellers with solicitations in the Culpeper newspapers. The trading firm of Isaac Franklin and John Armfield, with its northern base in Alexandria, pioneered and rationalized the grim business of selling human beings. Always looking for people to supply the labor demands of the Deep South, they recruited Jourdan

Michaux Saunders, who chose Fauquier County as his base of operations, scouring the nearby countryside where Strother's ancestors lived.[1]

The domestic slave trade and many other aspects of Virginia's antebellum world were swept away by the forces of the Civil War and Emancipation. Freedmen's schools rapidly grew as the formerly enslaved embraced their freedom to read and learn. Bondspeople became citizens, and 92,507 Black men (out of the 105,832 who had registered) voted in Virginia in 1867 to hold a constitutional convention. Some of these changes, such as access to limited education and property ownership, would be permanent; others, most notably Black officeholding and voting, would not outlast Jim Strother's formative years as the strictures of Jim Crow rose in the place of enslavement. And while Emancipation brought Black churches, schools, and a small degree of economic freedom, many of the essential patterns remained the same. Like his mother and older relatives, Jim Strother came of age in a world dominated by the land, backbreaking work, and a new but just as virulent system of racism. Seasons still dictated the pace of life — even social events. It was also a world still dominated by whites striving to restrict Black freedom. This was especially true for their desire to control Black labor.[2]

The prewar white elite largely retained their grip over the economy, society, and land throughout the South and Virginia. At the end of national Reconstruction, Culpeper had twenty-one farms of more than 1,000 acres. A majority belonged to men who had previously been the county's largest enslavers or their families. For example, in the Boston area in the Salem District of Culpeper, laborers on William T. Browning's property worked the same land that forty-four enslaved persons had farmed in 1860. Others had inherited land worked by forced labor. Samuel B. Chilton, who ran a 1,500-acre farm in the Jeffersonton area, does not appear on the 1860 slave schedules, but his father, Charles P. Chilton, does — he owned thirty-nine human beings before the Civil War. Such men now dictated the terms of free labor on their properties.[3]

The treatment of one branch of the Strother family reveals the ways in which former enslavers sought to control Black laborers and their lives during the tumult of Reconstruction. Harriet Strother and her children had little time to celebrate freedom or dream of the future in the aftermath of the Civil War. Hunkered down in the slave cabins on the border of Greene and Orange Counties, they faced a struggle for survival. (One wonders if Harriet was the "Hattie" referred to by Strother in his wistful version of

"This Old Hammer.") Orange County farmer Charles Tandy Graves also faced an uncertain future. A ruinous war of choice had destroyed the very thing that his class had fought to preserve—the right to own human beings like Harriet and her children. The Union military officers in Gordonsville struggled to maintain a fragile peace while watching warily over Graves and his fellow ex-Confederates. Violence, labor disputes, and legal wrangling kept the military district officers and the Freedmen's Bureau men busy.

Graves and his ilk wanted not only to reassert physical control over labor but also to dictate the terms of Black behavior, while freedpeople wished to control both their labor and their families. Harriet probably felt she had little choice when she made her mark on the labor contract proffered by Graves and sanctioned by the Bureau in December 1865. The contract included Harriet herself, daughter Jane Catherine, and sons Addison, Extra, and Lee. Echoing the language of slavery, Graves also included Harriet's unborn child in the list, noting that Harriet was "pregnant about six months gone." Graves promised thirty dollars, food, shelter, and fuel in return for the family's labor "inside and out." He also demanded that they "conform to the former habits & customs of the said Graves as regards the hours of labor and all loss time to be deducted." Graves further demanded that Harriet "not permit many visitors on the premises, and they to be of good character and use every precaution in keeping her children out of mischief." Violating this agreement would cost Harriet ten dollars.[4]

Just four years later, Harriet had somewhat broken this exploitative system, with the children staying "at home." Soon the entire family made their way to the southern part of Culpeper County and found a degree of independence. Son Addison Strother purchased land and farmed in the Buena settlement; others settled in Salem Township near the Madison County line.[5] Despite this modicum of mobility and freedom, Black Virginians still faced many obstacles. Racial violence loomed just below the surface of everyday life—at least two lynchings occurred in Strother's home county. The imposition of Jim Crow segregation limited social and economic opportunities, and most Black people still labored for white bosses in demanding agricultural or industrial settings.

The most obvious expressions of Strother's rural background and the conditions of Black labor are two songs from Strother's 1936 recordings at the Virginia State Prison Farm that strike very different moods. "Corn Shucking Time" and "I Used to Work on a 'Tractor" remind us that the African American songster or musicianer had to be extremely adept at "code-switching," adapting their material, delivery, and even style of composition to anticipate the preconceptions of their audience based on race, gender, age, and other considerations. Strother was both a folk artist working within his native communities and a commercial musician when performing on the stage, in the dance hall, and especially on the street. The whimsical "Corn Shucking Time" points back to an important celebration in the lives of the enslaved and forward to the evolution of minstrelsy in the days of Strother's youth.

[*Spoken by another man: "Go, man"*]

Corn shuckin' time, that corn shuckin' time
Ain't gonna bake that possum,
Tell you, friends of mine;
'Til that corn shuckin' time
Won't be having fun,
Ain't gonna bake that possum 'til that corn, corn shuckin' time.

Oh, Annie wanna go to heaven
But she says she is not gwine,
She says she is not going, 'til that corn shuckin' time;
For she knows she's gonna bake that possum,
And then get tipsy on wine,
She says she's ready to go to heaven after that corn, corn shuckin'
    time.

"Corn Shucking Time" is easy to dismiss as pure minstrel doggerel. It certainly conveys some of the familiar tropes of the minstrel and traveling-show "plantation songs": the African Americans' fondness for possum, their happy-go-lucky nature, and a comic reference to Black religion. While the subject matter echoes themes common in minstrelsy, I have not found a printed or recorded song that is a clear precedent musically or lyrically. The song reminds us that Strother grew up in an age when blackface performance flourished before white and Black audiences and was performed by both races. American minstrelsy had been pervasive for at least fifty years when Strother came of age. Performers such as Thomas D. Rice created popular stage caricatures of Black people in the 1830s, predating the full-blown minstrel show. Rice's "Jim Crow" became an enduring icon of blackface performance. Virginians also played a key role in minstrel-sy's origins. Joel Walker Sweeney, raised in Appomattox County, Virginia, brought the songs of the enslaved—and the banjo—to the American and British stage in the late 1830s. In the 1840s the minstrel show evolved into the first distinctively American form of musical theater, integrating music, dance, and comedic banter into a series of acts. After Emancipation, Black artists appropriated blackface performance for their own purposes. Black medicine-show musicians routinely "corked up" (applied burnt cork to their faces), and Strother no doubt followed this convention during his heyday on the road.[6]

A clear thematic connection can be made from Strother's "Corn Shucking Time" to the early compositions of Sam Lucas, a fascinating Black singer, composer, and performer who successfully negotiated the demise of minstrelsy and the rise of vaudeville and musical theater. Lucas, born in 1840 to enslaved Virginians, was brought as a child to Ohio after his parents' emancipation. Lucas reached the height of his musical powers and popularity during Strother's formative years. His 1873 breakout composition "Carve Dat Possum" became a sheet-music hit in the late nineteenth century. First aurally recorded in 1917 by white popular singer Harry C. Browne and the Peerless Quartet for the Columbia record company, it later flowed back into the repertoire of artists of Strother's generation, such as Uncle Dave Macon.[7]

Despite its nod to the romanticized life of the plantation imagined by whites, there are elements of Strother's performance of "Corn Shucking Time" that reach beyond the conventions of blackface minstrelsy. Strother does not sing the song in the exaggerated "Negro" dialect found in much minstrel performance; his delivery is relatively straightforward and even whimsical. One of the few nods to the minstrel stage is his pronunciation of "going" as "gwine," which stands in contrast to his more conventional articulation of the word in his proto-blues "Going to Richmond." Down-home and deeply ironic humor pervades the song.

While it may be disquieting to today's sensibilities, the song describes one of the few experiences in the lives of enslaved people that granted a brief respite from oppressive surveillance and physical abuse. Corn shuckings brought men, women, and children together from dispersed communities in a harvest activity of song, celebration, and solidarity. It was a rare moment in the year when families separated by sale or bequeathed to others in neighboring locales might see their relatives. The formerly enslaved and white onlookers described the scenes of "gangs" of Black people marching to the event by the light of pine knot torches from every direction late in the evening. Typically held in late November or early December, the corn shucking festival marked the end of a season of hard fieldwork and announced the beginning of the Christmas season. The enslaved transformed yet another aspect of their unending labor into a joyous social gathering that embodied community solidarity.[8]

Music was central to this yearly ritual. Song leaders or "captains" climbed high atop the massive corn piles and led call-and-response songs to coordinate the work. A Virginian recalled one such song: "Come to shuck that corn to-night / Come to shuck with all your might / Come for to shuck all in sight / Come to shuck that corn tonight." There were frequently competitions between rival song leaders and their teams. Obviously, enslavers promoted these corn shucking festivals for their own labor needs, but they also realized the value of the events as celebratory gatherings. They typically provided strong drink and a feast after the hard work of stripping the husks from the cob.[9]

After copious eating and drinking, the "frolic" began and continued deep into the night. The strong pulse of fiddles and banjos propelled dancers well into the early morning. Every conceivable rhythmic accompaniment assisted the string musicians; formerly enslaved people recalled tapping on the floor of a barn, "straw beating" a fiddler's strings as he played, clattering beats on animal bones, and creating intricate patterns on their own bodies—described as "patting juba." The frolic was an immersive and spiritual experience that involved every member of the extended Black community.[10]

The rural frolic lived on well into the twentieth century. Jim Strother refers to such an event in his song "Jaybird":

Jaybird died with the whooping cough,
Sparrow died with the colic,
I met a bullfrog with a banjo on his back,
Said he's going on down to the frolic.

African and African American folklore is replete with animal tales that encapsulate the experiences and foibles of humans. Although born a generation removed from slavery, Strother no doubt experienced the rural frolic in his youth. Later he would carry his own banjo to such gatherings.

The uneasiness that such songs evoke in twenty-first-century listeners rightly stems from disturbing stereotypes of Black people propagated for many years by minstrels and their progeny. Yet we should not assume that Strother's songs always operated in this way. For example, Strother's evocation of opossum as a holiday delicacy in "Corn Shucking Time" was not simply a minstrel fantasy. The famed Black abolitionist and author William Wells Brown specifically mentioned a song performed at his home farm during the annual event that echoes Sam Lucas's popular composition "Carve Dat Possum."

> De possum meat am good to eat,
> Carve him to de heart;
> You'll always find him good and sweet,
> Carve him to de heart;
> My dog did bark, and I went to see,
> Carve him to de heart.

Brown also described the gangs of men singing as they returned to their home plantations. A few, "having their dogs with them, would start on the trail of a coon, possum, or some other game, which might keep them out till nearly morning."[11]

The music of the corn shucking exhibited one other significant feature germane to Jim Strother's recordings and African American song in general. The corn shucking captain frequently made sly and subtle comments about enslavers and their families. "Singing the master," as Roger Abrahams called it, might include indirect, improvised references to the enslavers' domestic relations, the quality (or lack thereof) of his farm and the food provided for the corn shucking repast, and even his treatment of the enslaved. The captain, usually a leader in the enslaved community, knew all too well that the master and his family would be observing the festivities. These song leaders apparently knew exactly how far their clever wordplay and eloquence could go on this festive day. Likewise, the dance caller at the evening's frolic directed and sometimes commented on specific people in his audience. The practice of commenting on the foibles or circumstances of community members is, of course, characteristic of many African and African American cultural practices—from play-party songs to the back-and-forth insults of "playing the dozens" to stand-up comedians. Despite its obvious minstrel associations, "Corn Shucking Time" echoes realities of the antebellum experience and demonstrates Strother's ability to reach back to earlier musical modes and styles for his material.[12]

Strother's other musical account of farm life and labor could hardly stand in greater contrast to "Corn Shucking Time," evoking the everyday experience he and his contemporaries endured. "I Used to Work on a 'Tractor" reveals the nature of labor oppression in post-Emancipation Virginia in direct, compelling language. Unlike the clear but veiled language of African American protest songs, Strother called out a specific white Southern boss and the damage done to mules and men. Like many of Strother's other songs, a strong subtext of racial conflict and unfairness pervades his vivid recounting of his treatment under Jim Crow.

The upheaval brought by the destruction of slavery affected every relationship between Black and white people in Culpeper County and across the South. No longer able to exercise the direct physical control that slavery afforded, white planters and farmers quickly settled on new forms of coercion—restrictive labor contracts, the systems of sharecropping and tenancy, and hired day labor. This was the world of agricultural and industrial labor that Strother and other African American workers faced day-to-day. Strother evinced a sophisticated understanding of labor oppression and conflict in "I Used to Work on a 'Tractor." The song's title was initially misheard, but based on the lyrical content, folklorists have correctly interpreted "tractor" as "contractor"—in this case, the despised Mike Hardy. Backed by his banjo, Strother sang:

> Used to work on a 'tractor,
> Mike Hardy was his name;
> Wanted me to make four loads a day,
> Doggone mule was lame.
>
> Went out early in the morning,
> Got stalled and stayed all day.
> When I returned in the evening,
> These are the words he'd say.
>
> "Where in the world is you been all day,
> Here's your money, get away.
> With that mule and that *boy's* bushel corn."

Old Mike Hardy, he was mad,

Give my money and he got bad.

With that mule and that *boy's* bushel corn.

The song catalogs the plight of a landless laborer worked to the breaking point in an abusive system: sunrise to sunset toil, an impossible number of loads per day, a lame and overworked mule, and, in the end, a cash transaction. This is not the uncompensated work of the enslaved but the experience of landless Black people of the post–Civil War period still struggling in an unequal system of dependency and exploitation despite Emancipation. The confrontation with the contractor—and, later in the song, even Mike Hardy's brother—brings to the fore the abuse of both men and animals; in the minds of men like Hardy, there probably wasn't much difference. "I Used to Work on a 'Tractor'" recounts the hard reality of Jim Strother's early experience with "four loads a day."

The impoverished condition of Strother's family and their reliance on his labor are suggested by the fact that he could neither read nor write despite the presence of segregated African American schools in his community. Twenty-four African American delegates helped write the state's new constitution in 1868, creating Virginia's first statewide system of public schools. In the first year of the schools' operation, 131,000 students had enrolled in them, but many African Americans were unable to take advantage of formal schooling as a result of the economic demands on their time. While reality dictated that Strother and many others went without, Black leaders continually pushed for equal education in post-Emancipation Virginia. Despite their efforts, Strother came to adulthood in a state and region committed to eliminating the Black vote and imposing Jim Crow segregation. White supremacists would accomplish both goals largely through legislation and the 1902 state constitution that drastically shrank the Virginia electorate.[13]

Not all Black Virginians were landless. A remarkably high proportion of African Americans in Virginia actually owned land by the early twentieth century, but the vast majority—including the family of Jim Strother's second wife, Blanche Greene—still struggled to survive on their plots and resorted to sharecropping or sold their labor when necessary. By 1910, Black owners held around one-quarter of all farms in the state.[14]

While certainly a remarkable achievement for a people not long removed from being property themselves, landownership had its limits. The editor of the *Culpeper Exponent* trumpeted the fact that Blacks owned 9,952 acres of county land valued at $46,413 in 1902, yet it also reported that whites held 223,085 acres valued at $1,398,111. Most Black farmers owned small plots and could not afford improvements in machinery and tools, let alone livestock that could increase the value of their holdings. Many African American landholders still had to rely on day labor and renting to make ends meet. "Forty acres and a mule" certainly beat slavery, but it was not necessarily the way out of poverty when white farmers held far more and better land, enjoyed generous credit, and dominated politics.[15]

Black people did see a few other opportunities for economic advancement. County towns, transportation hubs, and regional cities all beckoned as possible places to make a better living. Even the town of Culpeper offered jobs in shops, maintenance, and a few crafts—perhaps even starting a business for fellow Black people. For Jim Strother, the town revealed new musical avenues and audiences.

5

The Wharf

There you can see clog and jig dancing, jay bird on the ash band, sand shufflers, negro singing, negro gags, banjo and all other kinds of picking, old plantation melodies, sung, danced, and picked, by home never-sweat talent, that is hard to beat.

—"HUSTLER," writing in the *Culpeper Exponent*, August 6, 1897

Despite the predominance of farm and field, Culpeper and the central Piedmont rapidly became connected to the wider world in the mid-nineteenth century. The Orange and Alexandria Railroad reached the county seat in 1851, fostering trade northward to Alexandria and west to Lynchburg. There, passengers and freight transferred to the Virginia and Tennessee line, pushing down the Valley of Virginia to the Tennessee border and beyond. Such rail connections provided an outlet for the agricultural and extractive industries in Culpeper, such as grain and lumber mills as well as a gypsum mill. Eventually the rail lines connected Piedmont Virginia with towns and cities north, south, and west.[1]

The long steel rails brought more than products to the town of Culpeper. Brass bands, ragtime strutters, minstrel shows, and, later, blues shouters traveled to the county seat. Here the worlds of folk and popular music collided and intertwined. Music also traveled with the railroad workers, peripatetic songsters, and Black excursionists who frequented the parks, streets, and alley "dives" in Culpeper County. Jim Strother and other central Virginia residents heard the full range of America's musical offerings. At one event in 1886, the town thronged with "a large crowd of colored people . . . from Madison C.H. [Courthouse] and Warrenton" celebrating the anniversary of the founding of the Black Odd Fellows Lodge in Culpeper. Appropriately, the Madison brass band enlivened the festivities. The next year the Old Dominion Negro Minstrels performed at the Culpeper Academy of Music. Admission cost eager patrons 25 or 35 cents, prices likely based on the separation of the races within the theater—where Black patrons were typically relegated to the balcony. These were the entertainments commonly mentioned by the editors of the local papers, along with society events, blackface minstrels, and guitar, banjo, and mandolin clubs, but another rich vein of music generally eluded their notice.[2]

Below the genteel surface was a wealth of Black folksong and popular music that traveled with country people and the workers and migrants along the rails and highways to the county seat. Locals dubbed an area just below the town's Black business district "the Wharf." Visitors who walked down East Davis Street passed the well-kept stores toward the train station and the venerable Waverly Hotel. Boardinghouses, warehouses, industrial buildings, and small businesses huddled against the railroad tracks. White politicians, policemen, and newspaper editors focused less on the area as a center of legitimate commerce and more on the Wharf's boisterous side. One wag writing under the *nom de plume* "The Hustler" described the area thus in 1897:

> The Wharf is not what it was in its palmy days, but she is, at times, a blooming daisy yet, and not of the Old field variety either. If you want to have a good time, you should make it convenient to land in that locality some time, when there are no officers about. . . . There you can see clog and jig dancing, jay bird on the ash band, sand shufflers, negro singing, negro gags, banjo and all other kinds of picking, old plantation melodies, sung, danced, and picked, by home never-sweat talent, that is hard to beat. Fishtown, Johnstown, Sugar Bottom, and Tin Cup Alley, are well represented, and the people at the Waverly; and others who are unfortunate enough to be domiciled in that locality, have no trouble in banishing sleep. Nobody especially is to blame for the high time that these people have, and I know the respectable people would not have it otherwise.[3]

Despite the obvious sarcasm, the anonymous chronicler perceptively cataloged the town of Culpeper's African American neighborhoods in close proximity to the Wharf. Just south was Fishtown, today the area along Commerce Street, Waters Place, and Locust Street, supposedly named for the open fish fries held by residents. Sugar Bottom sat along West Street near Antioch Baptist Church, so named for the location of a natural spring known for the sweetness of its waters. Tin Cup Alley meandered west across the railroad tracks into a bottom. It was home to domestics, laborers, and itinerant railroad workers. Jim Strother knew many people in these enclaves. His mother, Susan Strother, labored as a washerwoman in Culpeper Town during the heyday of the Wharf.[4]

While "Hustler" touted the "home talent" displayed at the Wharf, other reports of events in the neighborhood suggest that revelers came from far and wide to enjoy the musical offerings. "Hustler" witnessed a wide range of performers and styles of music. "[C]log and jig dancing" still persisted in Black folk culture, but it had long since made its way to the minstrel and traveling-show stage. The "negro gags" and "old plantation melodies," especially, seem like aspects of stage performance. Still, there are hints that traditional music had its place. "Jay bird on the ash band" is possibly a variation on (or mangling of) the title of an old fiddle tune, "Snow-bird on the Ash-Bank," a venerable reel dating to at least the American Civil War. This was fertile ground for Strother's musical education.[5]

One can easily imagine Strother's "Jaybird" performed on the Wharf. Elements of the song echo the minstrel stage as well as Black folksong:

> White folks in a parlor,
> Drink up all that dram,
> Darkies in the barnyard,
> Eaten up the white folks' ham.
>
> Jaybird trying to scratch back,
> Sparrow trying to crow,
> Young girls hop in the summertime,
> Blind man trying to sew.

Songs such as "Jaybird" had flowed between the minstrel stage and the folk stream well before they became fodder for musicianers such as Strother. Elements of Strother's lyrics appear in an early minstrel songbook but also in field collecting among Black people across the South. Charles Wolfe, in his edition of African American collector Thomas W. Talley's *Negro Folk Rhymes*, notes: "The first two stanzas of this piece have been widely collected from both white and black sources, and print versions are found as far back as 1846." Early field collectors found examples in coastal South Carolina, Mississippi, and Alabama. Likewise, some of the song's lyrics informed comedic tunes popular under the tents of traveling shows. Strother's opening stanza anchors the song "Ham Beats All Meats" as it appeared in Talley's 1922 collection. It quickly featured on several commercial recordings by Black songsters and white string bands in the 1920s. Those trying to parse this music as either commercial or folk music simply fall into the same trap as the folklorists who sought to define "pure" blues or "authentic" spirituals. Strother defied such categorization.[6]

A version of Strother's opening stanza, collected in Mississippi in 1909, suggests an origin among the enslaved and features the type of sly role-reversal seen in other songster material:

> Ol' Massa in de parlor,
> Ol' Missus in de hall;
> Nigger in de dinin' room,
> Farin' de best of all.[7]

The Black trickster yet again gets the best of the "Massa" and "Missus," just as in Strother's song the protagonist eats the "white folks' ham." Strother relied on Black folksong as well as popular forms of minstrelsy—performed by both Blacks and whites—to forge this genre of his repertoire. How he inflected this music when working before different audiences remains a mystery, but it's a good bet that he did so.

Culpeper County's residents were certainly no strangers to minstrelsy. Rixey's Opera House in the town of Culpeper featured such shows. An advertisement in the *Culpeper Exponent* screamed "New Jokes, New Specialties," promising vocal performances, "a powerful Quartette," and "The Trial of Joshua Beanhull, or a Scene in a Magistrate's Office." The pageantry of shows at the opera house jostled with smaller tent and medicine shows in Culpeper, no doubt influencing Strother in his youth. Those smaller shows were pushed to the outskirts of society—and of the town. In Culpeper, the "Negro minstrel shows played by the National Cemetery, just east of the railroad tracks; the lot was outside the corporate limits and they didn't have to worry about a license."[8]

Cedar Hill Park offered another opportunity for young Jim Strother to experience the sounds of Black music. Located about a mile south of the town center, the park offered a variety of recreational and entertainment possibilities. Henry Lightfoot, Cedar Hill Park's proprietor, led a fascinating life. He rose to political prominence as an active member of the interracial Readjuster Party in the late 1870s. The party's brief moment as a majority party in Virginia gave him local social and political clout that continued into the late nineteenth century, allowing him to serve on the town council; it also earned him the enmity of many whites.

Virginia's Readjuster Party, one of the most vibrant biracial political coalitions of post-Emancipation America, was improbably led by former Confederate general William "Billy" Mahone. The party sought to "readjust" the crushing state debt—essentially, to write off money owed to financiers from the prewar period. More importantly, the party defended African American rights to the ballot box and to public education that had been enshrined in Virginia's new constitution. The state debt threatened funding for public education and gave the Readjusters a powerful issue to unite African American and poor white voters. Yet, much like other movements in the South to foster biracial cooperation, the Readjuster Party fell apart in the 1880s as a result of sustained attacks from political elites and white intransigence regarding political and social equality.[9]

The hostility of the town elite toward the Readjusters and their leaders spilled over into the local newspaper's descriptions of Lightfoot and his entertainment grounds. The editors loudly publicized any violence at his events and dubbed the venue "Razor Hill Park," evoking the widely understood imagery of the then-popular "coon songs"—a derogatory term that the paper used liberally in describing the park's clientele. The editors most strenuously objected to excursions that visited the park by train, bringing, as they put it, "South Washington [DC] negro toughs" and the "drunken negro element from Washington."[10]

A correspondent to the *Culpeper Exponent* ascribed a political and economic motive to the town council's lack of action taken against the park and other places where Black residents and visitors congregated for entertainment despite the fact that the city fathers had recently campaigned against local saloons. "Why was Culpeper made the dumping ground of this?" the letter writer railed. "Methinks it must have been for the benefit of Razor Hill Park and its fat mulatto proprietor, the dives on the wharf, and the future claims of local politicians who, at the proper time, will have their arms around their necks, soliciting their trade and votes." In one of the paper's vilest tirades, a correspondent proclaimed that "I have seen, of late, many articles in the town papers in regard to saloons and their evils, but I have yet to see one line in regard to the influx of South Washington [DC] negroes that are given 'carte blanche' to crowd our streets, to disturb the rest of the people, use obscene language, force the ladies to stay in doors for fear of being insulted, to say nothing of the vile odor emanating from these coons that permeates and saturates the hitherto damp atmosphere, to the detriment of the Whole community." This letter writer invoked every fear and prejudice of Southern whites, especially the supposed impudence of Black men on the streets and the implied threat to white womanhood.[11]

The *Culpeper Exponent* published one more rather telling complaint: the effect of "city Negroes" on their rural Southern brethren. The excursions to Cedar Hill Park and "the dives of Black Belt . . . demoralize every negro in the town and county, who are bad enough at their best." This grievance was especially ridiculous because many of the people riding the trains from Washington, DC, to enjoy a summer excursion in the country had grown up—and decided to leave—rural Virginia. But in one sense the newspaperman was correct. Jim Strother and others certainly learned lessons from these tourists. One can imagine that Black Washingtonians—many with direct ties to relatives in Virginia—displayed a greater sense of their own self-worth and rights. Their example triggered a sustained exodus of Black people from Culpeper and rural Virginia, including many members of Jim Strother's extended family. As an aspiring musician, Strother would have been exposed to a wide range of musical styles and influences by the revelry at the Wharf, Cedar Hill Park, and other places of entertainment, but he also might have been inspired by tales of life in America's big cities as told by these visitors.[12]

Strother made his way to the steel mills of Sparrows Point and then the city of Baltimore during the heyday of the Wharf and Cedar Hill Park, probably lured by steady wages. Not long after Strother's departure, the mayor of Culpeper exerted the full force of Virginia's vagrancy laws against the inhabitants of these sections of the town. It presaged what Strother would experience as a performer in the medicine shows and city streets as a musician. Strother's rapid transition from steelworker to performer after his blinding is our best evidence that the Wharf and similar venues, and the traveling shows that visited Culpeper, served as his musical training ground for much of his popular, minstrel, and medicine-show repertoire. Strother drew on these sources as well as the rich vein of string music and religious folksong from his youth when, out of necessity, he turned to the life of a musicianer.

~BALTIMORE~

6

Sparrows Point

Strother had until recently been in perfect health and while working at
Sparrows Point, he was blinded by an accident.
—Baltimore American, January 27, 1915

In popular imagination, the "mug shot" is still to this day the defining image of the criminal. Television news, newspapers, and now the internet serve up a daily dose of booking photographs, traditionally two images—one in profile and the other capturing the prisoner's gaze directly at the camera. I've seen literally hundreds of examples in the Virginia State Penitentiary collection at the Library of Virginia. There's a certain numbness that comes with this familiarity. You tend to forget that these are human beings who had families, friends, and lives. And that is the point. The crisp black-and-white images mechanically fulfilled the carceral state's need to surveil, to catalog, and to dehumanize—the inmate number hangs loosely but conspicuously around the person's neck.

Yet James Lee Strother's photograph does much more. The finely detailed image memorialized the sudden violence of the industrial workplace and possibly the cumulative violence of altercations in house parties and alley dives. Strother's scarred face, photographed as he passed behind the gates of Virginia's prison system, gives testimony to a terrible moment of disaster. His eyes are cloudy and askew, staring blankly and not quite into the camera. Whether by intense heat or light, his blindness is apparent on close examination. A deep, poorly healed scar cuts across his right cheek, while other marks of trauma stamp the area above his right eye. I badly wanted to learn what life-altering event had left such an imprint on Strother.[1]

Jim Strother's "mug shot" reveals numerous scars and the damage done to his eyes at the Sparrows Point steel mill that left him totally blind. (Prisoner photograph of James Lee Strother, Records of the Virginia State Penitentiary, State Records Collection, Library of Virginia, Richmond)

Many previous writers assumed that they knew the answer based on the say-so of folklorist John Lomax, the man who first recorded Strother. Lomax asserted, "Years ago an explosion in a mine destroyed [Strother's] sight. Afterwards he earned a living as a street-corner entertainer." And who would question such an authority? After all, Lomax's companion on his trip to the Virginia State Prison Farm, Harold Spivacke, reverentially told how Lomax expertly prepared Strother for his recording session with hours of prefatory conversation. And claims that Strother had ties to Appalachia added to the plausibility of the mining accident story. There's only one problem—it isn't true. The real story is both more compelling and more revealing of the hardships Strother and other members of the African American diaspora endured in the early twentieth century.[2]

One of the first mysteries that I tried to solve was when Jim Strother lost his sight. The available evidence suggests that Strother's blinding occurred sometime before 1910. The census of that year places him in Baltimore with his first wife, Mary, and his profession is given as "musician." Maddeningly, a later scribe overwrote the census columns for disability with a series of numerical and letter codes. Beneath these later additions, one can faintly make out the census taker's notation "Bl"—blind. This entry, as well as Strother's profession, is our first indication that he had lost his sight; subsequent evidence, including his World War I registration card, confirms that he was "blind in both eyes."[3]

Time and place—these are two keys to unraveling a historical puzzle. When did Strother arrive in Baltimore? A tantalizing hint to the possible circumstances of Strother's loss of sight appears in the 1900 census, in which a twenty-two-year-old, Virginia-born "James L. Strather" is recorded as a furnace worker in the steel mills of Sparrows Point just outside the city. The available physical descriptions of Strother testify to a man who could withstand the rigors of demanding physical labor. Lomax called him "Big Jimmie Strothers," and his examiner for the World War I draft board described him as "tall and slender." By all accounts, he stood more than six feet tall and weighed around 165 pounds. Steel-mill work required both strength and agility, and Strother must have had both.[4]

I had always suspected that Strother's blinding occurred at Sparrows Point, but it wasn't until late in my research that a single newspaper article definitively confirmed my suspicions. A controversy in 1915 over his street performing led one of his defenders to write that he had been "in perfect health" but "while working at Sparrows Point, he was blinded by an accident." I have found no record of this "accident" that would reveal when, precisely, it occurred, but that isn't surprising. Only the most gruesome or dramatic episodes of destruction, usually with multiple deaths, made the newspapers. Accounts of industrial mishaps that killed or maimed a single individual might not even include the worker's name.[5]

Sparrows Point was both a welcome and an intimidating place for the Southern migrants who flocked to the industrial wages it offered. Incorporated in 1891 as the Maryland Steel Company, a subsidiary of the Pennsylvania Steel Company, the complex would eventually become the largest steel mill in the world after its acquisition by Bethlehem Steel in 1916. Its furnaces and mills provided the stage for many violent catastrophes, which happened with alarming regularity in America's emerging industrial landscape.

The carnage of the industrial age was on full display at Sparrows Point. In 1906, the *Baltimore Sun* reported one of many such incidents under the headline "Rush of Flame Kills 5." The victims were "literally cooked . . . as the result of a rush of flame and hot coke from a tuyere opening in blast furnace C." The *Sun's* reporter at least bore witness to the human cost by compiling a grim list of the dead and their Virginia hometowns:

Cyrus Street of Crewe
Matt Trent of Guinea Mills
Ben Booze of Zuni
William Alexander of Petersburg
Edward Redd of Farmville

Seven other men suffered serious injuries, but they remained nameless in the *Sun's* report. For all we know, one of them might have been Strother. The authorities held a coroner's inquest—prescribed by Maryland law in cases of violent or suspicious death. The jury of citizens predictably returned a verdict that the men "came to their death as the result of an unavoidable accident."[6]

The company specifically recruited African Americans from the rural South to man the blast furnaces that turned iron ore into steel, and large numbers of Virginians heeded the call. In 1904, Black migrants from the Old Dominion made up nearly 77 percent of the residents of Sparrows Point, with the vast majority of the remaining migrants coming from North Carolina. White inspectors of the Black sections of the company town found conditions even more dire than among Baltimore's other Black neighborhoods: "The manner of living of a large number of the negroes in this locality is not conducive to the uplifting of the race, numbers of them occupying shacks where three or four sleep, cook and eat in one room, thus engendering filth and disease." In 1900, Strother lived in a ten-by-fourteen-foot room with fellow Virginians William Moon, James H. Brown, and James Mitchell. Strother, Moon, and Brown labored in the furnaces and Mitchell at the dry docks. Reflecting the lack of any infrastructure, the street designation on the census simply says "Shanty."[7]

Sparrows Point—the mill and town—was largely the creation of two men: brothers Frederick W. and Rufus K. Wood. The sons of a manager at the legendary Boott textile mill in Lowell, Massachusetts, they both brought with them Yankee sensibilities about labor, industrial organization, and social hierarchy in a mill town. Frederick had graduated with an engineering degree from MIT, and he quickly rose through the ranks of the Pennsylvania Steel Company. He designed and constructed the Sparrows Point mill and became the first president of the Maryland Steel Company of Baltimore County in 1891. His brother Rufus designed and took charge of the company town. Rufus embodied the ethos of his Yankee ancestors: religiously devout, rigidly moralistic, educationally advanced, and devoted to a hierarchical social order. The rock-ribbed New Englander established public schools for both white and Black children as well as a kindergarten, a radical innovation in a state that at the time had no compulsory public education attendance law. He forbade the use of alcohol and succeeded in having a bar near the Point fined after it ensnared some of his workers, although his campaign against drink was largely unsuccessful.[8]

The Wood brothers wielded absolute authority over their workers and the town. The men had a gentleman's agreement with Maryland governor Elihu Emory Jackson that allowed them to control Sparrows Point's governance—no mayor or city council interfered in their affairs. The town itself reflected the influence of their native city, Lowell. The Woods designed a highly planned, self-contained company town laid out with a clear vision of social hierarchy. Houses lined a series of alphabetical streets proceeding from the harbor front; first were homes for company officers and superintendents, then for white workmen and foremen, and then, across Humphrey's Creek, for Black workers with families. The architecture of the succeeding blocks inscribed race and class in the landscape, from the fine homes of management to the brick row houses of white workmen to the rough, wooden double houses of Black families, each in turn closer to the mill.[9]

Jim Strother and his fellow Southern migrants—Black, single, and male—occupied the lowest rung of the Sparrows Point hierarchy: Shantytown. Constructed as a temporary labor camp in the early days of the mill, hundreds of ramshackle huts huddled up against the steelworks. Strother and his fellow laborers lodged four to a room with no running water and only outhouses. By the time Strother arrived at Sparrows Point, young Black men, overwhelmingly from Virginia, occupied about half of the shanties and paid a dollar a week for the privilege. An inspector for the US Bureau of Labor reported that the men had to provide their own bedding, stoves, and fuel for cooking. The bunks could barely accommodate a normal-sized man and the "furnishings are primitive in the extreme," the inspector wrote. As in most company towns, Jim Strother and his fellow workers used scrip, a form of payment only redeemable at the company store.[10]

Eastern European immigrants occupied the rest of Shantytown, but the managers of the hulking plant held a certain disdain for them; they

Strother and his fellow Black steelworkers lived in wooden shanties close to the Sparrows Point furnaces—the small white buildings in this image. Strother and three other Virginia laborers lived in a ten-by-fourteen-foot room in 1900. ("Furnaces of the Maryland Steel Co. Sparrows Point, MD" postcard, ca. 1901; courtesy of the author)

would not dominate the workforce as they did at steel mills in Pittsburgh and Chicago. Superintendent Axel Sahlin felt they lacked the stamina for much of the labor. For the heaviest and dirtiest jobs, he far preferred young Black men from the rural South. "I have personally known and supervised hundreds of coloured ironworkers," he reported to a British ironworking journal, and he found them "capable of competing with white labour in any country." Sahlin's preference for rural Black labor rested on obvious stereotypes. Sahlin asserted that Black men were uniquely suited for the intense heat, especially in the languid and humid Maryland summers, but that was not management's only consideration. Black workers and their families themselves knew why their white overlords chose certain workers over others. Florence Parks, whose family migrated to the Point from rural North Carolina, recalled that the "rule was, if you were a country boy from the farm, they wanted you, especially if you got relatives here. They didn't want the city Negro 'cause they thought he'd be uppity." No steelworks other than those in Birmingham, Alabama, employed as many Black workers as Sparrows Point.[11]

As bad as the living conditions were at Sparrows Point, the mill's furnaces posed a much greater threat to the steelworkers. Industrial work came with a significant threat to life and limb. One observant chronicler of Sparrows Point noted how the industrial age brought with it the concept of the industrial "accident." Earlier generations spoke of "acts of God" or natural disasters—events beyond the power of humans to control—but now manufacturers blamed industrial havoc on the processes and machines themselves, machines of such great power that they occasionally blew themselves up or flew apart in some inscrutable, inner rage.[12]

Mill owners and industrialists gratefully accepted such explanations for the carnage because it absolved them of any liability. Coroners' inquests, typically involving the "leading men" of a community, almost always considered these catastrophic events "accidents" and the cause "unaccountable and unavoidable." Not only did these judgments absolve the mill owners from responsibility and fend off lawsuits but they also gave industrialists little incentive to improve workplace safety. In 1912, the steel company compiled a financial accounting of workplace accidents. The list included artificial limbs, legal fees, and funeral expenses. The $9,141 cost of the 2,336 accidents paled in contrast to the company's $7.5 million in sales. In an age when Darwinism reigned as a leading social theory and when capitalists viewed labor as just another commodity, industrialists had little motivation to improve conditions on the shop floor.[13]

Strother was hardly alone. Maryland officials chronicled the frequency with which workers were burned, smashed, and maimed as well as the mill owners' relative inattention to such incidents. A report of Maryland's State Industrial Accident Commission reads like the matter-of-fact bureaucratese of a military after-action report, stating that "during the year ending October 31, 1917, there were filed with the Commission 37,434 reports of industrial accidents. . . . The maximum monthly record was reached in August when 3,708, or an average of 137 a day, were reported." Various tables calculated the grim toll, compiling such factors as the causes of injury ("Flying Objects," "Fall of Persons," "Drowning"), the nature of the injury, and "Parts of Body Injured." In 1917 alone, 3,384 unfortunate men and women in Maryland joined Strother as victims of eye damage.[14]

The Maryland General Assembly attempted to compensate for employers' lack of attention to these grim statistics. In 1914 they enacted a Workers' Compensation Act "to provide relief to the increasing number of workers in a rapidly expanding industrial society." The Act seemed relatively generous; negligence and fault were not considered for a claim, and a worker could receive cash benefits for lost wages, medical benefits, death benefits, and vocational training. Unfortunately, the Act came too late for Jim Strother, who had suffered his injury long before.[15]

It was at Sparrows Point that Jim Strother truly learned the full import of his song "I Used to Work on a 'Tractor." Despite the song's agricultural setting, it fully applied to the abuse and unfairness of Black labor in the industrial cities as well. His attempt to escape Culpeper taskmasters like Mike Hardy only brought him into the different but equally brutal Sparrows Point furnaces and shanties. White men still controlled his body and his labor—and eventually robbed him of his sight. A hard-hearted foreman asking the impossible "four loads a day" applied as easily to the mill as to the field. It was this alienation and bitterness that produced one of the most direct and evocative, but also matter-of-fact, labor statements in Black folksong.

Strother directly confronted the exploitation of his labor—but not his new disability—in his music. The only reference to blindness in his canon is a passing, comedic reference in his song "Jaybird." After a series of anthropomorphic absurdities, Strother sings,

> Jaybird trying to scratch back,
> Sparrow trying to crow,
> Young girls hop in the summertime,
> Blind man trying to sew.

Was Strother simply using a stock line of a well-known folksong trope, or was he referring to his own condition in a sly and subtle way? It seems likely that it is the former. Most Black musicians of this era did not sing about their blindness, despite their firm grounding in first-person descriptions of their lives and emotions. Some attribute this to the singers' feeling that it "othered" them, separating them from their listeners. One of the few but telling examples is John Estes singing, "When you lose your eyesight, your best friend is gone / Even your own dear people won't fool with you long." One of the most explicit examples, but one that is quite rare in its directness, is gospel singer Gary Davis's "Lord, I Wish I Could See." Davis echoed the sentiments of Estes, recounting abandonment by friends. He conveyed a sense of isolation and irony about the "trouble I see," singing "I'm away in the dark / got to feel my way." At the end of the song, he songspoke a brief exposition, telling his sighted audience that they should feel lucky: "You can see everything coming to you." The 1935 recording proved too maudlin and commercially risky for the American Recording Corporation A&R men, who did not issue it.[16]

After being blinded at the steel mill, Strother entered a new and perilous stage in his life. Black men in the age of Jim Crow had very few options for fair and lucrative employment—let alone those with disabilities. Yet Strother at least found a new source of support in these years. In 1908 he partnered with Mary Strother, settling with her in the city of Baltimore. Unfortunately, we know virtually nothing about her or her background. After his accident, Strother also relied on extended family. As we will see, the Great Migration provided him with a network of mutual support among extended kin. Strother was now eking out a living with his music and would spend at least two decades entertaining the throngs of Americans who crowded around the medicine-show stage, the dance hall floor, and the street corners of Baltimore. If nothing else, at least Strother had greater control over his own labor than he had had in the fields of Culpeper County and the furnaces of Sparrows Point.[17]

The Biddle Alley District

When I say that not all of the Negroes in Baltimore lived in the middle-class world that we did, I mean it. In the 1920s, there was an area in northwest Baltimore known as Lung Block. . . . [S]o many Negroes down there had tuberculosis.
—CAB CALLOWAY, *Of Minnie the Moocher and Me*, 1976

The first verifiable address for James Lee Strother in the city of Baltimore places him and his wife Mary on Walnut Street in the Seventeenth Ward. This area of northwest Baltimore had been one of the centers of African American migration in the preceding several decades as the city's population rapidly expanded. Unfortunately for Strother and his neighbors, it was also the most notorious neighborhood in the city, known for vice, crime, and disease. According to the 1910 census, Jim Strother now plied his trade as a musician. For "place of employment," the census taker simply wrote "Public"—a street performer. Strother entered this urban world at the very moment when the forces of the Great Migration, urban reform, and social welfare collided.[1]

The story of Black Baltimore did not start with the Great Migration. The city had the largest population of free people of color in the United States on the eve of the American Civil War. Likewise, Maryland led the states by a wide margin with some 83,924 free Black people, almost equal to the number of enslaved laborers in the state. Despite the centrality of African slavery to the founding of the Chesapeake colony, free people born of white mothers and Black fathers formed a distinct free class in early Maryland.

Later, the growth in the free population was driven both by Revolutionary-era ideals and lessened reliance on enslaved labor in staple agriculture. The presence of a large group of free people of color facilitated the development of strong Black institutions—churches, fraternal orders, and political organizations. A small but influential Black middle class emerged of craftsmen, shopkeepers, ministers, and eventually professionals—doctors, lawyers, and educators. The free population organized African American churches, societies, and organizations, and the city's Black community nurtured national leaders such as Frederick Douglass, Henry Highland Garnet, and many others.[2]

This antebellum experience shaped the impact of the Great Migration on Baltimore. Migrants joined a large, well-established Black community, and while the city welcomed rural migrants, many of them came from within the state. In 1920, three-quarters of the African American population of Baltimore had been born in Maryland, in striking contrast to the many cities that received far more migrants escaping the Jim Crow South. For example, only 8.4 percent of Detroit's African American community in 1920 had been born in Michigan. While the Great Migration did not have the impact on Baltimore in terms of the numbers that were seen in places like Washington, DC, and New York, it did bring an influx of a significant number of Virginia migrants. Strother's fellow Virginians made up the vast majority of that one-quarter of the Black population composed of non-Marylanders.[3]

Virginians contributed greatly not only to the economic and industrial growth of Baltimore but also to the leadership of the Black community in the late nineteenth century. Black Baptist ministers and their congregations were crucial to the Black freedom struggle in Baltimore, and many were Virginia natives, including Garnett Russell Waller (Trinity Baptist Church), P. H. A. Braxton (Calvary Baptist Church), and Ananias Brown (Leadenhall Street Baptist Church). The Reverend Harvey Johnson of Union Baptist Church became the acknowledged leader of civil rights activity in the city, mobilizing Black Baltimoreans to the battle. Born into slavery in Fauquier County, Virginia, in 1843, Johnson later attended Wayland Theological Seminary in Washington, DC. In 1885 he founded the Mutual United Brotherhood of Liberty with several of his fellow ministers to carry on the struggle for freedom and civil rights, fighting lynching, segregation in accommodations, and restrictions on Black voting. Johnson and his colleagues successfully beat back several versions of an amendment to the state constitution that would have restricted Black suffrage, just as most Southern states had already done.[4]

Still, the vast majority of new migrants to Baltimore were working people, like Jim Strother, who had witnessed many family members and friends make the trek northward. Among them were Susan and Charles Taylor, who owned property and had lived most of their lives in the Salem Magisterial District of Culpeper County. Jim Strother's link to the family came through Charles's mother, Mary Strother. Born enslaved around 1850, she belonged to the same generation as Jim Strother's mother, Susan. They were likely sisters, but the genealogical brick wall of slavery prevents us from verifying their exact relationship. Charles brought his family north-ward to work on the railroads. While Strother labored in the furnaces of Sparrows Point, the extended Taylor family lived just north of Philadelphia along the railroad lines that brought so many Southern migrants to mid-Atlantic cities. The Taylors brought their children as well as Susan Taylor's three brothers—Robert, Ernest, and James Toms—two of whom worked with Charles on the railroad repair crews. Charles's brother Andrew Taylor arrived in Maryland in the early 1890s, eventually settling in the railroad town of Ellicott City just south of Baltimore. Just as Strother would face white hostility in Baltimore, the Taylors and Toms experienced it on the railroad lines. When the Baltimore and Ohio Railroad introduced Black workers to work the lines at Ellicott City in 1905, white trackmen "refused to work with the negroes" and went on strike.[5]

The deep racism that Strother and his relatives faced in Maryland prob-ably didn't surprise them. Civil Rights attorney and US Supreme Court jus-tice Thurgood Marshall frequently and pointedly branded Baltimore "way up South." He knew from experience. Born in the city in 1908, he recalled that the white businesses downtown refused to serve Black people and re-membered the high degree of neighborhood segregation. Indeed, Strother witnessed the advent of *de jure* Jim Crow segregation of the public sphere in Baltimore. It was the progressive mayor of Baltimore, J. Barry Mahool, who signed into law the first residential segregation ordinance in the United States in 1911, prescribing separate blocks for residences, churches, and schools based on racial percentages.[6]

Mahool and the city's other elected officials reacted to long-standing white fears of "block busting" by African Americans. Under the heading "Feared Negro Influx," the *Baltimore Sun* reported in 1909 on the founding of the Harlem Improvement Association in the Harlem Park area: "Within the last three years the people of the white residential section of northwest Baltimore have had three examples of negro invasion of colored persons purchasing property in the finer residential sections." The article described attempts to fend off Black purchasers of homes on all-white streets. Ironically, these families were represented by lawyers and belonged to Baltimore's African American middle class, who themselves were escaping the emerging ghetto in an area known as "the Bottom" in the Fourteenth and Seventeenth Wards. Rural African Americans displaced whites, immigrants, and, in the case of the Seventeenth Ward, middle-class Black residents, who then pushed northwest into the Fourteenth Ward along Pennsylvania and Druid Hill Avenue. The Black population of the Seventeenth Ward exploded from 1,499 to 16,736 in the first two decades of the century, while the white population fell by nearly 80 percent to 3,900. Among these Black migrants was Jim Strother.[7]

Resistance to change took many forms. Neighborhood associations sprang into being to deny "undesirables," primarily Black and Jewish Americans, access to white enclaves. The use of restrictive covenants—clauses in deeds that prevented the owner from selling to a person of another race—became commonplace. Whites also resorted to the all-American solution to keeping their neighborhoods homogeneous and outsiders in their place: violence. Some Black residents who dared to break the city's racial codes faced beatings, mobbing, and destruction of their property.[8]

Such extralegal means of ensuring homogeneity in the city's neighborhoods became especially important for whites when, in 1917, the US Supreme Court struck down Jim Crow neighborhood segregation codes. (Paradoxically, the court did so to assert white citizens' right to sell their houses to any buyer; nevertheless, it was one of the earliest victories in the long struggle for civil rights.) Black Baltimore's experienced and well-established professional class took the lead. The city's merchants and professionals had the money to finance the fight and access to numerous Black attorneys who were more than willing to shepherd such cases through the courts. Influential ministers backed these efforts with the help of their large congregations.

This was the state of race relations when Jim Strother first came to reside within the corporate limits of Baltimore. He and his wife Mary jostled with fellow Southern migrants, rural Marylanders, and the remaining white families in the rough-and-tumble Seventeenth Ward. The Strothers lived in a brick row house at 514 Walnut Street in the heart of one of the most notorious "alley districts" in the city—so notorious, in fact, that it attracted the attention of Progressive reformers from the Association for the Improvement of the Conditions for the Poor and the Charity Organization Society. Commissioned to review housing conditions in the city's most blighted neighborhoods, white reformers combed selected districts of row houses and alleys to inspect sanitation, outhouses, leaky roofs, and the general conditions under which many immigrant and African American Baltimoreans lived.

Janet E. Kemp, an agent for the Charity Organization Society, summarized the findings in a 1907 publication. The study documented the appalling conditions that Jim Strother and his neighbors endured day to day. Kemp called the area the Biddle Alley District and reported that the neighborhood was "occupied largely by negroes with a sprinkling of native white families, and a remnant of the colony of the clean, hard-working, thrifty Germans, who seem to have constituted the original inhabitants."[9]

The 1907 study is a litany of Progressive concerns—poor public health, rampant disease, nonexistent government regulation of housing, and inadequate infrastructure. Construction had just begun on Baltimore's first sewer system after the Great Fire of 1904 spurred the city fathers into action. The catalog of deplorable conditions in the Biddle Alley District included 71 of 215 houses with leaking roofs; 74 percent of its cellars recorded as damp, wet, or containing water; and inadequate toilets. Perhaps the most shocking revelation of the study, and one that came to define the debates about Strother's neighborhood, concerned a rampant disease. Kemp reported that "the Biddle alley district, of all sections of the city, holds the record for a high tuberculosis death rate . . . there is not a house on Biddle alley in which there has not been at least one case of tuberculosis."[10]

The deadly reputation of the Biddle Alley District was well known to the city fathers and residents alike, especially African Americans. The famed musician, bandleader, and entertainer Cab Calloway, raised in a solidly middle-class section of northwest Baltimore, lived only a leisurely stroll from Jim Strother's home. Because Baltimore's residential segregation by race hemmed Blacks into certain neighborhoods, this meant that lawyers, doctors, and educators could only live so far away from their less economically successful brethren. Calloway recalled that the area was "called Lung Block because so many Negroes down there had tuberculosis." Medical reformers also called attention to the "lung block" and the overall plight of

Charity organizations graphically illustrated some of the worst housing and health conditions in Baltimore, notably in Strother's neighborhood. "Lung Block" in *Housing Conditions in Baltimore: Report of a Special Committee* (Baltimore: Federated Charities, 1907), 17. (Courtesy of University of Virginia Library)

African Americans, who suffered from tuberculosis at a rate far greater than the white population.[11]

Two images from the housing study dramatically illustrate the condition of the alleys and streets on which Jim and Mary Strother and thousands of other Black Southern migrants lived throughout Baltimore. One photograph captures a moment in the life of an alley connected to Hughes Street that sat just southwest of the inner harbor, near the current football and baseball stadiums. Butler Alley appears to be a rabbit warren of oddly angular, poorly built wooden structures mixed with small shops. A homemade sign advertises milk, soft drinks, and pig's feet. Two children and a young woman stare casually into the camera. A second image documents a street in the heart of the "Lung Block." While the brick houses are somewhat more substantial in construction, there is still an air of decay. Both images show a lack of basic sanitation, with open water standing on the street.[12]

If the deplorable living conditions of Baltimore's poorest residents shocked the conscience, the attitude of reformers regarding the victims of these conditions should have also caused widespread consternation—but they did not. Despite its scientific veneer, Kemp's report frequently devolved into diatribes about the morals and manners of the neighborhood's residents. While admitting that her work was "not a study of social conditions," she editorialized that it was "impossible to observe these gregarious, light-hearted, shiftless, irresponsible alley dwellers without wondering to what extent their failings are the result of their surroundings, and to what extent the inhabitants in turn react for evil upon their environment." Kemp's report was replete with similar attacks, which in some cases belied her own evidence. Despite admitting that the leaking roofs and wet basements "described might furnish further evidence of the connection existing between phthisis [pulmonary tuberculosis] and wetness of soil," Kemp gratuitously added that "[i]t must also be taken into consideration that most of the inhabitants of the district are negroes who live from the cradle to the grave in colossal ignorance and disregard of every known law of hygiene."[13]

Kemp seemed particularly obsessed with the morality of African Americans, "especially as regards the relation between the sexes." Her distaste for the common-law arrangements of many of the district's residents—and this probably included Jim and Mary Strother—comes through clearly in this diatribe: "Of course union without sanction of law or church occurs frequently among the negro race, and if the relationship is accepted as mutually binding and attains to a fair degree of permanence, it appears to entail no social or religious ban, but to be accepted as a sort of common-law marriage. But the short-lived, irregular and practically promiscuous pairings, which in the districts studied seemed to be more the rule than the exception, fall below the requirements of even this not ideal standard."[14]

In a clear case of cognitive dissonance, Kemp's own observations on her stated subject—housing—belie her moralizing about the Black family. Her study noted that the "great majority" of houses in the Biddle Alley neighborhood were "occupied by but one family"—in fact, "of the 215 houses of the Biddle alley district there were but 11 houses containing three or more families." This mirrored the situation of Jim Strother and his wife Mary, who lived on Walnut Street with extended kin and a musical partner, Eugene Carter. In fact, at the turn of the century Black Americans married and remarried at rates equal to or exceeding those of whites.[15]

What looked to an outsider as a lack of moral fiber and family cohesion was at least partially the result of the reconstituting of Black families due to migration, premature death, and the reality of a long-term reliance on extended and even fictive kinship networks. One of the few things that we know about Mary Strother is that she had had four children and that all had died before her. It is also worth noting that Strother and his fellow residents were only forty-odd years removed from the end of chattel slavery in Maryland and Virginia, a system that had promoted the breaking up of families as a matter of course and never recognized legal marriage between enslaved persons. Yet slavery did not define the Black family after Emancipation as much as new racist structures designed to control Black independence (and especially labor) did.

The reordering of families owing to the loss of relatives was an all-too-familiar occurrence for the Black residents of Baltimore. Crowded into the worst neighborhoods with poor or nonexistent city services, diseases took their toll. Yet despite the censure of welfare agencies that decried their moral failings, Black people formed meaningful and strong extended families providing mutual support. The language used to refer to relatives by the extended Strother family points to the adaptability of kinship that has always been a hallmark of the Black family in America. For example, William Taylor alternately referred to Jim Strother as either his cousin or his uncle in his letters seeking Strother's release from prison. He was actually more remotely related to Strother through his father's mother, but the relationship they established—almost father and son—dictated the more intimate terminology. Official records often obscure these relationships. Sarah Truman and her son Walter are both listed as lodgers in Jim and Mary Strother's household in the 1910 census, but both were in fact relatives of Strother's through marriage.[16]

The deplorable living conditions that Mary and Jim Strother endured on Walnut Street also alarmed Baltimore's Black professional and middle-class residents, who realized that the disorder of the Biddle Alley District threatened perceptions of all Black Baltimoreans. In 1906, a group of Baltimore's African American elite organized the Colored Law and Order League to combat conditions in some of Baltimore's poorest neighborhoods. League members, many of them neighbors of Cab Calloway's family in the Druid Hill Avenue area, viewed these blighted areas as threats to Black claims of respectability and progress. Dr. James H. N. Waring, a physician and principal of Baltimore's Colored High School, authored a League study in 1908 aimed at prompting city leaders to clean up the alley district that sat just below the homes and businesses of Baltimore's Black middle class. (Waring and his family lived in the Druid Hill neighborhood, making their home in a stately brick row house at 509 Mosher Street that still stands today.) Waring was highly qualified for the task. His credentials included degrees from Howard University and the Western University of Pennsylvania (later renamed the University of Pittsburgh) and significant experience as an educator and reformer.[17]

The Colored Law and Order League waged its campaign against the Biddle Alley District at the very moment that white backlash against Black home ownership in previously all-white neighborhoods became a consuming issue in the city. The Biddle Alley District epitomized what Black neighborhoods and Black people meant in the white mind—falling property values, disease, vice, and criminality. Black reformers were well aware of that fact, and they classed Jim Strother and his fellow musicians as part of the problem. After all, who provided the soundtrack—including salacious songs such as "Poontang Little, Poontang Small"—for the "crap shooters" and "dissolute women" who frequented the dives and street corners?[18]

The League's tract approvingly used material from Kemp's earlier study and in some cases echoed her judgments regarding the morals of Jim Strother and his neighbors. Waring quoted Kemp liberally, especially highlighting the vices of the neighborhood's denizens. The League reprinted Kemp's observation that "[f]rom morning to midnight the beer can circulates with a regularity that is almost monotonous" and further that "[g]ambling is also prevalent, and there is reason to believe that the cocaine habit hastens the premature decay of many of these degenerates." Waring characterized the Biddle Alley saloons as "meeting places for the idle, loafing element among the colored people, of the crap shooters, of dissolute women, and many of the saloon keepers did not hesitate to sell liquors to women and children." Despite such characterizations, the League also emphasized that the vast majority of the city's Black population behaved responsibly but were victims of inadequate education, the indifference of the police and city leaders, and even white promotion of vice.[19]

The Colored Law and Order League uneasily balanced these condemnations of "loafing" and "dissolute" Black Baltimoreans with the role that white interests played in the evils of the district—especially the complicity of the all-white police force. The League's researchers noted that the many white saloonkeepers who served the "colored trade" operated the "lowest possible type of saloon," where the "cheapest grades of liquors are dispensed." Such proprietors favored the remoteness of the alleys of the neighborhood where Strother and his neighbors resided. Waring and his associates also noted the complicity of the police force. It was widely known that "in this district detection and conviction seemed nigh on impossible."[20]

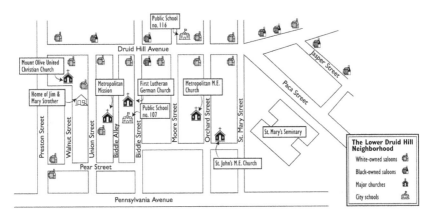

Black and white reformers emphasized the many saloons, run by both Black and white men, that crowded Strother's neighborhood, often near schools and houses of worship. This graphic locates Strother's home, major institutions, and saloons. One author noted that the district held "forty-two saloons, fifteen churches, twelve schools," and the Black YWCA and YMCA. (Adapted by Anna-Maria Crum from "Map Showing the Location of Saloons" in James H. M. Waring, *Work of the Colored Law and Order League, Baltimore, Maryland* [Cheyney, PA, 1908]; Biddle Street District map in *Housing Conditions in Baltimore: Report of a Special Committee* [Baltimore: Federated Charities, 1907]; and Sanborn Fire Insurance Map of Baltimore, Baltimore County, Maryland, 1914, vol. 2, sheet 168)

The League's leaders therefore attempted to control the liquor traffic in the Biddle Alley District, directly petitioning the Board of Liquor License Commissioners in April 1908. The Liquor Dealers' Association marshalled an army of lawyers to defend its interests, while the League relied heavily on the moral authority of Black men of the cloth from a variety of denominations as well as supporting petitions from prominent white leaders, including former mayor Ferdinand C. Latrobe, the Catholic bishop of Maryland, and Baltimore scion and US attorney general Charles J. Bonaparte. Members of the police force made a remarkable claim under interrogation before the commissioners. Not only did they swear that the liquor establishments "were quiet, orderly, and fully complied with every law and regulation," but some rather brazenly asserted that "the churches, and particularly the church on Orchard Street, gave them far more trouble than the saloons." The board of trustees of the Metropolitan Methodist Episcopal Church, the congregation in question, penned a blistering rejoinder to this accusation.[21]

In the face of such heated and contradictory testimony, the Board of Liquor License Commissioners decided to personally inspect the saloons and "dives" of the Biddle Alley District to see the state of things for themselves. It wasn't a pretty picture. According to the *Baltimore American*, board members found them "dirty and unsanitary in some cases; they found card playing going on in others, and white and black people of both sexes mingling and in one instance they found the law violated which prohibits a saloon from having entrance other than on a public highway."[22] Eleven saloons found their doors closed by the end of the day, and the police fell under intense scrutiny for their contradictory, if not mendacious, testimony.

The aspersions that the policemen cast on the neighborhood churches underlined a central reality of Black urban communities. Baltimore's first-in-the-nation racial segregation laws, the resistance of white homeowners, and Black poverty led to the marginalization and ghettoization of Black communities. White supremacy, as inscribed on the landscape, forced all classes of Black people to live and struggle in close proximity. The research of the Colored Law and Order League and the white charities highlighted the consequences of these policies on Jim Strother's neighborhood. Dr. Waring's report noted that the same community bedeviled by saloons, assignation houses, and alley dives also supported "fifteen churches, twelve schools, one home for old people, one home for friendless children,"[23] and the "colored" YMCA and YWCA. According to the League and Waring, this was the heart of the problem. Allowing evils such as drinking and prostitution in such close proximity to beneficial institutions, especially schools, would surely negate the latter's positive moral and spiritual influences. The League's focus on the Sunday closing laws reflected this concern.

Janet Kemp also noted the situation but cast it in cultural and moral terms—the juxtaposition of the sacred and profane, the moral and immoral—as yet another example of Black people's careless, irresponsible, and childlike behavior. Just as Waring did, she described the ubiquity of liquor and its consumption even on the street: "It forms the attractive center of every neighborly group, though its unstinted flow is apt to result in the sudden and violent breaking up of the group which collected to enjoy it." Kemp editorialized that such behavior was not "in any way impairing the social status of the combatants, who are probably found the next day joining with all the fervor of intense religious earnestness in the hymns and prayers of the revival services of the alley churches." Kemp's thinly veiled condescension toward Black behavior betrayed her lack of understanding of how the majority of working-class African Americans viewed their moral and spiritual universe and the strictures of Jim Crow.[24]

The performances of Jim Strother and his fellow street musicianers likewise reflected this seeming contradiction. How could a musician sing of his longing for Heaven and the proper path to get there but also perform material invoking sinful behaviors? How did a songster proclaim that listeners should "keep out the way of the gun-shot devils" but then perform for the dissolute while extolling the virtues of "poontang little, poontang small"? To answer these questions, we must look more deeply into the lived experience and world view of the denizens of the alley districts and the musicians who plied their trade there.

8

Rock Steady, Children

Gonna pull my dress up 'bove my knees,
Gonna give my poontang, who I please,
Oh my baby, somebody sold this thing.
—JAMES LEE STROTHER, "Poontang Little, Poontang Small," recorded 1936

John Lomax wasn't above prompting his informants to sing ribald and bawdy numbers. He once wrote a letter to federal wardens to gain access to their penitentiaries, emphasizing his interest in off-color material. "I am collecting for the Library of Congress the words and tunes of songs and ballads currently and popular among prisoners, or 'made up' by them and passed around by 'word of mouth' rather than by the printed page," he wrote, adding, "I wish to secure copies of them all, no matter how crude or vulgar they may be." While some wardens complied, others strenuously objected to Lomax's request. The warden of the South Carolina State Penitentiary in Columbus, who mistakenly received the letter, retorted that "in your damned letter you asked us to send the Library of Congress all the 'vulgar' songs these men know. What in the hell do you want with dirty songs? And do you think we would violate postal laws to send indecent stuff through the mails?"[1]

Jim Strother's ditty "Poontang Little, Poontang Small" certainly qualified. Of all the songs that Strother selected for Lomax's microphone, this one spoke directly to the illicit side of the Biddle Alley District and its residents as well as the Wharf in his native Culpeper. Not only did it frankly explore the world of prostitution in Baltimore but it also reflected the prominent place that music played in the marginalized world of working-class Black Southerners, urban or rural.

The dance halls, saloons, and "dives" within blocks of his residence on Walnut Street offered Jim Strother another opportunity to earn his daily bread. The rough and rowdy environs of the Biddle Alley District revealed the highly competitive nature of the musicianer's life. One confrontation at a saloon on Union Street, a mere block from Strother's home, is instructive. Bar patron Lewis Brown, who enjoyed "quite a local reputation as a picker of strings," became incensed when another man insinuated that he "could not play the guitar as well as the man who was employed to play in the saloon." After a war of words with his antagonist, Joseph Tilghman, the two squared off, with Tilghman besting Brown. Despite his victory, Tilghman ended up being arrested and surrendered ten dollars and court costs to the northwest district police court.[2]

Boasting, challenges, and exaggeration featured in the ribald songs of saloon and street corner songsters. Frank and sexually explicit songs had a long history among the American working classes, including Black folk. Historical musicologist Roberta Freund Schwartz persuasively argues that the bawdy "hokum blues" that appeared on commercial records in the 1920s and 1930s were not a corruption of earlier blues styles, as many white record collectors and revivalists have insisted, but rather a style rooted in Black folklife that had its own moral code and audience. She could have been describing Jim Strother and his fellow Southern migrants to Baltimore when she stated that "[m]uch to the consternation of the black middle class, many of the new arrivals were hesitant to relinquish the folkways and expressive culture that defined them."[3]

Bawdy material abounded in the rural South and early professional traveling circuits of African American performers. As Howard Odum and Guy Johnson noted in their 1925 *The Negro and His Songs,* "It is to be regretted that a great mass of material cannot be published because of its vulgar and indecent content." They wrote that the "prevailing theme is that of sexual relations" in such songs: "Children of ten or twelve know scores of them, varying in all degrees of suggestiveness." Anyone familiar with early Black folkloric material is well aware of the ubiquity of such material, and of course Jim Strother's repertoire was no exception.[4]

Such material was hardly confined to African American culture. Except for the extremely religious, people of all colors in the rural South or in most American working-class cultures knew bawdy jokes, quips, and songs. Even Americans in the Victorian era enjoyed such taboo material, spawning underground literature and early cylinder recordings that equal the bluest comedians today. Kinney Rorrer, a relative of the great string band musician Charlie Poole, once regaled me with some of the unexpurgated verses of one of Poole's all-time hits, "Take a Drink on Me." Yet few white musicians in Strother's time recorded such lyrics. If they did, it was typically while covering songs from the Black songster repertoire. For example, brothers Austin and Lee Allen recorded a version of the venerable "Salty Dog Blues" in 1927. Austin exclaimed, "I got a gal, she's raised in the sticks / She does her lovin' in a Packard twin six / She ain't nothin' but a salty dog." Black performer Papa Charlie Jackson had recorded his own version three years before.[5]

While Strother played the old minstrel songs, spirituals, and "plantation melodies" for white passersby in Baltimore's markets and commercial districts, his "Poontang Little, Poontang Small" gives us a glimpse of the material that he performed for Black audiences in the heart of Baltimore's alley districts and likely on the rural roads in front of male audiences, white and Black. The song lays bare one aspect of the rough-and-tumble of the Black working class with remarkably frank sexual language but also contains nuances that would have been largely lost on white audiences. In the world of sexually explicit songs emphasizing double entendres, one wry and knowledgeable observer rated the tune as "one-and-a-half entendres." The Library of Congress even marked the catalog card for Strother's song with a Greek delta, "indicating material of an erotic nature"![6]

I had heard a version of the song on several published compilations, but I knew that John Lomax and Harold Spivacke had captured two takes at the prison farm. I searched commercial releases for the other version without success. Was this take simply so scandalous that it was too hot to handle? A provocative thought, though doubtful—if Lucille Bogan's unexpurgated version of "Shave 'Em Dry" had made it to vinyl and CD, surely Strother's tune was not off-limits. As far as I know, this significantly longer take remains unissued. It's a shame. The twenty-two stanza, four-minute recording is more reminiscent of a street performance, with Strother several times imploring his audience to "Rock steady, children." It also contains verses absent from the reissued recording. As always, the staff at the American Folklife Center came through with a digitized copy.[7]

The origins of the term "poontang" are obscure, but its meaning is not. Gershon Legman, one of the first Americans to conduct serious research into sexually explicit and taboo folklore, wrote one of the few scholarly articles on the word. Legman concluded that it was a Creolized version of the French term "putain" (whore). Others have proposed alternate origins, but its usage in the twentieth century is largely agreed upon—and capacious. It has been used to refer to a prostitute, a woman's genitalia, and the act of sex itself. Strother's wordplay encompassed all of these meanings.[8]

Not surprisingly, the term "poontang" appears in Southern literature in the works of Thomas Wolfe and Tennessee Williams. Wolfe gave it a transgressive, racial cast, referring to white men having illicit sexual encounters with Black women. Notably, this white author did not feel the need to explain if the act was consensual. In Jim Strother's South, such acts were often coerced and frequently violent. Two elderly Black people whom I interviewed openly discussed the threat and reality of white-on-Black sexual violence. One described a brutal gang rape near the town of Buena in Culpeper County, where a young woman was left tied to a mail post. Another informant explicitly noted that his mother's family intentionally moved north when the girls in the family reached an age at which they might receive unwanted attention from young white men.[9]

Black usage of the term "poontang" varies widely. There are examples from the African American toasting tradition that associate the term with male sex workers, but these versions are relatively recent. The earliest commercial recording to use the term is by the classic blues singer Clara Smith, who exults, "Oh, oh, Mister Mitchell / I'm crazy about your sweet poontang / Oh, oh, Mister Mitchell / I'll tell the world that it's a wang." She seems to imply a role reversal, with the man supplying the "poontang":[10]

> Miss Lindy Lou, she takes this brand new confection,
> Mr. Mitchell called it sweet poontang;
> And when Miss Lindy Lou with it made good connection,
> This is what she yelled before the gang.
> Oh, oh, Mr. Mitchell, I'm crazy about your sweet poontang.
> Oh, oh, Mr. Mitchell, it's got me going with a bang.
> Your cherry pie is juicy, so is your jelly roll
> But when you give me poontang, I just lose control.
> Oh, oh, Mr. Mitchell, I'm crazy about your sweet poontang.

Strother's song is lyrically and musically far different from Smith's jazz-inflected version. He eschews the banjo for the guitar, a marker of the newer blues styles prevalent in Black music, and gives the song a vigorous ragtime feel. The lyrics to Strother's "Poontang Little, Poontang Small" are not only quite explicit but also among the most difficult of Strother's recordings to decipher. The inferior recording technology and Strother's delivery inhibits the decoding of his words. Here I must thank some of the denizens of traditional music online forums, such as Mudcat and Weenie Campbell, for their valiant attempts to untangle Strother's lyrics. All mistakes here are my own.

First, let's consider Strother's opening stanza:[11]

> Poontang a-little and poontang small
> Poontang stretches like a rubber ball,
> Oh my babe, somebody sold this thing.[12]

Here Strother objectifies the woman by defining her by her "poontang" and implicitly by her ability to satisfy a partner. If the song simply recycled such tropes, it would be uninteresting indeed. Luckily, Strother's narration moves beyond extolling the virtues of "poontang small" to capture other elements of the world of the alley. He next casts a critical eye on the men who solicit her favors:

> Gonna hang my poontang upon the fence
> So the man come and get it ain't got no sense,
> Oh my babe, somebody sold this thing.

Suddenly the singer switches perspective, assuming the voice of the woman who has previously been merely a sexual object. In most songs of sexual desire in the blues and ragtime idiom—and many such songs made it onto field recordings and commercial records—the singer remains in his or her identified gender. Both men and women sang such songs, but rarely did they switch gender perspectives. Lucille Bogan's X-rated version of "Shave 'Em Dry" is sung completely from the woman's perspective; likewise, Bo Carter, infamous for his double-entendre performances, voices a male character for all of his most memorable ditties, such as "Please Warm My Weiner." Even performers who routinely complicated gender roles by dressing in the manner of the opposite sex typically maintained the "voice" of the assumed gender.[13]

Strother's narration switches back and forth between the perspectives of a man and a woman, the hustler and the hustled, although who is doing the hustling becomes somewhat unclear. Gender-bending, he sings,

> Gonna pull my dress up 'bove my knees
> Gonna give my poontang, who I please,
> Oh my baby, somebody sold this thing.

> Gonna pull my dress up to my thighs
> I'm gonna give my poontang exercise,
> Oh my babe, somebody sold this thing.

This is no song of male boasting or domination. Here the woman claims her freedom to do as she pleases with her body. Although somewhat more graphic, it echoes songs such as Ida Cox's "Wild Women Don't Have the Blues" in its assertion of female sexual freedom. Later in the song, the female persona asserts the right not only to have both a husband and an outside man but also to choose, at her discretion, whoever can satisfy her.

> My man has gone, couldn't do me once,
> I'm gonna *dup* my husband 'til my man comes,
> Oh my babe, somebody sold this thing.

These stanzas stand in striking relief to Strother's commentary on two-timing, duplicitous women in his songs "Going to Richmond" and "Daddy, Where You Been So Long." These songs assume the more traditional male viewpoint of blues narratives—a man done wrong by a cheating woman. One other moment in "Poontang Little, Poontang Small" stands out as one of the few moments of unrestrained levity in Strother's recorded songs. He audibly chuckles—cracking himself up after this verse:

> Got a humpback livers and kidney feet
> —*his shackles* on a streetcar seat, [chuckles]
> Oh my babe, somebody sold this thing.

While Strother delivered comedic lines in songs such as "Tennessee Dog" with energy and brio, this is the only moment in his recorded repertoire where he genuinely seems amused—tickled by his own music. It stands in stark contrast to some of his darker moments, when the ring of his banjo and the sinister words of his songs create strong cultural and musical tension.

The female persona singing in "Poontang Little, Poontang Small" could easily have been one of the many Black sex workers who labored in the Biddle Alley District. The police allowed the trade to flourish there just as they tolerated the saloons, dives, and dance halls. Baltimore cops and the city fathers chose neighborhood containment and haphazard enforcement rather than an all-out war on vice. Those arrested were largely Black and poor and received longer sentences than their white counterparts. Strother also worked the streets and knew the sting of being "moved along" by a beat cop. His gender-bending proclamation of a woman's sexual freedom seems a fitting tribute to the women with whom he shared Baltimore's alley districts.[14]

Indeed, of all of Strother's recorded songs, "Poontang Little, Poontang Small" is the most invested in the life of working-class Black people. Strother invokes a Black folk practice—hoodoo—in an obvious sign that this song is meant for his own community. He relates the woman's use of a "lucky hand" to apparently coerce a public worker (and in Baltimore at the time, such workers were all white men).

> Oh I b'lieve to my soul she had a lucky hand
> 'Cause she said to give her thanks [*thing?*] to the streetcar man,
> Oh my babe, somebody sold this thing.

This verse evokes the role of Southern Black folkways in the migrant city. A "lucky hand" is mentioned by many blues artists as a familiar element in hoodoo conjuring. Perhaps she had placed some "lucky oil on [her] hand" (as in Rosetta Howard's "When I Been Drinking") to get the desired result. Or she may have placed a lucky hand root—the long, hand-shaped root of several species of orchids—in her mojo bag for good luck in love, gambling, or another purpose. Whatever she got from the streetcar man, her use of hoodoo rooted in African and African American cultural traditions did the trick.

The practice of hoodoo, root work, and conjuring remained widespread in the South and in the cities inhabited by Black migrants well into the twentieth century. One of the most prominent of Baltimore's street vendors used his knowledge of potions and conjuring to keep his stable of horses healthy and strong. The community recognized his special skills with ad-miration and some apprehension. Strother's musical partner at the Virginia State Prison Farm, Joseph Lynn Lee, was himself a local conjure doctor and root worker in the area around Danville, Virginia. No doubt many migrants reinvented themselves to fit into the more sophisticated ways of the city, but many retained their Black folkways. Nor did most residents see these folk beliefs as contradicting their religious practices. This acceptance of folk practices and down-home culture extended to embracing frank talk about worldly things.[15]

Music with suggestive and playful sexual lyrics was part of a vibrant street life in Baltimore. Black performers and their working-class audiences "[n]ot only claiming but also actively exaggerating such [sexual] imagery served as a reminder to the black bourgeoisie that sexual expression was an important component of African American self-identity and culture." Black author Ralph Ellison commented that "sex means far more than poontang, but the good life, cunning, the wholeness of being colored, the beauty of it, as well as the anguish, and the deep capacity of [a person] to stand for, to symbolize it all." Similarly, Black theologian James H. Cone asserted the naturalness and spirituality of Black sexuality in the face of modern West-ern bourgeois notions of religion and respectability. After quoting the rib-ald lines of the blues song "Peach Orchard Mama," Cone asked, "What are we to make of such blatant descriptions of sexual love? Theologically, the blues reject the Greek distinction between the soul and the body, the physical and the spiritual. They tell us there is no wholeness without sex, no authentic love without the feel and touch of the physical body. The blues affirm the authenticity of sex as the bodily expression of Black soul."[16]

Musician Dom Flemons sees another aspect of the most explicit songs—as a reaction against the hypersexualization of Blackness by whites. "In a world where Black people are seen as subhuman . . . underneath the mainstream of social life, there is a certain expectation that most Black people just have explicit thoughts and only think about dirty things," he muses. "So there is a certain aspect of Black humor that plays to the super explicit things—not just slightly explicit but the fact that you can go as far explicit as you possibly can. That is part of the art." From "Shave 'Em Dry" to "WAP," Black artists have reveled in transgressive assertions of their sex-uality.[17]

Black and white reformers both associated certain styles of Black mu-sic and dance, especially jazz and blues, with vice and unbridled sexuality.

The Colored Law and Order League reported that Strother's neighborhood "was honeycombed with gambling dens, known not only to the initiated, but carrying on unblushingly a business that was known to the citizens if not the police. There were numerous dance houses, clubs and billiard halls, which were in actual practice only assignation places for girls and young women, and to which many of them owed their downfall." They described the unsavory situation in one of the Biddle Alley District's saloons where, "in addition to the bar, a dance hall was run by the proprietor. Nightly orgies of half-drunken men and women made this neighborhood particularly objectionable to surrounding residents."[18]

Even some of Baltimore's Black musicians made the association between music, moral turpitude, and class. Thomas Henderson Kerr, an Eastern Shore native, led a popular Baltimore dance orchestra; he performed and composed ragtime numbers, tunes from musicals, and popular songs. He strongly objected to the music popular with the lower classes. In an interview with a reporter for the *Baltimore Sun*, Kerr emphasized that his band played respectable places, and he added, "No Jazz. I never did like that jumpy kind of stuff. I like society kind of music, not the kind the riff-raff would enjoy." It's not hard to imagine what his reaction to Strother's repertoire would have been.[19]

Class divisions regarding music manifested themselves in other Southern cities, too. In Durham, North Carolina, working-class Black residents "warmly recalled street singers," but those aspiring to middle-class status preferred the sophisticated sounds of bands such as Duke Ellington and Cab Calloway. Helen Jackson Lee, a resident of Jackson Ward in Richmond, recalled the neighborhood music she enjoyed as a child from her room's window. Queenie Ross, "a frail-looking, yellow-skinned hunchback," banged out ragtime tunes on the piano at the corner saloon. Queenie sometimes competed with the powerful sounds of a "Holy Rollers" storefront church in the next block, where congregants "shouted, stomped their feet, clapped hands, rang cowbells, and banged tambourines." Her Methodist mother disapproved of both Queenie, a "loose woman" fond of makeup and whiskey, and the Pentecostals' behavior—and their music, because it "wasn't cultured."[20]

Lee's parents aspired to respectability, although "race records" were allowed in the home. "Most of the race songs in fact had sexy words, and a lot of Negroes didn't allow them to be played in their homes," she recalled. "They felt it demeaned their racial pride to listen to the coonshouters sing about long, tall, seal-skin browns making a preacher lay his Bible down, and praying for the lights to go out in the church so they could roll on the floor together." Yet this impulse toward respectability clearly did not apply to working-class Black men and women who largely ignored the niceties that failed to describe their lived experience.[21]

Yet another apt example of the reaction of the Black middle class to the realities of working-class Black life occurred with the publication of Langston Hughes's poetry compilation *Fine Clothes to the Jew*. Hughes's work drew heavily from the folk culture of African Americans without judgment about its language, themes, and attitudes. Yet the editors of the most prominent Black newspapers savaged Hughes for casting an unfavorable light on "the Race."[22]

While "good Christian people" and the "talented tenth" might have looked askance at Jim Strother's scandalous material and his easy combining of sacred and secular material, such a view was outside the mainstream of Black folk thought. Many Black authors argue that African Americans held a holistic approach to life that did not recognize arbitrary boundaries between the worldly and spiritual. Theologian James H. Cone and music scholar Jon Michael Spencer are but two examples. Spencer specifically dismisses the "devil at the crossroads" myth that promotes a blues versus sacred dichotomy. Strother's Black audience understood a spiritual world that encompassed the blues, balladry, hymnody, and much more.[23]

Virginia street singer Calvin "Big Boy" Davis seamlessly bridged the world's secular and spiritual sides in his recordings for Hampton Institute (now University) professor Roscoe Lewis as part of the highly successful *Negro in Virginia* project. Lewis likely found out about Davis from Black author Sterling Brown, who worked with Lewis's brother at Howard University and also edited African American content for the Federal Writers' Project. Brown immortalized Davis in "The Odyssey of Big Boy," published in 1927 in his first poetry collection, *Southern Road*. Brown's students at Virginia Theological Seminary and College (now Virginia University of Lynchburg) had brought Davis to Brown's attention in 1927.[24]

"Big Boy"—otherwise unidentified in the cataloging—recorded several songs for Lewis as part of the Virginia project, and the discs were later transferred to the Library of Congress. Music researchers puzzled over his identity, and some even speculated that Strother was the mysterious Big Boy. While the documentary and aural evidence contradict this guesswork, there are obvious similarities between their experiences. Both men had been injured in industrial accidents (Davis in a West Virginia mine), both took to the road as itinerant musicians, and both were natives of Virginia.[25]

Davis's powerful rendition of a sacred song inspired Brown's poem "When de Saints Go Maching Home." Later, Roscoe Lewis preserved the song for posterity on the recording machine he had borrowed from the Library of Congress. Brown poignantly describes Big Boy's profound connection to his listeners as he weaves together a holistic worldview integrating the secular and the sacred through a shared lived experience:

> He'd play, after the bawdy songs and blues,
> after the weary plaints
> Of "Trouble, Trouble deep down in muh soul,"
> Always one song in which he'd lose the role
> Of entertainer to the boys. He'd say,
> "My mother's favorite." And we knew
> That what was coming was his chant of saints,
> "When de saints go machin' home . . ."
> And that would end his concert for the day.[26]

Davis performed another song for Lewis that similarly elided the boundaries between the secular and sacred. First released under the uninspired title "Blues," Davis's song tells of his attempt to catch a freight train. Davis mimics the train's whistle and bell, deploying his metal slide across the strings of his guitar in one of the street singer's favorite tunings— "Vestapol," pitched to an open D chord. Davis first discovers that the conductor is a "religious man," so he delivers an inspired version of "Nearer My God to Thee." Davis next encounters the brakeman, who is "a bluesman." Without breaking the stride of his muscular and insistent alternating bass line, Davis sings, "I'm standing here wondering will a matchbox hold my clothes / For I haven't got many, got so far to go." A Black listener would easily recognize this stanza, a classic blues trope employed by many performers, such as Georgia's Ma Rainey, Texas's Blind Lemon Jefferson, and South Carolina's Willie Walker. Davis's use of the slide guitar technique to expound on the traveling/train theme can also be heard in numerous commercially recorded blues, including Blind Willie McTell's "Travelin' Blues" and Booker T. Washington "Bukka" White's "Panama Limited."[27]

Like Calvin Davis, Jim Strother did what Black songsters had always done—weave a wide range of folk and popular source material into a com-

plex, fresh composition. One last example from "Poontang Little, Poontang Small" reveals the tangled web of influences that Strother recast in this
provocative song:

> Oh wire, brier, limber, lock
> How many geese is in our flock?
> Oh, my baby, somebody sold this thing.
>
> Oh, one flew east and a-one flew west
> One flew over in the cuckoo's nest,
> Oh my babe, somebody sold this thing.

In the context of the song, the "geese" might well be interpreted as sexual
partners in the woman's "flock." The second stanza then implies a somewhat nomadic clientele. Strother here signified to his fellow countrymen
and -women through the salacious use of a common children's counting-
game rhyme. What they may not have known is that the rhyme originated
in the British Isles and became ubiquitous in the United States and Canada
by the early 1800s. It entered the lexicon of Black Southerners in an ironic
way. Several formerly enslaved African Americans recalled learning the
rhyme and game from their enslavers' children.[28]

Jack Maddox, who had been born enslaved in Georgia but was then
taken to Texas, recounted the rhyme under its traditional name "William
Tremble Toe":[29]

> William, William Tremble Toe,
> He's a good fisherman . . .
> Wire, brier,
> Limber, lock
> Three geese in our flock;
> One flew east,
> One flew west,
> One flew over in the cuckoo's nest.

White and Black children often played together and exchanged such
rhymes. Dink Walton Young was one of several hundred people enslaved
by Major Jack Walton in Talbot County, Georgia. She played with the Walton children, "often joining and playing with them in such games as 'Mollie

Bright,' 'William Trembletoe,' and 'Picking Up Sticks.'" Young's patron-
izing interviewer related that "until the white boys and girls were ten or
twelve years of age, their little Negro playmates, acolytes, valet de cham-
bres, bodyguards, and servants usually addressed them rather familiarly
by their first names, or applied to them nicknames that amounted to titles
of endearment." The author then acknowledged that "when the children
became of age, this form of familiarity between slave and White was termi-
nated," with little reflection on what that experience would have been like
for Black children.[30]

"Wire, brier, limber, lock" frequently turns up in collections of Black and
white folklore from the American South. In fact, it was collected by ballad hunter John Stone for the Virginia Folklore Society in Strother's home
county of Culpeper while Jim was still entertaining at the local dance halls.
Bruce Stringfellow performed the ditty for Stone in 1934, recounting that he
had sung the rhyme as a child. A fifty-five-year-old white insurance agent,
he was roughly the same age as Jim Strother.[31]

Thus are the often convoluted and sometimes perverse transformations
of folk culture and expression. Toasts, play party songs, children's rhymes,
vernacular sayings, and much more flowed in and out of folk and popular
usage, gaining an accretion of meanings. Jim Strother and his fellow musicians deployed them in clever and ironic ways, always with an eye on their
audience. In this case, a child's rhyme became fodder for the medicine show
or the street corner.

9

The Medicine Show

WANTED: GOOD BANJO PLAYER *Must sing strong. Balls for Open Air, Medicine Man. Work all summer. Call this address:* 1036 PENNA. AVE. RED. SYN. MED. CO.

—Advertisement in the *Baltimore Afro-American*, June 3, 1921

It's tempting to imagine Jim Strother wending his way the few blocks from his Baltimore home to the Red Syns Indian Medicine Company's offices and offering his services. Mary Richardson, the proprietor, might have requested an impromptu audition. Strother, banjo at the ready, likely would have performed his signature showstopper, "Tennessee Dog," which found its way onto the metal discs at the Library of Congress. But the truth is that numerous hawkers of cure-alls combed the ranks of the city's musicians anxious to find a performer of Strother's caliber. Baltimore had a thriving industry in "patent and proprietary medicines," boasting around one hundred such companies when Jim Strother arrived in the city. These firms manufactured and peddled ointments, bitters, syrups, and pills containing various roots, herbs, and often alcohol. Not all took their shows on the road—but some, like the Red Syns Indian Medicine Company, did. Whatever the case, Richardson's advertisement, placed in a major African American newspaper, succinctly outlined the requirements for an American medicine-show performer: instrumental prowess, a voice that could be heard for blocks, and the toughness to endure heat, rain, and whatever else Mother Nature threw at you.[1]

It was on the medicine-show stage that James Lee "Jim" Strother transformed himself into "Blind Jimmie Strother." Borrowing heavily from minstrelsy and other forms of American popular culture, the shows highlighted America's addiction to patent medicines advertised in newspapers and songbooks. Minstrel tunes and comedic skits continued to be staples of the medicine-show stage, and "blacking up"—performing in blackface—was a common convention. Strother's rural Virginia background gave him access to a variety of songs rooted in earlier Black musical traditions that flowed into his performances in traveling shows. Songs from the older fiddle and banjo traditions, such as his "Thought I Heard My Banjo Say," were the kind of lively numbers that could attract a street-corner crowd in small Southern towns or even in the cities to which so many Americans had migrated. Religious songs—or parodies thereof—might be employed to good effect, too.

When singing clever, evocative tunes such as "Tennessee Dog," Strother played the role of musicianer, trickster, and popular entertainer. His job was not just to entertain but to *sell*. Crowds of men, women, and children of both races gathered on the streets and corner lots to hear him. Jim Strother's jaunty banjo and wordplay could excite and amuse children while provoking knowing smiles from worldly men—and allow white audiences to indulge in racial fantasies about happy-go-lucky Black people while Black men and women heard other messages about the realities and dangers of the world. There was much complexity lying beneath the minstrel veneer.

Strother's specific wanderings in his early adulthood, and the circumstances of his eventual migration to Maryland and Baltimore, are largely lost to history. The cryptic stories associated with these years of his life come largely from the work of folklorists John and Alan Lomax and Benjamin Botkin. These men established Strother's background as an itinerant musician familiar with the medicine show and the life of the street. Botkin wrote that "Blind Jimmie Strothers [*sic*] learned his hearty minstrel style of gospel-singing while traveling with a medicine show. Joe Lee sings jubilee songs in truly spiritual fashion. Both have considerable showmanship." Botkin's contrast of Strother's style with that of fellow inmate Joe Lynn Lee is a striking nod to notions of authenticity, a prime preoccupation of folklorists.[2]

Charlatans had pitched cure-alls and nostrums in America for hundreds of years, but the heyday of the traveling medicine show coincided with Jim Strother's youth. The largest and most famous medicine shows had elaborate setups. The Kickapoo Indian Medicine Company and Hamlin's Wizard Oil Company were two of the largest, traveling across America in the late nineteenth century. Providing entertainment to lure the masses was key to the show's success, and the offerings ranged widely. Curious onlookers witnessed magic acts, acrobats, ersatz cowboys and Indians, comedic patter, and always music. The major shows also sometimes featured large instrumental ensembles such as brass bands.[3]

By the turn of the twentieth century, these elaborate medicine extravaganzas had begun to die out. The large traveling tent shows had to some degree displaced them. Among these large revues were Silas Green from New Orleans and Wolcott's Rabbit's Foot Minstrels, companies featuring comedy and minstrel sketches and incorporating some of the earliest female blues divas. The medicine show of Jim Strother's era was largely regional and smaller, occupying street corners, fairgrounds, and local halls in rural communities and small towns. Evidence suggests that small circuits still thrived primarily in the American South.[4]

The medicine show was a staple of the mid-Atlantic region that Strother inhabited. One western Maryland newspaperman marveled at the ability of the Clifton Remedy Company's traveling show to extract "a considerable amount of money from the people of Emmitsburg [Maryland]." He continued: "It cannot be said that Emmitsburg is lacking in physicians and drug stores, and this makes it hard to understand why people of intelligence will at times be led into the error of ignoring the local doctor or druggist in favor of strange decoctions which are sold by 'Vaudeville performers' to the accompaniment of so-called 'popular song' and questionable jokes." While elites looked down on the shows, local people still flocked to them. If newspapers of the period are to be believed, sales were brisk. In Seaford, Delaware, a fire broke out at the local opera house packed with "nearly 600 people" attending a medicine show. Luckily, quick thinking by the stage manager averted a disaster.[5]

Herman Miller, a longtime resident of Cumberland, Maryland, and an amateur historian, vividly described the visit of such shows to his hometown in the western Maryland mountains. Miller recounted street-corner hustlers selling cures for corns and bunions, tent shows that set up their small stage and wares in vacant lots, and "one of the most colorful of all sellers of cure-alls . . . a snake oil dealer" who rented a downtown room. Holding a few defanged rattlesnakes aloft and draping them around his neck, the "Doctor" would assure the audience that the concoction would "cure everything from toothache to the common cold, bruises, sprains, skin diseases, and other ailments"—all at a mere dollar a bottle.[6]

Ben Shahn took a series of photographs of a medicine show in Huntington, Tennessee, in October 1935. While he did not capture musicians, Shahn documents key elements of a typical medicine show in its last days: the street-front, open-air setting; the pitchman making his appeal; a Black man in blackface (perhaps a comedian); and an "Indian" ready to testify to the remedy's healing powers. One wonders what the two Black men in the foreground are thinking as they stare back at the camera. (Ben Shahn, photographer, United States Resettlement Administration; Farm Security Administration—Office of War Information Photograph Collection, Library of Congress, Washington, DC)

Music was essential to the medicine show's appeal. Miller recounted that most of the shows that passed through his western Maryland town "had Black musicians and entertainers." The medicine show inherited the legacy of small traveling circuses, tent shows, and even vaudeville, all of which drew on the jokes, music, dance, and performance styles of blackface minstrelsy. Countless country, blues, and jazz performers cut their teeth in such shows—artists as varied as eastern Tennessee mountain singer Clarence "Tom" Ashley, Piedmont South Carolina songster and bluesman Pink Anderson, and even Baltimore native and stride piano master Eubie Blake. The young Blake took various musical jobs in his native Baltimore, including performing with a street-corner vocal quartet, tickling the ivories at one of Baltimore's most popular bordellos, and "playing melodeon and buck dancing in a medicine show throughout Maryland and Pennsylvania." He didn't last long in "Dr. Frazier's Medicine Show," however; after not being paid for engagements in neighboring Pennsylvania, he and a few friends made their way back to Baltimore.[7]

In the confines of Strother's Baltimore, such entertainments persisted. Ralph Matthews, a "wandering reporter" for the *Baltimore Afro-American*, observed both the familiar and rapidly changing elements of the city in 1927. He recounted a familiar sign of spring as residents removed snow guards from the marble steps of the city's iconic rowhouses. A realtor's sign on Woodyear Street lured clients by announcing "Buy here, this block is 100% white," jarring testimony to the ongoing process of neighborhood blockbusting and segregation. Another sign of change came in the form of a radio installed in Matthews's favorite barbershop on Dolphin Street, allowing patrons to "wait to jazz or waltz time." Yet another musical element evoked a not-quite-bygone era, made the more unusual by its location on the main entertainment drag of Black Baltimore, literally blocks from Strother's stomping grounds. Matthews wrote, "A medicine show is packing them in on Pennsylvania Avenue . . . same old stuff, a couple of blackface comedians with banjos, a barker and the usual crowd who buy patent medicines."[8]

A second example of city residents' enduring taste for impromptu sidewalk amusements was provided by Baltimore's Red Syns Indian Medicine Company, the firm that advertised for a banjo player in the *Afro-American*. The company's headquarters stood in the 1000 block of Pennsylvania Avenue, just a few streets from Strother's home in the majority-Black Seventeenth Ward. Proprietor Charles H. Richardson, a native of South Carolina, had arrived in the city sometime in the late nineteenth century. He seemed to have had considerable skills at selling but also a propensity for getting into trouble with the law. In 1903, Richardson appeared in the southern district police court on the charge of conducting a Punch and Judy show on Light Street without a license. The crowd of men and boys attending the street performance "cheered wildly" when two policemen placed Richardson in handcuffs and threw him in the patrol wagon, thinking that his arrest was part of the act. He argued that he had been conducting such entertainments for eight years without a license, but Richardson's ignorance of the law did not sway the judge.[9]

Richardson apparently learned his lesson. Two years later he received a permit for a tent at Monroe Street near Christian Street. But a far more serious charge leveled against him in 1906 sent him to the state penitentiary. He had been convicted of bigamy. The newspapers speculated that he had not just two but three wives. Richardson appealed all the way to the state's supreme court, but his conviction was affirmed. Yet all must have been forgiven—or brushed over—because he, his wife Mary, and several children lived together at the company's headquarters on Pennsylvania Avenue in 1910. Mary began managing the company after her husband's death a few years later, and it was she who placed the advertisement for a "banjo player" in the *Afro-American*.[10]

While medicine shows still amused crowds in larger towns and even cities into the early twentieth century, performers increasingly trod the old turnpikes and remote country roads. Assuming that Jim Strother used central Virginia and Baltimore as his base of operations during his time as a medicine-show performer, we can easily document a range of shows traveling the region through newspaper accounts. The Alfareta Indian Medicine Show appeared in Long Green Valley, Maryland, northeast of Baltimore in 1902; Dr. Spangler's Indian Medicine Show played to full houses in Middletown, Maryland, and was reported to be on its way to Burkittsville, also in Washington County, for a week's engagement in 1899; and the Wells' Medicine Show announced its arrival in Monterey, Virginia, in 1917 with a notice in the *Highland Recorder*, complete with testimonials from local residents.[11]

Strother's medicine-show background shines through in several songs in his repertoire. The most distinctive and best known today, "Tennessee Dog," would become a favorite performance piece for musician and folklorist Mike Seeger. Strother's song about a ravenous canine is both a bit of doggerel and an exercise in clever wordplay. Strother banjo struts as he sings in rapid-fire fashion:

> Anybody here want to buy a little dog?
> Come right here I'll sell you.
> Ain't no catfish, ain't no hog,
> And I'm right here to tell you.
>
> *Chorus:* That dog, talking about that dog.
> Oh his head is long, his ears is flat,
> He never stops eatin' 'til he balls that jack.
> That dog [*spoken:* "Lay down there, I tell you"], mean little dog,
> He's the meanest dog that come from Tennessee. [*Repeated after each verse*]

Now he can eat more meat than any butcher dog,
Eats steaks, pork chop, and liver.
He catch more rats than any other cat,
On this side the Mississippi River.

Does anybody here want to buy a little dog?
I'm right here to sell you.
Ain't no catfish, ain't no hog,
And I'm right here to tell you.

I say come here to me Tabby
Balls right up and shivers,
He catch more rats than any other cat,
On this side the Mississippi River.[12]

Strother's stylized, rolled "r" on the word "river" and his syncopated, ragged-out banjo give away the flamboyant stage origins of his voracious dog. His duple and triple syncopations provide a different energy and drive to the tune. The connection of such a song to the four-string banjo is obvious and likely reflects Strother's observations of traveling-show musicians who integrated ragtime and early jazz styles into their performances. Full of absurdist humor, animal tropes, and sly innuendo, "Tennessee Dog" was a sure showstopper.[13]

Strother proclaimed that "ballin' the jack" was the only thing that satisfied the appetite of his hungry canine, and it's a wonderful bit of wordplay that's worth exploring in detail. The phrase had an accretion of meanings that evoked a panoply of possible associations for the listener. The railroad men who worked the tracks snaking northward from Strother's birthplace toward his adopted home in Baltimore "balled the jack" as they set their locomotives in rapid motion. In its simplest usage, the "high ball"—typically a large, colored ball suspended high above the ground—signaled the engineer that the line ahead was clear. He then throttled up his locomotive (the "jack") and "let his drivers roll" to his next station. This trope suggests that the Tennessee Dog "never stopped eating" until signaled (or forced) to roll on to his next destination, certainly an appropriate allusion for a man constantly on the road.

Strother and his audiences also understood an added, even more dominant, meaning. Brave (or foolhardy) engineers expressed their obsession with timetables and speed by driving their iron horses to the brink. A guide to railroading slang explained that "ball the jack" meant to "work an engine hard." A frustrated railroad man bemoaned yet another task added to his colleague's run, "right when he has to get to ball the jack on his other duties, but still *everything* has to be done, and right then." Yet another engineer was told that thirty minutes had been put down on his delay sheet, and he should "just ball the jack as fast as you can." Thus "balling the jack" could mean moving fast and energetically—at "full throttle." Perhaps the Tennessee Dog wasn't leaving after all; maybe he only stopped "eating" when he fell down from exhaustion![14]

This popular meaning is reflected in a musical song-and-dance craze that exploded into the American popular imagination in 1913. Lyricist James Henry "Jim" Burris and composer Christopher M. "Chris" Smith set an African American dance called "Ballin' the Jack" to sheet music, causing the kind of major musical sensation that seemingly always ensues when white Americans "discover" a previously "unknown" (to them) art form. Already setting bodies in rapid motion in Harlem (and likely across the country) before its publication, the sheet music spawned hundreds of ragtime, popular, and jazz recordings. The song and dance appeared in a Black musical production called *Darktown Follies* at the Lafayette Theater in Harlem. Impressed, Florenz Ziegfeld of the eponymous Follies bought the rights to several numbers and integrated them into the show's 1913 season to great fanfare. The song also set the traveling tent show circuit on fire. Black newspapers attested to its popularity in the 1914 and 1915 seasons. In just one example, eager West Virginia audiences called for multiple encores of the song from "female impersonator" and comedian Leroy Knox of Wolcott's Rabbit's Foot Minstrels.[15]

Smith and Burris knew both their source material and the publishing world well. Smith was a Black medicine show and vaudeville veteran from South Carolina, and he collaborated with a number of other noted songwriters and performers, including Richard Cecil McPherson (known professionally as Cecil Mack) and stride piano pioneer Charles Luckyth "Luckey" Roberts. Both he and Jim Burris wrote for the great Black vaudevillian Bert Williams. There is little doubt that both men knew this dance long before they committed it to sheet music. Tennessean Burris cleverly integrated the dance's movements into his lyrics, promising to "show this little dance" to his audience. The knee-swaying, body "twists," and arm gesticulations described by the lyricist called forth movements commonly found in Black folk dance. Burris even name-checked another well-known dance, the "Eagle Rock." Lead Belly waxed "Eagle Rock Rag" at his 1944 Capitol recording session, and Georgia bluesman Blind Willie McTell invoked the Eagle Rock in his spirited "Georgia Rag," itself a cover of Blind Blake's "Wabash Rag." There are many other examples by blues, ragtime, and jazz musicians.[16]

The association of such dances with sexual movements created yet another layer of meaning for Strother's audience. The deep current of double entendre embedded in secular Black song, especially blues, gave alternate meanings to expressions such as "ballin' the jack." In a recording studio in New York City in 1926, Bessie Smith sang:[17]

> He can be ugly, he can be black,
> So long as he can eagle rock and ball the jack;
> I want to be somebody's baby doll so I can get my lovin' all the time,
> I mean to get my lovin' all the time.

Black Americans had recognized the sexual connotations of this expression long before Bessie Smith intoned these words in 1926. The editors of the *Indianapolis Freeman,* one of America's most prominent African American newspapers, commended a dancer for not succumbing to her audience's "repeated calls" to "Ball the jack!" "Put it over, kid!" "Let us have it." The editors of the *Freeman* archly echoed the Black bourgeoisie's rejection of such material, insisting that "we want no more *'Balling the Jack'* or any other vulgar contortions." Black audiences begged to differ, however. The clever, playful, and openly sensual nature of this dance song sprang from a rich Black culture comfortable with adroit and evocative expressions of everyday life.[18]

Like many tent and medicine-show tunes, "Tennessee Dog" and its associated imagery moved silently and easily between the musical world of the popular stage, song sheets, and 78-rpm recordings and the local milieus of the alley "dive," house party, and street corner. Even the songs of rural children reflected these tunes' endurance and ubiquity, right down to their salacious content. The editor of the *Kentucky Folklore Record* recorded "a tuneful little ditty collected from an eleven-year-old Negro girl" in 1964 that clearly mirrors some of Strother's lyrics:

Does anybody here want to buy a little dog?
I've got one to sellum.
If you don't believe it's a he or a she,
Pull up his tail and smellum.
My little dog is a good little dog,
Eats beefsteak and liver.
Kills more rats than a thousand cats
From here to the Mississippi River.[19]

The trickster humor, clever innuendo, and absurdist imagery of the medicine-show musician allows those of us at a distance of time, place, and race to imagine a carefree musical world sanitized by the grinning, burnt-cork mask. The truth is that Jim Strother's comedic songs disguised the underlying reality of violence and exploitation that all Black people faced when traveling in the segregated South—or living in a segregated city like Baltimore. Exposure to mortal danger was very real while traveling the back roads of rural America. With a medicine or minstrel show there may have been some limited safety in numbers, but that was not guaranteed. The self-proclaimed "Father of the Blues," W. C. Handy, recounted harrowing tales of violence while traveling with minstrel tent shows across the segregated South. In one case, angry locals literally fired into the passenger cars carrying his troupe; in another, a mob beat and lynched a fellow musician for defending his girlfriend from abusive whites. We can only imagine the stark terror of a lone musician traveling into the wrong town or crossing the wrong track.[20]

No doubt Strother and his fellow itinerant performers shared stories of sundown towns, locales where Black people risked their lives if they stayed after the setting of the sun. Before the advent of printed guides such as the *Negro Motorist Green-Book*, such knowledge was part of the necessary folklore that was passed from person to person to keep Black travelers safe. I have personally heard the stories about "sundown" towns and entire counties in Virginia, especially in the Appalachian region, where African Americans put their lives in danger after sunset. Yet Strother's references to these realities in song, such as "Don't let sundown catch you here" in his "Thought I Heard My Banjo Say," seem relatively unusual among musicians of his era. These may have been songs that most Black performers would not entrust to a white folklorist or commercial record company.[21]

The spirited ring of Strother's banjo could not hide his haunted vision of these dangers. He paints a dark picture of his life in "Thought I Heard My Banjo Say," evoking none of the fun and wit of the standard renditions collected by ballad hunters or inscribed on early 78-rpm records by white songsters. While these artists enthusiastically sang about going to Cripple Creek "to have some fun," seeing their gals, and drinking moonshine liquor, Strother's lyrics evoked a vision of a violent and threatening landscape strangely set against the sprightly gait of this traditional banjo piece.[22]

White musicians rarely mentioned leaving Cripple Creek; Strother always coupled going and leaving, and he comments in the song on the transitory life of the itinerant musician:

> Goin' to Cripple Creek, goin' to town,
> Leave Cripple Creek, goin' to roam.

Strother later states that his exit isn't simply wanderlust. Singing "gonna leave this town for times getting' hard," the musician intimates that taking to the road is not voluntary. Then the itinerant songster leaves no doubt about the reason he must move on. While transcribing the words to this song, I was at first stunned at the directness of his lyrics:

> Thought I heard my banjo say
> . . . my banjo sound
> Goin' to Cripple Creek,
> Leaving Cripple Creek.
> Read and run, nigger, read and run,
> Drinking whiskey, drinking beer,
> Don't let sundown catch you here.

No African American would have been surprised at these sentiments. Far from the carefree place of drinking and socializing celebrated by white performers, Strother's "Cripple Creek" is a threatening place where "shootin' off heads" was a commonplace. Strother's song contains two expressions found on signs posted at the outskirts of so-called sundown towns— "Don't let sundown catch you here," preceded by a racial epithet—that many older African Americans remembered. An elderly resident of Garret County, a mountainous area in the far western end of Maryland, recalled a less common expression that makes Strother's lyrics even clearer. He related the story of a jazz musician almost lynched in 1960 in the town of Oakland and his father's comments on the sundown town and its residents:

> Mr. Les [Clifford] was "up Oakland," a town full of crackers and red-necks, if ever there was one, located on Deep Creek Lake, 25 or so miles from Piedmont. They hated niggers up Oakland . . . NIGGERS READ AND RUN, Daddy claimed a sign there said. AND IF YOU CAN'T READ, RUN ANYWAY.[23]

Itinerant musicians had to be especially attuned to these dangers. Howard Armstrong, better known as "Louie Bluie," the famed African American string band performer, openly discussed the trials of performing in the lumber and coal camps of the mountains as a Black man. A veteran of street performing and medicine shows, he told the tale of traveling with Carl Martin, himself born in Big Stone Gap in the southwest Virginia coalfields. The duo asked a depot master how far their available funds would take them north. He sold them tickets and the duo ended up in a small mining town. Armstrong told Martin, "Carl, this looks mighty . . . I don't feel right here." Martin either didn't sense the danger or was hungry enough to try his luck; he convinced Armstrong that good money might be had busking. Armstrong's instincts proved correct. As he put it, "It was a town where they don't even like a black cat to walk down the street, let alone black people." Before they could flee to safety, a group of young men arrived. Speaking to an elderly bystander, one said, "You know we don't allow their kind here. There's been a long time since we hung one of 'em up, too." Luckily, the locals noticed their instruments and asked them to play. Their talents, especially their ability to perform old-time mountain music, saved their skin. Still, they were required to leave the town by sundown.[24]

Strother knew of such encounters from firsthand accounts—and, no doubt, from experience. Like any Black man of his time, he understood that being in the wrong place at the wrong time could result in death. In fact, an extrajudicial murder occurred in his home county during his lifetime. Allie Thompson was lynched on November 24, 1918, for allegedly attacking a married white woman. A group of masked men went to the county jail and supposedly duped the jailers into opening Thompson's cell. A Richmond newspaper matter-of-factly reported that "at sunrise the body of Thompson was found dangling in a tree down the Rixeyville Road, three miles from Culpeper." Jim Strother and his family were quite familiar with this violent form of Southern "justice."[25]

Strother's troubling vision of the world's dangers also inhabits his most commented-on religious song. The verses of "Blood-Stained Banders" are dark, menacing, and full of the evil and violence in the world. He opens the song with a glimmer of hope in fairly stock religious language, telling us what we must do to "go to heaven, over on the other shore," but he then immediately invokes the degradation and temptations of the world. The world is bloody, full of violence and death. His invocation of the "gun-shot devils" reminds us of influential Black theologian James H. Cone's assertion of the grounded realism of the religious music of the enslaved. Cone, relying on his deep knowledge of Black religiosity, argued that for Black people, "Satan is not merely an abstract metaphysical evil unrelated to social and political affairs; he represents the concrete presence of evil in human society." For the enslaved, the "earthly representatives" of such evil were "slaveholders, slave catchers, and slave traders."[26]

Singing in the post-Emancipation era, Strother could be referencing the violence he experienced as a musician on the streets or as an itinerant traveling musician, or perhaps the threatening world he encountered in his first neighborhood in Baltimore, or the depredations faced by Black people across his native South, including several lynchings in his home county. His invocation to "keep out the way of the long-tongued liars" echoes other common gospel song expressions, such as "you better leave that liar alone," but also has direct parallels with his own life experience. The mistrust of those who might abuse him at work or on the street and the constant danger of unreliable strangers and white violence were all reflected in Strother's songs and his own words.

As with so much of Strother's music and life, the surface playfulness of his instrumentation and vocal delivery hid dark realities that his Black audiences would have readily comprehended but that white audiences might not have. This type of lyrical sleight of hand, along with the songsters' ability to "code-switch" based on their audience, was not merely a commercial ploy allowing musicians to connect with their hearers and gain greater remuneration for their efforts. Being able to "speak" to hostile whites in a mountain town in their musical language likely saved the lives of Carl Martin, Howard Armstrong, and countless other traveling musicians. Similarly, Strother reinforced a potentially life-saving lesson about traveling in rural America as a Black person as he "spoke" to members of his own community in "Thought I Heard My Banjo Say."

10

The Street

Baltimore has always shown itself hospitable to street musicians. Even at Lexington Market there are beggars with concertinas and banjos and "mouth harps."

—MARION GRUBB, "Little Brothers of Business," *The Commonweal*, 1930

Luckily for James and Mary Strother, their domestic circumstances improved not long after they settled in the Biddle Alley District of Baltimore. By the mid-1910s, they had moved into north-central Baltimore into a neighborhood today dubbed "Old Goucher" by realtors, yuppies, and preservationists. Lying east of Jones Falls on the Patapsco River, the neighborhood was a study in contrasts. The Jones Falls area was a mix of industry and became a locus of African American migration. European immigrants also came to the neighborhood, even while it still stood outside of Baltimore City. Only two miles north of the harbor and main commercial district, the area followed the pattern of the earliest suburbs before de jure and de facto segregation. Before its annexation in 1888 it was touted as the "richest and most populous" district of Baltimore County, yet working-class white and Black residents already populated the outer margins and alleys of the neighborhood.[1]

Mary Strother now walked every day from her two-story brick row house just a few blocks to the much more opulent residence of her employer, William F. Stone, at 2612 North Charles Street. Each morning she joined an army of Black women who left their homes on small alleys and side streets and trudged to the residences of Baltimore's elite to sew, launder, cook, and respond to the general whims of white families. While certainly healthier than Walnut Street, the Strothers' neighborhood still comprised cramped quarters on narrow streets. Notably, all of the addresses the Strothers occupied in this district of the city are now mere alleys—if they exist at all. Mace Street is a narrow passage flanked by parking lots and the backs of businesses or industrial buildings. Nothing is left of Ware Street save thirty-odd feet ending in a chain-link fence next to a storage company.

The neighborhood did have its advantages. The proximity of wealthy residents meant that city services could be counted on and public health maintained. Several prominent institutions sprang up to serve the Black community. Oak Street AME Church stood in the middle of the neighborhood, and Trinity Baptist Church at Twentieth and Charles Streets became an important center of Black activism. The Reverend Garnett Russell Waller built the small congregation into a large, dynamic house of worship. A native of Virginia's Eastern Shore, he migrated to Baltimore and worked as a shoemaker before attending Lincoln University in Pennsylvania. After pastoring several Northern congregations, he returned to Baltimore and not only advocated for civil rights in the city but also became a national civil rights leader. If Jim Strother stayed in the denomination of his ancestors, he may have attended Waller's church.[2]

Strother could see the advantages of his new locale as well. The church people in the neighborhood and the Goucher College students likely responded positively to his sacred repertoire. If not, several public venues, such as Union Station, were a comfortable walk away, where he could deploy "plantation songs" for the better-heeled white crowd. Even the rough haunts in the Seventeenth Ward could be easily reached by foot. By this time Strother was well prepared for his role as a street singer. His ability to convey different meanings and emotions to his audiences was vital. It goes without saying that a professional songster had to sing convincingly and powerfully, melding lyrics, vocal inflection, and tone color into a compelling and emotional vocal performance that would loosen a listener's purse strings. Street singers also had to be loud enough to be heard over the din of the street with no amplification. Modern-day songster Dom Flemons specifically mentions Strother's subtle merging of language, inflection, and emotion that gave meaning and power to his performances. Strother no doubt "read" his varied audiences well, maintaining a rapport with his listeners. The reinforcement of listener applause, shouts of encouragement, and other forms of call and response shaped his music as surely as his own inner artistic sensibilities. Lacking the ability to time-travel back to the streets of Baltimore or the medicine-show stage, we must be satisfied with the few examples of his art on record that likely only hint at his performance skills on the street.

Beyond the technical limitations of early field recording technology, assessing Strother's vocal approach leads us into the difficult terrain of timbre, sound color, and vocal expression, including enunciation, accent, and dialect. Numerous authors have bemoaned the impoverished state of our descriptions of vocal qualities such as timbre. Consequently, there is little consistency in how scholars—let alone laypeople—describe voices. Yet the sound qualities of the human voice are central to how we listen to, interpret, and even define twentieth-century popular musical styles—the blues "growl" and the country nasal twang being perhaps the most obvious examples.

We also know that vocal timbre and accent have been (and still are) highly racialized by listeners in America. For example, modern aficionados of early blues music routinely judge the authenticity—essentially the "Blackness"—of a performer by assessing certain vocal characteristics. The moaning, growling sounds produced by some Mississippi Delta bluesmen are frequently held up as the most authentic; thus the fixation on artists such as Charley Patton and Howlin' Wolf. This, despite the fact that early blues performers demonstrated a wide range of vocal approaches and colorations, from Tommy Johnson's use of a "cry break" or sudden leap into falsetto (similar to the "yodels" produced by early country artists such as Jimmie Rodgers) to Mississippi John Hurt's "light," almost delicate singing. Early mid-Atlantic and Virginia songsters have especially suffered on this scale of perceived "vocal Blackness." All I can do here is describe what I hear in Strother's voice, understanding that it is ultimately subjective and contingent.

Strother's baritone voice is distinctive in character and tone, but he deftly modifies his approach depending on his material. This includes his pronunciation, timbre, and melodic sensibilities. Strother delivers his comedic showstopper "Tennessee Dog" in a direct, clearly articulated vocal style, rolling the letter "r" on the word "river." Strother's performance still feels more natural and restrained than the stylized shouting and declamatory approaches of Black vaudevillians. Witness, for instance, the vocal lead on "Oysters and Wine at 2 a.m." by Polk Miller's Old South Quartette, a roughly contemporary group from central Virginia. Did Strother "dial back" his performance to better suit the wishes of John Lomax? It remains a possibility.[3]

Strother was especially adept at conveying emotional states to his listeners through his vocalizations. His understated and rhythmically loose approach to "This Old Hammer"—quite different from the song's use as a hammer song or from later, driving string-band versions—conveys a state of resignation and almost wistfulness that is in full accord with the lyrical content. In the opening stanza of "Thought I Heard My Banjo Say," Strother pushes his voice to the upper brink of his range, never quite breaking into falsetto. At the edge of his range, he seems to be "crying out" as he sings the words of the song's title. In the "B" section of the tune, he drops down into a darker, lower voice that effectively matches the menace and alienation described in his lyrics. Strother deployed his full bag of tricks to reach the multiplicity of audiences walking along the streets of Baltimore. After all, his survival and that of his family depended on it.

The Strother family's relocation to Mace and later Oak Street brought the Strothers not only closer to a variety of audiences and useful busking locations but also closer to his extended family. His connection to the Taylor and Johnson families came through Andrew Taylor, the son of Jim's relative Mary Strother Taylor. Andrew Taylor, like Jim Strother, had come northward in the Great Migration from Culpeper County and married Basil and Hannah Johnson's daughter Frances Jane ("Fannie") in 1894. The couple lived in Howard County near Ellicott City before moving to Baltimore to be closer to Frances's mother.

The birth of the couple's son William Taylor in 1907 must have been a joyous moment, but tragedy soon followed. Fannie Jane Johnson Taylor developed a bacterial infection, likely strep or scarlet fever, that resulted in "acute articular rheumatism"—fever, swollen joints, and arthritis. Heart disease followed, and Fannie died when William was just three months old. Andrew Taylor completely disappears from the record around the same time.

In the wake of this tragedy, the resilient Strothers, Taylors, and Johnsons reordered their lives and households. Hannah Johnson took her grandson William Taylor into her home at 204 Ware Street, just around the corner from his parents' former residence. The sixty-eight-year-old widow labored as a laundress, "working out" in Baltimore City. Jim and Mary Strother took in William's aunt, Sarah Johnson Truman, and her young son Walter while still living in the Biddle Alley District on Walnut Street in 1910. Sarah Truman's husband, James Truman, had likely also died recently, and she redistributed her own children. Her daughter Lillie lived with grandmother Hannah Johnson along with William Taylor.

Hannah Johnson, the Taylors, and the Strothers all lived on Ware Street at various times and later occupied houses next door to each other on nearby Mace Street—although not at the same time—in the period from 1915 to 1920. William Taylor and Jim Strother developed a close personal bond that would have a profound effect on Strother's ultimate fate. Mary's employment with political power broker William Stone added much-needed stability and a steady income. Jim Strother continued to contribute to the family financially, by performing on the streets of Baltimore, and emotionally, by mentoring young William Taylor.

Despite this fortuitous change in their domestic situation, both Strothers still plied demanding and difficult trades. Mary answered to a powerful white employer and spent long hours away from her own home, shopping in the markets and preparing and cooking the Stone family's meals. Jim Strother busked on the streets, exposed to every extreme of the elements there. He also faced the uncertainties and dangers of periodic forays into the countryside and surrounding towns with small traveling shows. Simply moving through the noisy, crowded Baltimore streets proved a daily challenge. Rumbling streetcars, the newfangled and largely unregulated automobiles, and old-style horse-drawn hacks and carts created a panoply of dangers to the pedestrian.

Other dangers plagued the street singer aside from runaway traffic. The possibility of violence in white sundown towns had its urban equivalent in street theft and harassment. While the idea of blind performers packing weapons may seem absurd to us, it provided at least enough of a threat to discourage a thief or make a heckler move along. Blind Boy Fuller, Gary Davis, and a host of other street musicians carried pistols. Strother himself owned a .38 revolver. The Reverend Gary Davis, legendary ragtime and blues guitarist and gospel singer, carried a .38 Special and a knife to protect himself on the rough-and-tumble streets of Durham, North Carolina, in the 1930s. In one instance, a man snatched away a five-dollar bill being handed to Davis by a benefactor. During the ensuing dispute, Davis stabbed him twice with a small blade, sending him to the hospital. The judge let Davis off with the admonition to not cut anyone else. Davis's younger protégé, Blind Boy Fuller (whose real name was Fulton Allen), shot his wife in the leg in what was almost certainly an accident and then memorialized the act in his "Big House Bound": "I shot the woman I love / ain't got no one to come go my bail."[4]

The street posed the threat of conflict and violence, but poverty and marginalization always loomed as an existential, day-to-day concern. Blind Lemon Jefferson's "Tin Cup Blues" succinctly describes the challenges facing the blind street singer, even one supported by a partner in the domestic trades:[5]

> I stood on the corner and almost bust my head [2x]
> I couldn't make enough money to buy a loaf of bread
> My girl's a housemaid and she earns a dollar a week [2x]
> I'm so hungry on payday, I can't hardly speak.

Jefferson clearly elucidates the marginal situation of Black street singers and their families. Black women had very few employment options beyond domestic work at low pay. The uncertain nature of street performance meant that such families lived on the edge of survival.

On the bright side, Jim Strother's adopted city, Baltimore, seems to have been relatively open regarding street performers at the turn of the century. In 1893, a British consul, Captain William Francis Seagrave, whose diplomatic purview included Maryland, Virginia, West Virginia, and Kentucky, reported on the situation in the city to London's *Musical News*. Seagrave declared that Baltimore had "no restriction on hand-organs and other forms of street music" and that "any individual may start a barrel-organ" and play "when and where he pleases." Nevertheless, the city fathers banned street bands except in the case of parades. The law failed to define exactly what constituted a parade, however, prompting the *Music News*'s editor to sardonically declare, "Truly a delightful law!" By the time that Jim Strother arrived in Baltimore a decade later, the rules had become somewhat more stringent, with permits required of musicians.[6]

Even as late as 1930 a vigorous street culture seemed to prevail. Author Marion Grubb painted a decidedly romantic view of Baltimore's street life, lauding cities such as Charleston, New Orleans, and Baltimore, "where time stands still withal and living is an art, not a utilitarian enterprise." "It is pleasant to find anywhere in this time-ridden world," she mused, "an order of human beings who refuse to be enslaved to regular hours and routine tasks, yet manage to earn a living while taking their time from the sun."

She described a rich mixture of street vendors, artisans, and musicians on Baltimore's streets, notably the Irish, Bohemian, and Italian vendors as well as African American carters. Grubb's invocation of Charleston and New Orleans as sister cities is intriguing. Baltimore's industries and large foreign-born population might seem to militate against such a comparison, but the city's culture was strongly influenced by the legacy of enslavement as well as being a major port with an expressive Black street culture.[7]

Strother and other musicians contributed to this lively street life and soundscape. His baritone voice, accompanied by banjo, guitar, and perhaps fiddle, mingled with the calls of vendors, sidewalk preachers, and even brass bands led by Black musicians, such as the Baltimore Colored City Band and Harris's Famous Commonwealth Cornet Band. African American cart vendors, known locally as Arabbers, gathered at their stables early in the morning to bring out their horses. They haggled for their wares at the city markets and then carefully arranged them on their colorful carts. Fanning out into the neighborhoods, they called housewives from their kitchens with piercing calls declaiming the superiority of their produce. These were family businesses passed from fathers to sons (and sometimes to daughters).[8]

There is no doubt that Jim Strother had strong competition in winning donations from the city's pedestrians. Grubb described a few of the typical musical entertainers: "Baltimore has always shown itself hospitable to street musicians. Even at Lexington Market there are beggars with concertinas and banjos and 'mouth harps.' Still, the hurdy-gurdy business is falling off; it is three years since I have seen a monkey; and for months there has been no piano man."[9] Even Grubb, while extolling the independent life of the men of the street, still considered these musicians to be beggars. For the blind African American street performer, the association with beggary only compounded multiple existing disabilities—blindness (and ableist assumptions about it) and, especially, the pervasiveness of Jim Crow segregation and violence. As Jim Strother would soon find out, Black street musicians occupied a decidedly liminal space in Progressive-era America.

The status of street musicians has historically been quite fluid. Traditional cultures have often treated blind itinerant musicians as honored and respected members of society. In fact, they were sometimes considered to have supernatural gifts. From Irish bards to Japanese biwa singers to Ukrainian minstrels, each figure had its own trajectory. Early minstrels and bards performed important storytelling, genealogical, and sometimes religious functions for their communities. In addition, in the Western tradition, the giving of alms to mendicants was a religiously sanctioned act.[10]

In modern times, especially in cultures undergoing rapid industrial, urban, and capitalist transformation, ideas about begging, dependency, order, and institutionalization changed dramatically. Often this meant the institutionalization of "dependent" people, suspicion of anyone who was itinerant, and the assumption that street performers were little more than beggars. In Spain, the blind had traditionally been employed on the streets as musicians, singers, balladeers, and sellers of chapbooks and other printed materials. They organized themselves into brotherhoods for mutual aid and protection in various Spanish cities and even gained official state sanction. Yet by the nineteenth century these brotherhoods had died out, and "the blind were largely reduced to begging."[11]

These forces of change can be seen in non-Western cultures as well. The traditional blind biwa singers of Japanese feudal society had clear and honored roles in their world. As masters of the biwa, a short-necked, fretted lute, they performed narrative songs at Shinto temples and served in the courts of the samurai. They handed their profession down to other sightless persons. Despite this long tradition, the biwa singer's status began to change by at least the nineteenth century. Several of the few remaining Japanese biwa singers whom author Hugh de Ferranti tried to interview in the late twentieth century turned him away, while others revealed a deep ambivalence about their profession in their answers to his questions. The association of itinerant biwa performance with beggary seemed to be at the root of these feelings of reluctance and shame.[12]

Itinerant musicians, blind or sighted, came under increased scrutiny across America and Europe beginning in the eighteenth century. The rise of modern cities drew people from the countryside in large numbers, causing city leaders to struggle with questions of "mendicancy, poverty, and begging." As historian John E. Zucchi writes, they occupied a netherworld where "the line between mendicancy and work was not clear," and they "requested money from people in a manner that resembled begging. They did not have a scale of charges or established prices for their services." Musicians and other itinerants were the "other." Rootless, not bound to the community by family ties, they were often foreign and possibly a threat. City fathers in Europe and America saw disorder and chaos in such a mass of humanity, including the disturbance of public (and possibly political) order; disruptive noise, particularly in middle-class neighborhoods; and the perceived pathology of simply being poor and dependent.[13]

A London music journal's survey of itinerant musicians conducted through the British diplomatic corps underscored the universal nature of street performance and governments' attempts to regulate it in the late nineteenth century. Prompted by calls for regulation of such musicians in Great Britain, the *Musical News* recruited none other than the prime minister, Lord Salisbury, to canvas consular offices throughout Europe and the United States regarding legal restrictions on the practice. The article's anonymous author drew some crucial distinctions regarding the status of street musicians that revealed common attitudes of the time that still persist today.[14]

While asserting that a street performer was not "a musician in the true sense of the word," the writer made allowance for what we would today call traditional or folk artists. He held up the example of "the harpists of Wales who render their native airs with touching effect" as musicians worthy of exemption from legal sanction. The replies to Lord Salisbury's consular inquiries reinforced this distinction. Officials in Spain reported that itinerant musicians were divided into two classes: "those playing the national instrument, the guitar, who are apparently treated with leniency, though even in their cases a license is required; and those provided with 'grinding organs or pianos,' who are treated very harshly." Likewise, Russian policy declared that "those who are of foreign nationality are not permitted to pass the frontiers of the empire." Such a judgment was not surprising. The music of the native "folk" had become a key element in the rise of cultural nationalism across Europe, advocated by philosophers such as Johann Gottfried Herder in the German states and actuated by collectors and compilers such as Scotland's Robert Burns.[15]

The American situation, the author reported, was considerably more complicated, and significant variations existed from locality to locality: "In many of the States, licenses are required, and street musicians are permitted to follow their avocations only so long as they do not become a nuisance. In other parts no street music of any kind is heard." Still other cities had virtually no restrictions at all. Following the general example of Russia and Spain, Richmond, Virginia, was said to act on "distinct protective principles": "The city accepts street music only from its natives, foreigners are not allowed to perform." This standard gave some legitimacy to Jim

Strother and his fellow Southern street musicians. Their music provided a familiar and even romanticized soundtrack to cities filled with rural migrants singing spirituals, "plantation melodies," ballads, and other materials from the common stock. As with everything related to Black life, this tolerance could quickly be overturned by the capricious application of the law, however.[16]

The fate of a street singer in Richmond, Virginia, illustrates the busker's dilemma. In 1910, the *Richmond Times-Dispatch* reported on the case of "Samuel Russell, who although unknown by name is yet known to every man and woman in Richmond as the blind negro player who pipes on his accordeon [*sic*] every day and night." Russell stood before "Justice John" Crutchfield in Richmond's police court on the charge of "refusing to move when ordered to move by an officer." Russell performed mostly on Broad Street, Richmond's main commercial thoroughfare—a bustling landscape of theaters, department stores, and streetcars. The location was no doubt lucrative, as his "plaintive music . . . brought many small coins in the little tin cup on top of his instrument." Despite Russell's claim that he had a permit "to play and sing and beg," a policeman determined that he had become a "nuisance" and "ordered him to move on." Judge Crutchfield, despite his well-earned reputation as a virulent racist, decided to let Russell go "on account of his blindness." Crutchfield was notorious for operating on the same principles that the British consul had described. Black Virginians— "our people," as many Southern whites would have put it—might expect some leniency in his police court, but outsiders received no such benefit of the doubt. "Justice John" was notoriously hard on Black people from North Carolina.[17]

One of Jim Strother's competitors faced a similarly revealing situation in Baltimore's southern district police court. Lucy Scribner stood before Judge Paul Johannsen on a charge of being drunk on the street. The magistrate demanded that Scribner "render some darkey melodies" in order to win his release. Scribner obliged, taking a "seat in the courtroom with a mouth organ fastened to his shoulders, so that he could play it, which he accompanied with a guitar." His performance won him his freedom. This coercive episode not only reveals the ways in which white authorities arbitrarily exercised their power but also suggests what they considered the proper musical domain of Black Americans. The situation in this Baltimore courtroom eerily duplicates the strategies used by some folklorists when faced with recalcitrant subjects in Southern prisons. The Lomaxes consciously played on some prisoners' beliefs that compliance might bring release and sometimes recruited wardens to enforce their authority. Jim Strother and his fellow musicians would hardly have been surprised at the demands of Lomax and others—the folklorist was simply another white authority or "boss man."[18]

Jim Strother, Samuel Russell, and Lucy Scribner knew the tenuousness of their situation. The authorities could always decide, as they did by arresting Russell, that a blind street singer could no longer perform. Stripped of their livelihood, what were they to do? The Richmond newspaper reporter casually noted that Russell "may go to the colored almshouse if he wishes." Perhaps he did, or, more likely, he found another city or town to ply his chosen occupation rather than be institutionalized. He may have come to Richmond from Norfolk in the first place. In 1899, a street musician named "Sandy Russell" was "arraigned for disorderly conduct, and in default of a fine of $5 was committed to jail" in the port city.[19]

The police often prescribed where musicians performed on the streets of the South. Fulton Allen, known professionally as Blind Boy Fuller, had a permit to perform on the streets of Durham, North Carolina, but only in certain places. Durham's superintendent of welfare recommended to police chief G. W. Proctor that Allen be allowed to perform in public "at a place designated by you." It was well known among Durham musicians that the police would move musicians blocking public ways along and that certain areas of town were reserved for African American musicians.[20]

Baltimore's police force had numerous laws empowering them to move people off the streets with impunity. Criminal dockets filled up with infractions: "Acting in a Disorderly manner on the public streets of Baltimore City," "Obstructing the free passage of persons on the public street," "Being Drunk upon a public street," "Begging from persons along a public street," and "being a Vagrant, having no visible means of support or permanent place of abode in Baltimore City." There is also abundant evidence that the weight of these arbitrary laws fell most heavily on Black people.[21]

Just as turn-of-the-century urban reformers had racialized neighborhood disorder and disease by focusing on Black people as the primary culprits, now the police, city leaders, and the Democratic Party fixated on Black criminality. The Baltimore dailies used terms like "negro rowdies," "toughs," and "coons" to describe Black people, echoing the language of Strother's hometown newspapers when reporting on Black visitors to Culpeper's entertainment grounds. Magistrates in the city's police courts notoriously levied excessive fines on African American defendants. The police made punitive sweeps for "disorderly" behavior with little reason except to exercise control and clear the streets.[22]

Despite this oppressive and growing regime of control, in the early twentieth century musicians like Strother could still secure a permit to entertain on the city's streets. Strother did so with the help of his wife's employer, William Stone. Despite this support, he soon found his livelihood threatened by the politics of Progressive reform. A very public dust-up about his ability to perform on the streets of Baltimore would reveal attitudes about race, the disabled, and what constituted legitimate work and mendicancy. Reformers now posed a direct threat to Jim Strother's livelihood as they sought to clear Baltimore's streets and public spaces of disorder and "beggary."

11

The Politics of Race and Disability

[Institutionalization] would save him from the humiliating experience of being led about the streets as a blind musician, and therefore, of necessity, as virtually an object of charity.

—JAMES W. MAGRUDER, Federated Charities, commenting on Jim Strother in the *Baltimore American*, January 27, 1915

William F. Stone strode with purpose toward the offices of Baltimore's charity agency on a January day in 1915. Stone was extremely hot under his double round collar. The bespectacled collector of the Port of Baltimore soon found himself in the presence of his new nemesis, James W. Magruder, a minister and secretary of the city's Federated Charities. The wily older politician eyed the young reformer with some disdain and demanded answers.

Mary Strother, William Stone's cook, had pleaded with Stone to secure her husband a permit to play his "string music" on the streets after years of such performing. Stone "appealed to the police department for a permit for the man to play a fiddle on the street as a means of livelihood and he was referred to Mayor Preston, as all such permits are issued from the office of the municipal executive." Little did Stone know that the Federated Charities and Magruder had insinuated themselves into the city's welfare bureaucracy. Learning that Magruder had stymied his efforts, he decided to pay this young busybody a visit. William F. Stone wasn't one to take "no" for an answer.

Stone's unsatisfactory interview with Magruder and his subsequent letter to Mayor Preston—copied to the Baltimore dailies, who gladly reported his scathing comments—set off a brief firestorm. The blazing column header in the *Baltimore Sun* proclaimed, "PLEA FOR BLIND NEGRO: Collector Writes Indignant Letter to Mayor Preston." The *Sun* breathlessly reported that "Collector of the Port William F. Stone has complained to Mayor Preston that James Strothers, colored, the blind husband of his cook, has been refused a permit to play music on the streets solely because he is blind." Not to be outdone, the *Baltimore American* boldly declared, "Mr. Stone Flays Charity Methods: The Collector Bitterly Arraigns J. W. Magruder." Magruder penned a retort on the decision to deny Strother his permit that appeared just below Stone's tirade, denouncing such "begging" as beneath the dignity of the blind.[1]

The spectacle of two Baltimore elites engaging in a heated debate about the fate of a "blind Negro" musician in the pages of the city's major newspapers likely prompted various reactions. White citizens reading the headlines might have been puzzled and slightly amused at two city leaders arguing about the propriety of allowing a blind Black street singer to ply his trade. Black citizens probably nodded their heads in silent recognition of another indignity to their race. The politically astute might have assumed familiar battle lines—the grizzled machine politician of the old order against the young, idealistic reformer. The heated exchange was, of course, about much more than that. The fight revealed a deep ideological divide among the city's patricians and progressives regarding the poor, race, and the enforcement of social control. One side viewed the issue from an older, patriarchal perspective, while the other relied on a respectability politics that delineated the "deserving poor." Jim Strother and his fellow blind street performers sat uncomfortably between powerful forces that would either allow them to continue to ply their trade or institutionalize them.[2]

Jim Strother had a powerful ally in William Stone. The acknowledged leader of the Republican Party in Baltimore and Maryland, he wielded enormous influence. Stone began his career as a modest clerk and bookkeeper, rising from the bottom rungs of the Republican Party ward machine in Baltimore. First elected in the fall of 1881 to the position of president of the Seventh Ward, his political ascendancy in Baltimore became complete when he was appointed chairman of the Republican committee for the city in 1893. Indicating his status among national Republicans, President William McKinley appointed him to the federal sinecure of collector of customs of the Port of Baltimore, a post he held for many years, "eclipsing the record of any other man who has held this office." Stone still enjoyed this patronage position when penning his letter on behalf of Jim Strother to Mayor Preston.[3]

How much the issue of race played into Stone's intervention on Strother's behalf is difficult to say. Stone had long supported Black political rights, a fact not lost on the city's African American leadership. Baltimore's *Race Standard* pictured Stone, then city registrar, on the cover of its 1897 issue celebrating Emancipation. Likewise, *The Commonwealth,* a weekly African American newspaper, lauded Stone as "one of our staunchest and sincerest friends, who does not wait until political campaigns are on to show his interest and friendship in the welfare of the race." Yet a Democratic resurgence in the city and state strained the alliance with Black voters as Republican leaders retreated from a full endorsement of social equality.[4]

Not surprisingly, opinions among African American leaders regarding Stone and the Republican Party soured. The *Afro-American Ledger* opined after a 1913 electoral defeat that it was time for "William Stone and his henchmen" to bow out of the leadership of the Republican Party. A year later, the same newspaper asserted that Stone and the Republican machine's "only interest in the colored man is his vote on election day." Feeling betrayed, Black leaders in Baltimore independently marshalled their own political forces, creating the Suffrage League and mobilizing boycotts against the new segregation laws.[5]

Despite these criticisms—or perhaps because of them—Stone attacked Magruder directly on race. In his letter to Mayor Preston, he pointedly asked "where the difference came between a white person playing music on the street and receiving compensation for it and a person who had been afflicted by the hand of Providence doing the same thing." Stone also raised the issue of sighted "foreigners" who received permits to play on the streets while Black, unsighted musicians were left out in the cold. Stone's hostility to the foreign born was a not-so-subtle reference to the marshalling of ethnic voters by the Democratic Party.

Stone likewise ridiculed Magruder's claims about the wonders of institutionalization and the paltry amount offered to the street singer. Magruder had sniffed, "We arranged with the Maryland Workshop for the Blind to take in James Strothers and train him as a piano tuner or for some other regular and remunerative occupation; the workshop to pay him one dollar a week during the period of his training, and the Federated Charities to pay him an additional amount sufficient to keep him until he could become self-supporting." Stone responded forcefully. "They offered to put Strothers in some blind asylum at $1.00 a week," he scoffed, "which, of course, is ridiculous, but will not give him a permit to play upon the street, though they will give permits to anybody else who can see." Stone's acidic tone conveyed his anger, but underlying his complaint were long-standing tenets of American Republicanism. For Stone, a key element of manly independence was the ability to control one's labor; independence and citizenship went hand in hand, whereas dependence was servility.

Stone then went a step further and accused Magruder of un-Christian behavior toward the disabled. As the American's reporter declared, "Strother had until recently been in perfect health and while working at Sparrows Point, he was blinded by an accident." Stone viewed such an event as many Christians had for centuries—a tragedy, but part of God's inscrutable plan. He skewered Magruder's position with unconcealed sarcasm: "In other words, if God in His infinite wisdom has afflicted a person then that person is not entitled to a permit to earn his living upon the public highway, while the person who has not had a visitation of affliction by Providence may be given the privilege. I told Mr. Magruder that I considered this action arbitrary and autocratic in the extreme and that it was a travesty upon charity." He concluded: "If this is consistent, then God preserve me from such consistency." Magruder reacted angrily to Stone's imputations of racial discrimination and un-Christian thinking in the pages of the American and the Sun, insisting that "no distinctions are made between white and colored applicants for permits."[6]

Magruder had a very different view of the blind and their presence on Baltimore's streets. He approached his work informed by the new sociological perspectives of "scientific charity." After graduating from Ohio Wesleyan University, the young minister pastored a church in Cincinnati where, as one reporter noted, "sociological work counts more than preaching." In his posts in Cincinnati and in Portland, Maine, Magruder collaborated extensively with academics at Johns Hopkins University and other academic centers of economic and social work research, such as the Center for Philanthropy in New York. He lectured widely and authored tracts on a variety of social reforms. The young minister arrived in Baltimore in 1907 ready to take up the mantle of scientific philanthropy.[7]

Magruder threw himself headlong into every aspect of the reform crusade in Baltimore. His drive to restrict the ability of blind musicians to ply their profession on city streets was part and parcel of his campaign to restrict beggary and vagrancy in the city. Magruder served notice in 1910 that he intended to eradicate "the evil of street begging, house-to-house mendicancy, and irresponsible soliciting of all kinds." Magruder argued that "there is absolutely no occasion in Baltimore or the surrounding suburbs for any man, woman or child to resort to these practices. Most of them are already known to us. One of the reasons why they continue to beg is that it pays. And there will always be as many mendicants as almsgivers are ready to pay for." Magruder's solution naturally involved the intervention of the Federated Charities.[8]

To accomplish this goal, Magruder would transform the Federated Charities into an arm of the state. At a dinner attended by "magistrates, members of the police department, social workers, and others," Judge J. Abner Saylor described some of the difficulties of law enforcement officers who were "called upon daily to dispose of scores of beggars and vagrants." Magruder spoke next and "outlined a plan for solving the problem," which was largely implemented. At his prompting in 1912, the Baltimore City Police assigned a plainclothes "mendicancy officer" to warn beggars that they were violating the law and subject to arrest and to report them to the relevant private relief agency for aid. A second transgression set the courts in motion, and law enforcement and a representative of the relief organization now became witnesses against the accused. The authorities seemed to have liked the plan; the number of officers was quickly expanded to nine.[9]

It wasn't long before Jim Strother and his fellow blind musicians became a target of Magruder's crusade to eliminate "irresponsible soliciting of all kinds." In his response to Stone, the Progressive minister argued that blind people themselves "earnestly object to having blind peddlers and blind musicians on the streets for the reasons that the spectacle of them playing musical instruments and peddling has the tendency to bring upon the blind on account of their affliction a certain stigma of dependency." Magruder asserted that Strother's institutionalization at the Maryland Workshop for the Blind would "save him from the humiliating experience of being led about the streets as a blind musician, and therefore, of necessity, as virtually an object of charity." The reformer's words—humiliation, dependency, stigma—unfortunately still echo today.[10]

The blind street singer as a pitiable figure, robbed of sight and reduced to street-corner singing, has long been a familiar trope of the disabled musician. One examination of the oral autobiographies of Chicago street singers Arvella Gray and James Brewer describes several such popular tropes, including the "mostly negative image . . . of the suffering blues singer begging with a tin cup. This formulation casts blindness as the mark of a cruel fate which caps the singer's degradation and alienates him from his community." Folklorists John and Alan Lomax both described Jim Strother in these terms. John emphasized Strother's inability to see "the beautiful valley of the James River" at the state prison farm owing to the cruel accident that had "destroyed his sight." Alan echoed Magruder's invocation of the "humiliating experience of being led about the streets" in the introduction to one of Strother's songs in *Our Singing Country*. Alan describes the life of the "itinerant street singer": "Usually blind, piloted by his wife or by some little boy, he inches along through the streets and down the alleys of Negro working-class neighborhoods." Both paint a picture of tragedy and pathos when describing Strother's circumstances—of someone dependent, robbed of agency by fate, and forced into the life of a street performer.[11]

Jim Strother himself contradicted this maudlin tableau in a letter to Virginia's chief executive. Petitioning Governor James H. Price, he explained, "Your Excellency need have no fear of my being able to travel alone if I can secure my release. I have been going where ever I wanted to go practically ever since I lost my sight." Strother surely had traveled many miles with the medicine shows, on Baltimore's streets, and along the byways of rural Virginia. Clearly, he valued his independence, although he also had every reason to exaggerate his ability to navigate the world to press his case for a pardon.[12]

The uncanny ability to freely negotiate and "sense" the world has become one of the most repeated bits of folklore associated with blind songsters and musicianers. To some degree, it harks back to earlier ideas of blind minstrels as seers with almost supernatural powers. Writers often marvel at Georgia songster Blind Willie McTell and Texas troubadour Blind Lemon Jefferson, who traveled widely without the aid of an assistant—but this was hardly universal. Other musicians employed "lead boys" to help them navigate the world. Such stories laud the disabled for essentially being "normative," performing tasks that the sighted accomplish routinely. Societal attitudes about the disabled shaped such tales, and even those subjected to ableist tropes might internalize such attitudes.[13]

The legend of Blind Lemon Jefferson best illustrates this problem. A seminal artist in the commercial recording of early blues, the Texan was exceedingly peripatetic. Fellow Texas bluesman Lightnin' Hopkins asserted that Jefferson "didn't allow no one to lead him" and that the older bluesman fiercely defended his independence to the point of denying his disability:

"He say then you call him blind. No, don't call him Blind. He never did feel like that." Yet Huddie William Ledbetter, better known by his stage name of Lead Belly, also knew Jefferson well and portrayed the situation quite differently. In a musical tribute to his fellow songster, Ledbetter cried, "Blind Lemon was a blind man, He'd holler—'Catch me by the hand'—oh baby, 'and lead me all through the land.'"[14]

It may well be that Lead Belly was engaging in poetic license or that this was simply a plea for female companionship. Whatever the case, his tribute to his musical mentor alludes to the tradition of some blind musicians employing a "lead boy" to navigate the streets and byways. Perhaps the best account of the lives of "lead boys" and the musicians they worked for comes to us from Josh White. White became an important performer and political activist during the 1940s and '50s folk revival, but he began his musical career in the 1920s as the lead boy for as many as forty-odd blind musicians both in his home area of Greenville, South Carolina, and extensively on the road. White worked with Blind Joe Taggart, a street evangelist who recorded for the Vocalion and Paramount record labels; John Henry Arnold; and the incomparable ragtime-blues guitar player Willie Walker. The experiences of lead boys varied considerably. While some musicians treated their young charges as valued apprentices and fictive kin, the relationship could also be abusive and exploitative.[15]

We don't know if Strother had a "lead boy" to guide him through Baltimore, and his own words suggest that he did not, but he likely had a musical partner who was also a mentor. In the 1910 census, a boarder named Eugene Carter was recorded as living with the Strothers. Like Strother, his occupation is given as "musician" and the place of employment as "Public." Born in Virginia and twelve years Strother's senior, Carter may have assisted Strother in learning the ropes in a new city. Strother's young relative William Taylor might have also assisted the older musician.

No matter Strother's specific situation, his ability to practice a marketable profession—and society's acceptance of that ability—set him apart from many of his peers, who were hemmed in by ableist assumptions. Magruder and his fellow reformers did not seem to grasp that Strother practiced a well-honed skill for remuneration and thereby increased his independence—a rare thing for a blind Black man in that era. Or perhaps that was actually the problem. Americans have lionized independence as a central pillar of citizenship and democratic society since the days of Jefferson, but there were always those who were explicitly and implicitly written out of that social contract. Magruder's blindness to Strother's independence as an economically productive citizen is striking but not unusual for Progressive reformers. As historian Thomas C. Leonard has shown, many Progressives "were so sure of their own expertise as a necessary guide to the public good, so convinced of the righteousness of their crusade to redeem America, that they rarely considered the unintended consequences of ambitious but untried reforms." Strother's situation was a clear case in point.[16]

Just as troubling was the Progressive movement's targeting of those with disabilities. While we typically think of American eugenics as a bunk "science" of racial superiority, purveyors of its economic incarnation also attacked the "crippled" as inferior workers who brought down the wages of American laborers. Magruder and most of his fellow Progressives advocated for the institutionalization of the disabled or their relegation to a few trades, thus removing them from competition with the general workforce. This view of the disabled as a drag on American progress and economic productivity was a favorite theory of the leading lights of economic Progressivism, including John R. Commons and Richard T. Ely. Both men taught at one of the hotbeds of intellectual Progressivism in America, which just happened to be in Magruder's and Strother's backyard—Johns Hopkins University. Magruder and his fellow Baltimore reformers enthusiastically allied themselves with these scholars and their ideology.

Strother, then, suffered from multiple disabilities in the eyes of the Baltimore reformers. His blindness made him "unfit" to participate in the larger labor market; his means of labor was reduced to mere "begging"; and his presence in the public square—a Black man occupying the city's main thoroughfares—was in itself a cause of public disorder. Just as neighborhood segregation and sundown towns delimited the geographic space that Black people could occupy—enforced by the constant threat and reality of violence—the law of mendicancy and disability layered itself on top of the laws of neighborhood segregation, vagrancy, and other strictures, all attempting to relegate Jim Strother to his "proper" place behind the brick walls of the Maryland Workshop for the Blind. These beliefs drew from stereotypes that pervaded turn-of-the-century America but were magnified and given official sanction by Progressives.[17]

Strother's predicament mirrored the experiences of other disabled African American musicians who depended on the street for their daily bread. Musician and evangelist Gary Davis, who would become one of the guiding lights of the 1960s folk revival, faced similar discrimination. Davis fre quently clashed with welfare workers in Durham, North Carolina, regarding his street performing and the amount of relief he received. In 1935, during the depths of the Great Depression, welfare officials referred his case to the Federal Emergency Relief Administration (FERA) project in Raleigh. The FERA experience only lasted a week. An agency caseworker suggested that Davis "put bottoms in chairs and repair mattresses, etc.," — surely not the kind of work that a successful and highly skilled musician would want or accept. Not surprisingly, Davis rejected the offer. Strother faced the same dilemma when challenged by Magruder and the charity establishment.[18]

Jim Strother and Baltimore's working-class Black community understood intuitively that Progressive campaigns inevitably involved questions of disability, race, and class. William Stone's accusation that race played a role in Strother's banishment from Baltimore's streets no doubt rang true for many, despite Magruder's protestations otherwise. Baltimore's *Afro-American Ledger* admitted as much the very year that Strother's troubles came to light. The newspaper approvingly reported on Magruder's alliance with Black community leaders in establishing a board of "colored workers" predictably focused on reform efforts in Strother's first neighborhood—the Biddle Alley District. Black reformers sought to "spread their belief . . . that the Federated Charities Association deserves the confidence and cooperation of everyone in the community." The *Ledger*'s reporter admitted that in the past, charity workers were "looked upon with distrust and, among the poorer Negroes, with perhaps suspicion. . . . and vague rumors were current that an unfair distribution of the funds was made so that few if any Negroes in distress were helped." This distrust was well earned. The alliance of charity workers with the police, the segregationist policies of many Progressive leaders, and the regressive charity policies of the agencies all gave less fortunate Black Baltimoreans plenty of cause for skepticism.[19]

Most Black citizens still hewed to a view of disability and mendicancy based in their Christian faith and biblical precedent. Such attitudes cut across class lines, despite the conversion of some to "scientific charity." Even the daughter of a solidly middle-class Black Richmond family was taught to give alms to the disabled. She recalled "lazy summer days when Brother and I ran into the street at the alluring sound of Blind Tom's high, sweet tenor and the strumming of his guitar. At the first twang we grabbed pennies Mama kept on the hall table and as Blind Tom passed by led by a young boy, we dropped the coins into his cup. Mama told us never to pass a blind person without giving him a token of money."[20]

Theologian Howard Thurman's meditation on the meaning of the spiritual "The Blind Man Stood on the Road and Cried" can perhaps give us some insight into this attitude toward the blind among Black residents. The song is based on the biblical account of a blind beggar's entreaties to Jesus to heal him near the town of Jericho. In the Bible story, his cries are heard and he is healed. A typical verse of the spiritual goes thus:[21]

O, the blind man stood on the road and cried,
O, the blind man stood on the road and cried;
Cryin' O, my Lord, save-a me.

Thurman posed a profound question about the song: "The slave singers did a strange thing with this story. They identify themselves completely with the blind man at every point but the crucial one. In the song, the blind man does not receive his sight. The song opens with the cry; it goes through many nuances of yearning, but it always ends with the same cry with which it began." How to explain this remarkable omission? Thurman's answer is simple but elegant: "The people who sang this song had not received their 'sight.' They had longed for freedom with all their passionate endeavors, but it had not come." The song reflected the unrelenting pain without recourse suffered by the enslaved: the brutality of punishment, family separation, and the auction block. Despite these trials, Thurman asserted that the enslaved somehow found the will to go on and that this is the true meaning of the song: "a complete and final refusal to be stopped," a victory for the "dignity of the human spirit."[22]

While Jim Strother's world was not that of his enslaved forebears, it was still a world of violence, discrimination, and a deep-seated "trouble in mind" for Black people. Just as Strother's ancestors could relate completely to the blind beggar's pain and cries, so too could the crowds on city streets who encountered Strother himself. Their vicarious understanding of his intense alienation and marginalization, coupled with their strong religious conviction, kept the coins flowing into the musicianer's cup.

The appearance of James Strother in the pages of Baltimore's most prominent newspapers was fleeting. While no further newspaper articles provided a resolution to the debate between Stone and Magruder, the attitudes toward blindness that the imbroglio provoked continued to echo in the experiences of blind musicians, their music, and in the tropes folklorists used to describe them.

There are two scraps of evidence that hint that Magruder's view prevailed—one of Strother's own letters to Virginia governor James Price and a single census entry. Whether this incident prompted it or not, Jim Strother did at some point enter the Maryland Workshop for the Blind. In his later bid for a pardon, Strother wrote Price that "I am completely blind & of no use to the State" and that he had "formerly worked and supported myself at the Maryland Workshop for the Blind." A single entry in the 1940 census confirms his occupation as a chair caner after his release from prison. As we will see, this evidence by no means establishes that Strother's musical career was over, but at least for a time he did enter Baltimore's Progressive welfare system. Strother would remain in Baltimore for at least another eight years, but a new family would soon find him Virginia bound.

~≈~ VIRGINIA BOUND ~≈~

12

Blanche Greene

My man is gone, Virginia bound
—JAMES LEE STROTHER, "Poontang Little, Poontang Small," 1936

Like so many periods of James Lee Strother's life, his whereabouts from around 1917 until 1923 are difficult to pin down. In 1917 he appeared in the Baltimore City directory residing at 2025 Oak Street in Baltimore. The next year he stood before the World War I draft board in Culpeper County and gave his home county as his residence. The next official sighting of Strother is his marriage to Blanche Greene in Alexandria, Virginia, in 1923, using Oak Street in Baltimore as his address. He eventually moved with his second wife back to Culpeper County. (What became of his common-law first wife, Mary, is unknown.) It is likely that he still traveled with local medicine shows in the early years of his marriage. One of his pardon documents suggests that he did not move back to Virginia until 1929. An unfortunate event may have prompted his permanent return. That same year, a doctor diagnosed Strother's mother, Susan, with "sarcoma of the jaw." Strother settled with Blanche just two houses away from his elderly mother and her husband.

Blanche Greene grew up in very different circumstances than her husband. The large, dark-red bindings of the county land books revealed to me the history of a proud, landholding family. Opening the volume's "Colored" section for 1919, I found her father, Robert Lee Greene—listed as Lee, as he was commonly known—owning two lots in Culpeper County. His home sat about four miles southeast of the county seat in the Cedar Grove community near Mount Pony. The county authorities assessed this 3.5–acre lot at $270, including buildings and improvements. His main farmland sat on a modest 14.5–acre plot with a value of $3.10 per acre. The Greenes fell within the roughly one-third of African American farm owners in the state with holdings of fewer than 20 acres. Maintaining ownership was a struggle, however. Lee Greene and his father both appeared on the lists detailing delinquent land taxes published in the Culpeper newspapers, although both managed to retain their property. By 1920, Lee Greene owned his own farm free and clear in the Cedar Mountain District and lived there with his son and three daughters as well as two grandchildren.[1]

The Greenes' tradition of land ownership began with Lee's father, Noah Greene. The elder Greene had been born enslaved in adjoining Madison County. He had several children under slavery with a woman named Betsy Brock, but what became of her after Emancipation is unknown. In 1867, he married Martha Champ while living in Locust Dale, Madison County, close to the Culpeper County line. Noah Greene did what his parents could not, providing for his family's education and acquiring property. In 1886 Noah purchased land near Mount Pony in Culpeper County. Unfortunately, his wife Martha did not make the move with the family—she had died in 1874. Lee Greene, Noah's son with Martha Champ, then purchased a plot of land in the neighborhood, moving close to his wife's people, the Deane and Hawkins families.[2]

When Noah Greene dictated his last will and testament, he did so with both of his wives' families in mind. At his death in 1893, he left his property and possessions for the use of his mother-in-law, Mary Champ, for as long as she lived. The patriarch did not forget his children born in slavery to Betsy Brock, but he remembered them unequally. Upon Mary's death, Noah declared that his daughter Rebecca should receive $1, while Helen would gain a third of his property. Daughter Ella and son Robert Lee, both from Noah's second marriage, also each received a third. Mary Champ must have died sometime within the next decade, for in 1905, Lee, Helen, and Ella agreed to distribute the property left to them. Both Ella and Helen had made their way to Pennsylvania during the Great Migration.[3]

Noah Greene understood not only the value of land but also the power of the ballot and education. While he had been enslaved like Jim Strother's parents, his experience after Emancipation was very different. His name appears in a Madison County poll book from the first election in Virginia's history to enfranchise African Americans. The 1867 campaign elected twenty-four Black men as delegates to the post–Civil War state convention, whose members rewrote Virginia's constitution and established the first statewide system of education in the Old Dominion's history. Although he and his wife Martha could neither read nor write, Noah saw to Robert Lee Greene's education.[4]

Alice Deane had a very different family experience than her husband, Lee. Alice's parents, Robert Deane and Lucy Hawkins, reported their marriage on the "Register of Marriages (Colored) Under Act of Assembly of Virginia, February 27, 1866." Most registers of this type solemnized and gave legal force to previous marriages of the formerly enslaved, but what makes this list so special is that it features many surnames common in Culpeper's free Black community, such as Deane, Fields, and Bundy. In addition, unlike most cohabitation registers, the document does not have a column for the names of former enslavers. Indeed, Lucy Hawkins and her mother, Frances, appear on the schedule of free inhabitants in the 1850 Culpeper census. Robert Deane likely had been enslaved at some point but may have gained his freedom before the Civil War.

The Deane family therefore belonged to the small number of free people of color who lived in the county before the Civil War. Their numbers had dwindled considerably since 1830 as Culpeper's white citizens actively sought to remove them, charging that they "congregate in and about our little Towns and by idleing [sic] their time indeed entirely neglecting to work they show no visible means of support, and must steal or perish." White people alleged that free people of color received goods from the enslaved that had been stolen from their enslavers. (The enslaved had a different view of who owned the product of their labor.) Free people felt under siege, and many packed their bags for cities in the North and West. One Culpeper free person, Dangerfield Newby, would join John Brown's attack on the Harper's Ferry arsenal in 1859 in a desperate attempt to end the system of slavery that kept his family in bondage.[5]

A very few owned businesses. Willis Madden, for example, established a tavern and campground on his land at Chinquapin Neck. Well positioned on the eastern end of the county on the road from Fredericksburg, Madden's enterprise became one of the most successful businesses in that section of the county. But Madden was the exception. The vast majority of his fellow free people of color did day labor and agricultural work. Many lived in "The Flats," an area of poor land that one wit claimed was "so wet in the winter . . . he believed it never leaked" and "so dry in the summer that you can't drive a nail into it without greasing." Indeed, free status did not confer access to education or land. Neither Lucy Hawkins, who had been born free, nor her freed husband, Robert Deane, could read or write, and they owned no property in the 1870 census. Robert worked as a farmhand. But like Noah and Martha Greene, they made sure their daughter Alice attended school and gained literacy.[6]

Lee Greene wed Alice Deane in 1890, and they had five children who lived to adulthood; of these, Blanche was the last, born in 1902. The Greenes followed the example of their parents and saw to the education of their son and daughters as far as the local schools allowed. In 1910, all five children, ranging from fourteen-year-old Clifton to seven-year-old Blanche, had attended school the previous year at the Eckington School, a one-room frame schoolhouse built in 1895 near Free Union Baptist Church. The "ungraded" school reflected the traditions of the nineteenth century, with all ages in a single room and the adherence to racial segregation common throughout Virginia. During the Eckington School's inaugural year, 1895–96, the county recorded a total school-age population of 2,639 white students and 3,203 Black students, but "only 1549 white and 1231 Black pupils are listed as actually attending school, while seating capacity was given at a total of 1380 for white students and 750 for Black students."[7]

The Greene and Deane families seem to have been reasonably prosperous. The *Culpeper Exponent* noted the family patriarch's aptitude for agriculture, reporting that "Uncle Lee Green, quite a respectable colored man of Cedar Grove, has broken the record on fine hogs—he butchered one that wighed [sic] 428 lbs." This short notice reflected the casual racism with which the white-owned newspapers described "respectable" Black people. Positive articles about African Americans inevitably labeled their subjects "aunt" or "uncle" and typically reported an unusual occurrence or the death of someone closely tied to a white family. Whites defined respectability in various ways: religious devotion (Lee Greene was a deacon at Free Union Baptist Church), land ownership, and definitely knowing your place. The use of the phrase "respectable colored" to describe such individuals was so ubiquitous that using this terminology became one of my go-to strategies in searching digital newspapers for African Americans. It worked exceptionally well.[8]

True to form, the *Culpeper Exponent* reported the death of Blanche Greene's grandmother Lucy Hawkins Deane under the heading "Death of Respected Colored Woman." "The white people of this section of the county thought there was no one like 'Aunt' Lucy," the reporter gushed, "and manifested their appreciation by turning out in large numbers at her funeral." One wonders what the reaction to this display of paternalism was within the congregation at Free Union Baptist Church. Nevertheless, Black Virginians' connections to influential white people could yield a certain amount of useful social capital with the white community.[9]

Another newspaper notice regarding Blanche's grandparents illustrates the larger community's admiration for family devotion while demonstrating how the shadow of slavery still loomed over Blanche as a child. When Lucy Hawkins Deane died in 1912, she left behind Blanche's grandfather Robert Deane. That fall, the eighty-seven-year-old man mounted his horse and rode the eight miles to the county courthouse. There he requested a license to marry a woman named Ellen. In a remarkably frank article—and without a hint of irony—the *Culpeper Exponent* described Robert's situation as follows: "His wife, he said, was sold long before the war and he had married again as she had also, but now that the respective husband and wife of each had died he 'wanted to marry his wife again.'" The newspaper reporter's glib recounting of the breaking up of a Black family seems incomprehensible except in the context of a society that had convinced itself of slavery's benign nature.[10]

By 1920, seventeen-year-old Blanche Greene still lived with her parents and had already had a child, eight-month-old James C. Greene. The official records do not hint at a family secret regarding James's parentage. According to family lore, a newcomer to Culpeper married the Greenes' oldest daughter, Martha, and had three children with her. The interloper also cast an eye on the other Greene girls and, whether by seduction or brute force, proceeded to impregnate two of the younger sisters—including Blanche. The story goes that when he made advances on his own daughter, the family reached a breaking point. His wife reputedly slowly poisoned him. His death certificate records eight days of sickness leading to his death from a cerebral hemorrhage. Family tales also claim that Blanche's daughter, Dorothy, born in 1922, was also a product of this man's advances, but that remains unconfirmed by other sources. Her birth occurred at a time when Jim Strother and Blanche Greene had likely already met. Strother would later insist that neither child was his.[11]

Blanche moved to Alexandria to work as a domestic soon after Dorothy's birth. One of the few occupations open to African American women with limited education other than farm labor, domestic work at least afforded indoor employment. Nevertheless, it was both psychologically and physi-

Robert Lee and Alice Greene raised their daughter Blanche in this house in the Cedar Grove community. Several relatives built homes nearby on Woolen Lane. Greene family home, Woolen Lane, Culpeper County, Virginia. (Photograph by Corlis Kimball Chamberlain)

cally demanding. At the beck and call of white women and often exposed to the unwanted advances of white men, domestic workers laundered clothes, cooked meals, and cared for white children in the Jim Crow South. Black women typically contributed essential income to their households, especially at a time when most Black men faced low wages and sporadic work.

Both of Strother's wives, Mary and Blanche, labored as domestics for well-to-do families, and bluesmen and songsters often extolled the advantages of such unions. In his 1927 Victor recording of "Cocaine Blues," Lynchburg's Luke Jordan boasted, "I've got a girl, she works in the white folks' yard," a sentiment expressed in numerous African American songs. According to Jordan and other musicians, having such a woman meant good food from the white people's table, economic stability, and the freedom to pursue music and other endeavors. Strother certainly benefited from this arrangement, although he also brought money into the household.[12]

Yet Jordan's positive sentiment was not universal. Louisiana bluesman Willie Thomas expressed the downside of such an arrangement: "You see, a woman could get a job at that time, but a man couldn't hardly get it. Want a little money, had to get it from her. And it gave a man the blues: he's been the boss all the time and now the Depression come and she's washin' at the white folk's yard. And she's cookin' there and she can get a little money but she's feedin' him, so he can't cut up too much." Jim Strother probably saw both good times and bad in the always tenuous situation of a street musician and dance-hall and medicine-show performer; his wives' income surely sustained him during the bad times. Whether this was part of the resentment that eventually troubled his relationship with Blanche remains unknown.[13]

Strother was still living on Oak Street in Baltimore at the time of their marriage, while Blanche resided at 319 North Columbus Street in Alexandria, Virginia. She does not appear in the Alexandria city directories, but the white family living at that address does. Miss Frances Pauline Harrison, a thirty-three-year-old "ladies tailor," lived in the row house with her extended family and ran her business from the residence. Blanche no doubt assisted with the management of the household, which included Harrison's elderly parents; her older brother, a mill manager; and her sister. Railroad workers, watchmen, salespeople, teachers, and retail workers populated the overwhelmingly white blocks of North Columbus Street and adjacent streets and neighborhoods. Blanche's marriage certificate implies that she "lived-in," but the city directories suggest that many other servants lived in nearby Black enclaves apart from their employers. The place where Blanche toiled at washing, cleaning, and other domestic duties is now part of the upscale Historic Old Town Alexandria neighborhood.[14]

The Reverend Samuel B. Ross of the Third Baptist Church officiated the marriage of James Strother and Blanche Greene on November 19, 1923, in Alexandria, Virginia. Their age difference is notable, though hardly unprecedented—she was 20 and he around 42. Less than two months after their marriage in Alexandria, Blanche and James lost a male child as a result of a premature birth in Culpeper. Obviously, their relationship had begun sometime before their marriage. How this union of a Baltimore street musician and an Alexandria domestic worker developed can only be speculation, but their shared origin in Culpeper and Madison Counties is the most likely answer. Thornton Strother and Noah Greene, the respective grandfathers of both parties, had lived close to each other in Locust Dale in the 1880s. Perhaps a more obvious link is through Jim Strother's first cousin Lizzie Strother Green, who taught for a time at the Eckington School that the Greene children attended.[15]

Eventually, Jim and Blanche Strother settled into a small cottage in the town of Culpeper that sat on "Barbour Alley in the rear of the Gertrude

Armstrong residence on Railroad Avenue" near the city's Black business district and the Wharf. The census taker who visited the home in 1930 recorded Strother's profession as "musician" and his place of employment as "dance hall." Scattered along the streets and alleys of the Black enclaves in Culpeper, such establishments provided a welcome relief to the long workweek. Still in the last stages of America's Prohibition experiment when Strother returned to town, these small venues might provide illegal liquor and allow gambling. Fatal violence erupted at one such dance hall on Culpeper Street in the Fishtown neighborhood in 1925. Barber Lewis Ellis brought a pistol to the dance hall and confronted "Frog" Williams in an adjacent alley, shooting him three times. Such episodes made the newspapers and unfortunately offer what few insights we have into the life and location of such establishments. The areas of Black entertainment, especially the Wharf and its surrounding neighborhoods, changed very little between Strother's youth and the civil rights era. Zann Nelson, a Culpeper native and historian, remembered a Black nightclub in the area still going full tilt in the 1970s.[16]

As a working musician, Strother would have traveled into the countryside to Black settlements and their places of entertainment. Virginia had a well-established tradition of house parties, as did many other Southern states. Host families rolled up their rugs and moved furniture to make room for a night of music and dancing. Virginia bluesmen readily recalled these down-home frolics. John Cephas served an apprenticeship under Caroline County's David Taliaferro, who taught him much of his Piedmont guitar style. The two men traveled the "house-to-house circuit" mostly in the Bowling Green area, but sometimes they ventured as far away as North Carolina and West Virginia and even to cities with large populations of Southern migrants. The host family typically provided food, home brew, and corn liquor; frequently this served as the musician's payment. Revelers danced the buck dance, the slow drag, and "kicking the mule," depending on the tempo of the music. Cephas nostalgically recalled the neighborliness and sociability of these house parties, heralding the closeness that these events fostered within rural communities. He recalled that "everybody, they would gather around different family members and friends' houses . . . we'd all get together and drink corn liquor and play guitar and have a real good time, you know, like a country breakdown."[17]

Cephas also acknowledged that the presence of alcohol fueled jealousies and could turn revelries into brawls and scenes of violence. Drunken men sometimes targeted the musicians out of jealousy. "A lot of times I have almost gotten in fights over women," he recalled, "but especially if you're an entertainer or you're in the limelight." Songsters faced a decision when the atmosphere of the room clearly augured violence: slip away from the whole mess before things got out of hand, or get ready to fight. Black people knew that the police would not intervene at a rural brawl in their community unless someone got "serious hurt," Cephas remembered, "and then they'd come the next day." He concluded that "nine times out of ten the police were scared to come in the Black community" during such an affray.[18]

The northern Piedmont and Blue Ridge counties had a long history of rural frolics, dances, and house parties. Most never came to the attention of white Virginians unless they ended in violence. In 1907, the *Culpeper Exponent* reported the shooting of Henry Jett, a Black resident of Rappahannock County, at a Saturday dance in Frytown, a Black settlement near Warrenton. The following year the editors took notice of two calamities near the Wolftown settlement in Madison County: the burning of Edmond Jackson's home while he attended "a festival given by one of the neighbors" and the shooting of Crit Spotswood by William Strother—no relation to Jim Strother, as far as I can tell—at a "colored dance" at the farm of W. M. Early.[19]

Corn liquor circulated freely at these rural parties and town dance halls. Well before Virginia's experiment in Prohibition, Powell Green stood before the mayor's court on a charge of bootlegging while an anxious crowd "gathered around the Mayor's office to hear the trial." (I haven't connected him to Strother's Greenes, but who knows?) He apparently had an established reputation in the business. The court took the testimony of several people that he was "known as a go between or silent partner in the illegal disposal of liquor, and that he as a first aid to Hannah Jones could easily supply the material for allaying the thirst of he who was dry." A marked 50-cent piece used to buy the whiskey proved to be his undoing. Green's lawyer "tried to prove that while Green was not known to have any employment, yet he was considered as a pretty good sort of a fellow and not known to have any bad habits." The mayor clearly was not impressed, and Green and Hannah Jones both received $100 fines and a sixty-day jail sentence, which Green appealed. Two prominent Black citizens, Henry Smith and E. H. Grasty, paid Green's $200 bond. Obviously, he was also well liked in the Black community.[20]

Culpeper County always had its fair share of bootleggers and moonshiners providing illegal liquor to whites and Black revelers alike, and this tradition continued well into the twentieth century. Jeffrey Scott, born and bred in Culpeper, regaled me with vivid stories of the liquor trade. Despite his considerable musical talents—he learned at the knee of songster John Jackson or, as he calls him, "Uncle Johnny"—Jeffrey has been a trucker, mortician, farmer, and deputy sheriff. In that last line of work, he crossed swords with several local bootleggers, including some modern-day Strothers. He expressed the lament of many local cops in a small community: he ended up arresting friends and kin whom he knew well. Jeffrey also remembered his uncle's accounts of good-time house parties broken up by jealous fights and drunken brawls—scenes with which Jim Strother would have been all too familiar.[21]

While Jim Strother made his money at the dance halls and byways, Blanche Strother went to work in the home of Culpeper resident Nannie J. Lacy, who lived with her three adult children on East Street. The Lacy siblings were all professionals. Harry B. was a dentist, daughter Leslie taught voice, and William L. was a physician. Nannie and her husband, William B. Lacy, farmed considerable and valuable land in the Locust Dale District of neighboring Madison County until William's untimely death in 1922. Both were old enough to have known Blanche's grandfather Noah Greene, who lived and worked as a farmhand in the same district of Madison County into the 1880s. Perhaps this accounted for the family's strong devotion to Blanche in her later time of need.[22]

While Blanche enjoyed a good relationship with her employers, things at home were less than satisfactory. Based on later accounts, the couple had a tumultuous relationship as they tried to negotiate the hard times of the Great Depression and Jim's sporadic work. The two children were surely victims of the disorder in the house. They likely spent considerable time with their grandmother at the home place in Cedar Grove as Blanche labored long hours in the Lacy household and Jim cobbled together a meager living performing wherever he could. Teachers dismissed their son James as "worthless" and unteachable. Despite two generations of literate Greenes, he never learned to read or write. As time would prove, his deficit was not due to a lack of intelligence or drive but to the obvious dysfunction of the family. The violence within the Strother household would explode into public view in 1935. The unintended consequences of these events resulted in the thirteen recordings that traditional music fans value today.[23]

13

Murder on Barbour Alley

Yes, your fair brown will tell you
That she'll love you all her life [spoken: "poor boy"],
Meet another dude 'round the corner and retell that same lie twice.
—JAMES LEE STROTHER, "Going to Richmond," recorded 1936

Jim Strother shot and killed his wife Blanche on Tuesday evening, April 2, 1935, in their home on Barbour Alley in the town of Culpeper. According to official reports, the deed had no witnesses except the shooter and his victim. (It's not clear where Blanche's two children were that night, but neither newspaper accounts nor court reports mention them as witnesses.) Strother never disputed these bare facts, but the circumstances and causes of the murder depended on who told the story. If the town's lawmen knew of the killing that evening, as they likely did, they displayed little urgency in attending to the crime. Town Sergeant Joe Bowers didn't arrest Strother until Wednesday morning. Strother handed Bowers his .38 revolver "on demand" and surrendered without incident. According to Bowers, Strother recounted that visitors had been to the Strother home that evening. After her guests retired, Blanche sat down at a table and began writing a letter. Jim Strother, armed with his pistol, approached her from behind, firing at least three shots. The first bullet was fired from point-blank range into the top of her head, penetrating into her body; remarkably, she survived for several days.[1]

Strother made some rather damning admissions that morning, according to Bowers. The lawman claimed that Strother "expressed no regret for his rash act and admitted his guilt" and "meant to kill her." Early newspaper accounts spoke of Strother's jealousy and drinking as the kindling for the shooting. Bowers also remarked that Strother "appeared to be badly frightened," a natural reaction for a Black man who would likely be charged with a serious offense.[2]

As news of the murder spread throughout Culpeper County and the surrounding region, Blanche Strother still clung to life. Local physician D. W. Kelly initially treated her but, seeing the severity of her wounds, quickly transferred her to the University of Virginia Hospital in Charlottesville. Throughout this ordeal Blanche remained conscious. Culpeper's *Virginia Star* newspaper conspicuously noted that the Lacy family, who employed Blanche Strother as a domestic, visited her frequently there over the subsequent days.[3]

The judicial system acted with more dispatch than Sergeant Bowers had. Jim Strother was arraigned before Judge C. Everett Reams Jr. on the day of his arrest, April 3, and he admitted to the shooting, "which he said was the result of a quarrel with his wife over her absence from home for several hours Sunday." Like most African American defendants, Strother stood alone before the bar while making this incriminating statement. He was bound over to the grand jury and remanded to jail "pending the result of his wife's injuries."[4]

While Jim Strother awaited his appearance before the grand jury in his jail cell, Blanche Greene Strother lay in a bed some sixty miles away in the University Hospital at Charlottesville. Her death certificate only hints at the terrible suffering she must have endured. Doctors performed an exploratory laparotomy to repair perforations to her intestines from one of the gunshots on April 3. Four days later she had developed hypostatic pneumonia. A day later she was dead.

On April 11, the *Virginia Star* reported that Blanche's "body was brought back to Culpeper and the funeral services will take place from the church of Good Hope." Good Hope Baptist Church stands about four miles northwest of the town of Culpeper in the Norman community, making it unlikely to be the final resting place of Blanche Strother. Mount Pony's Free Union Cemetery holds the remains of Blanche's mother and at least two of her siblings; it was surely here that Blanche was laid to rest.[5]

On Monday, April 15, Strother arose and took the short walk from the county jail to the Culpeper Courthouse. Inside, he faced Judge Alexander T. Browning, Commonwealth's Attorney R. A. Bickers, and an all-white

A grand jury indicted James Lee Strother for the crime of murder in the Culpeper County Courthouse in April 1935. Soon thereafter he stood before Judge Alexander T. Browning and pleaded guilty to second-degree murder. I spent many hours in the courthouse's record room searching for Strother and his relatives. (Photograph by Corlis Kimball Chamberlain)

grand jury. While they were not a jury of his peers, Strother certainly knew some of the men who would pass judgment on him, and they knew him as well. Popular Southern courtroom dramas often play into stereotypes of tobacco-chewing rednecks sitting in judgment of Black men. The citizens impaneled to rule on Strother's true bill, in contrast, mirrored the classic—if no less racist—county-town Southern bourgeoisie. These were stolid, conservative townsmen of some means, men who took religion and the racial and social order seriously.[6]

L. Frank Smith, the jury's foreman, ran a wholesale grocery business in the town and served as the founding secretary of the Culpeper Silk Mills, one of the few manufacturing enterprises in the county. Thomas W. Hendrick, the superintendent of the Culpeper school system, also sat in the jury box, along with Robert W. Early, proprietor of the venerable Waverly Hotel; Walter W. Brown, an insurance man; and Henry P. Walton, a retired postal agent. Rounding out this slice of Culpeper's professional and middle class was farmer Harry T. Bowers. These men knew who came and went in front of their establishments in the small Southern town—including street musicians like Strother and his wife Blanche as she passed to and from her employer's place and shopped in the segregated stores.[7]

We do not know what witnesses appeared before the grand jury or what courtly, bespectacled Commonwealth's Attorney R. A. Bickers told the assembled men. We do know that Jim Strother testified before the all-white panel but changed his story considerably from his earlier admissions. Now Strother insisted, as he did in his subsequent pardon pleadings, that the killing was an accident provoked by Blanche's anger. He had fired his pistol in self-defense, he claimed, and only intended to scare his wife by firing at her feet. Newspaper reports played this admission for ironic-comic effect, calling it "rather an extraordinary plea in view of the fact that the defendant is blind."[8]

The six white jury members brushed aside Strother's claims that Blanche attacked him and that he fired in self-defense without murderous intent. They unanimously indicted the blind musician for murder. Strother now faced trial for a crime "that may be punishable with death." Due to the seriousness of the charge, Judge Browning appointed local attorneys Charles M. Waite and Burnett Miller Jr. to defend Strother, noting that "the accused has no counsel and no means of employing one." The judge set a trial date and the clerk wrote it down: April 22.[9]

Strother's legal team was certainly competent, if possibly going through the motions. Waite, in his mid-sixties, had practiced in Culpeper County during a long career filled mostly with the usual work of a small-town lawyer—estate matters, property disputes, and land deeds. Still, he had considerable political and legal experience. He had been mayor of Culpeper in the 1890s, advancing several improvements in the town. He also had had a brush with one of the most sensational murder trials in Virginia history while serving as Culpeper's commonwealth's attorney. Two Strothers—both prominent white men—had murdered family confidant and well-known Culpeper citizen William F. Bywaters at the Strother family seat, "Rotherwood," for "ruining" their younger sister in 1907. Newspapers across the nation published the lurid case details of illegal abortions, a deathbed shotgun wedding, and family betrayal. Waite never tried the case. In an explicit recognition of the entangled nature of Culpeper's ruling elite both socially and through family ties, Waite and the presiding judge declared themselves hopelessly conflicted and withdrew. Authorities appointed the commonwealth's attorney of Fauquier County to prosecute and brought in a jury from Shenandoah County.

In the end, both Strothers went free. A law review article concluded, "There is little doubt that, with possibly one or two exceptions, the plea of emotional insanity, interposed by the defendant Strothers, had no weight whatever with the jurors, and that the acquittal was based solely upon the unwritten law, which has prevailed in every Southern state since the memory of man runneth not to contrary, that the despoiler of a woman's virtue shall atone for his crime at the muzzle of a double-barrelled shot gun."[10]

Waite probably didn't find much irony in catching a case of murder committed by a Black Strother less than thirty years after he stepped away from a too-hot-to-handle homicide by two white Strothers—but I did, at least initially. What could be more striking than the contrasting fates of defendants with the same name across the color line? Were the Strothers of Rotherwood the enslavers of the ancestors of Waite's client? Such questions initially fired my imagination, but then reality set in. Culpeper and the surrounding Piedmont counties were thick with Strothers of both races, no doubt a legacy of slavery but nearly impossible to untangle. Waite wouldn't have given it a second thought, nor would he have worried much about the racial disparities of a legal system he considered fair and just.

Waite's fresh-faced co-counsel may have been from a younger generation, but he also had a respectable training and background. Burnett Miller Jr. had graduated from the University of Richmond's T. C. Williams Law School just four years prior. Well educated, young, and ambitious, he had recently been elected to the Virginia House of Delegates while still in his mid-twenties.[11]

When Strother and his white lawyers walked into the Culpeper Courthouse and stood before Judge Browning on the appointed trial date, the prisoner pleaded guilty to second-degree murder. The court handed down a sentence of twenty years, which the commonwealth's attorney, the judge, and Strother's court-appointed attorneys no doubt considered both fair and justified. In their minds, the court had efficiently dispatched a case that in the end was simply a domestic dispute between Black people turned violent. The court closed the books on the case by authorizing payment by the county of "the statutory fee of Twenty-five Dollars" to attorneys Miller and Waite "for their services in defending the defendant." A decade after he entered the Culpeper Courthouse to represent Jim Strother, Burnett Miller would take Judge Browning's seat as the judge of the Ninth Judicial Circuit.[12]

Underlying this unanimity was the incestuous nature of the bar—and elites in general—in small-town Virginia. The tight-knit fraternity of white, male, and prosperous lawyers extended beyond the courtroom. Less than three months after Judge Browning handed down Jim Strother's sentence, Eliza Grimsley Miller, the sister of Strother's co-counsel, married the judge who had arraigned him, C. Everett Reams Jr. In the chummy world of county politics and law, the decision of someone's fate could be pre-ordained. Nobody in the system thought a prolonged trial to attempt to reduce the charge—let alone argue self-defense—was justified.[13]

There had been no witnesses to the shooting other than Strother himself and his wife. Still, he must have realized how tenuous his situation was, given his prior statements—made without benefit of counsel. It is likely that his lawyers convinced him that a plea deal was in the interests of all concerned. While there is no question that Strother shot Blanche, the legal proceedings epitomized the dark efficiency of the Jim Crow justice system. It also demonstrated the relative lack of concern most white people had when one Black person shot another. Suffice it to say that if Strother's victim had been white, the story and his sentence would have turned out very differently.

We are still left with the key question—what really happened on Barbour Alley in the weeks and days before the murder and on that fateful early morning of the second day of April? The wheels of justice turned too quickly for the courts to create more than the most *pro forma* record of Strother's indictment and plea. The Culpeper County Courthouse holds no police evidence, records from the grand jury, or even Strother's own testimony. Our only window onto the facts of the case comes from often-inaccurate press reports and Strother's later pleadings with Virginia governor James H. Price for a conditional pardon. Strother was an experienced performer, crafting compelling musical narratives in medicine shows, dance halls, and on the streets for white and Black listeners alike. No doubt he was a master of gauging his audience. Now he played to an audience of one for his very freedom. This performance was as serious as any he had ever attempted, but this time he could not rely solely on his own invention and mother wit.

To argue his case for Governor Price, he needed help. Unable to read or write, he likely turned to a fellow inmate or a sympathetic guard to craft his appeal. As all historians know, legal petitions are as formulaic and predictable as any culture-bound narrative form—like a British ballad or kabuki theater. Such petitions are morality plays that are meant to convince in the most obsequious manner possible. While Strother's letters are appropriately deferential to the governor, he stubbornly insisted that he was the victim. Strother claimed that the "evidence and facts showed conclusively that my act was committed in self defense," and another plea provided a similarly cryptic account: "I was being attacked by my wife, who had been unfaithful to me, & shot her in defense of my own life."[14]

Strother dictated the most detailed account of his relationship with Blanche Greene, her supposed abuse, and the circumstances of the murder in his very first letter to Governor Price:

> In March 1935, in order to protect myself from the fury of my wife, I fired my pistol and happened to hit her and she later died from the wound. This sounds strange, but I am totally blind. I married a woman who had had two children out of wedlock before I married her. After our marriage she continued to see the father of one of her children. We had some arguments over her acts, and on previous occasions she had hit me over the head and knocked me down, one time she used an iron poker and the other time a radio stool. I still have a hole in my head from one of these blows. On the occasion of the shooting she had been out with one of her children and on her return she told what neighbors she had been to see, when her own child spoke up and told me that his mother had left him at that neighbor's home and had gone across the road and spent a long time with the man who was the father of one of her children. This information brought on an argument and she jumped up and said she would swat me again. We had been sitting on the side of the bed and when she ran toward the fire-place, as I thought to get the poker, I reached under the pillow where I had kept a pistol for several years and got my gun and shot toward the fireplace to scar[e]. She had stopped [sic] over and the bullet hit her on the head from which wound she later died.[15]

Here Strother set forth the fullest explanation of the killing that we have, both the causes and mitigating factors: infidelity, spousal abuse, and even his blindness. This version is wildly different than the initial reports gleaned from Sergeant Bowers's interview with Strother and his first court appearance. With little physical evidence or testimony other than Strother's word, the two tales are difficult to reconcile. Still, Occam's razor might suggest which account rings true. The physicians at University Hospital clearly recorded a shot fired into the top of Blanche's head that ended up in her abdomen. Which story is more likely? A blind man randomly firing at the feet of a stooped-over wife? (Wouldn't Blanche, threatened with a gun, flee the house?) Or a calculated, close-range execution carried out by a man capable of negotiating dense city streets? In the end, of course, the details of the case made little difference to the county. The state had a confession; a Black person was dead at the hands of a jealous spouse; and a guilty plea had been efficiently obtained.

Strother's account of the murder and the circumstances that precipitated it did not go unchallenged. R. A. Bickers, the commonwealth's attorney who prosecuted Strother, had a very different view of the matter. Noting that "there were no actual eye witnesses to the shooting," Bickers questioned Strother's claims of self-defense and wondered that he "could make no explanation why he had the gun so conveniently at hand to commit the offense." Perhaps sensing that the lack of evidence or a trial made for a less-than-convincing argument, Bickers went further. He hinted at a darker motive for the slaying, recounting that "at the time of the trial and prior thereto a great many intimations came to my office that Jim Strother was jealous of his wife, and that he had treated her very badly for some considerable time." Was Strother under the watchful eye of officials in Culpeper? It is not out of the question. Employed in a dance hall in a small town where people knew each other's business, Strother may have attracted the notice of police and other officials.[16]

But who had made these "intimations"? Newspaper accounts suggest an answer. The reporter for the *Virginia Star* who summarized the case after Strother's conviction concluded—probably as a nod to the supposed impartiality of white people's treatment of the affair—that Blanche was "visited each day by members of the family of her employers in Culpeper, all of whom spoke in the highest terms of her and who expressed the opinion that the shooting had been entirely unprovoked." It is almost certain that Bickers received his intelligence regarding Strother's behavior and culpability from other members of the white gentry rather than from the Black community, and certainly not the people who frequented Strother's dance-hall performances. In the case of Strother versus Strother, Blanche likely benefited from the secondhand social status and respectability bestowed on her by her association with the "better class" of white people in the Culpeper community and her family's long reputation as "respectable colored people."[17]

That a commonwealth's attorney would defend his handling of such a case is hardly surprising. What gives Bickers's account a bit more weight is the fact that he ultimately argued for the musician's release. Replying to Governor Price's request for his thoughts on the matter, Bickers, after scoffing at the veracity of Strother's pleadings, remarkably concluded, "I feel inclined to recommend a conditional pardon to him provided he would return to Baltimore, which was the original place of residence before he came to Culpeper." Jim Strother would be Baltimore's problem.[18]

One fundamental reality of this whole sordid story gnawed at me. While standing at the cemetery at Free Union Baptist Church, I realized that I was mere miles from the Library of Congress's Culpeper facility, the place that carefully preserves the words and art of James Lee Strother in its audio-visual archives. Yet Blanche Greene's voice had been silenced—as quiet as the grounds that held the remains of her damaged body. I knew nothing about her beyond cryptic mentions in newspaper reports, government reports, and the words of Jim Strother himself. And what of her children, James C. and Dorothy Greene? A partial answer to this conundrum came through the exertions of local historian Zann Nelson. While it did not give voice to Blanche herself, it at least provided some closure to the tragedy of her murder.

Zann took the initiative. Mining her extensive local connections and considerable research skills, she found a phone number for a person in South Carolina who might well be a relative. She cold-called a man who turned out to be Blanche's grandson: James "Jim" Greene. After several conversations, she arranged for Mr. Greene and his wife to visit us in Virginia.

On a brilliant fall day in 2020, I drove from Richmond to Culpeper to meet Jim Greene and his wife, Shirley. An uncomfortable combination of excitement and nervousness filled me as I navigated the Piedmont's back roads. I was an outsider stepping into another person's story of family trauma. I felt lucky that the Greenes were even willing to talk to me. I understood from thirty-five years of doing public history in Virginia that I had no right to expect trust, especially from elders who had suffered under Jim Crow.

Zann and I met the Greenes at the train station in the heart of what had once been the center of Culpeper's vibrant Black community. We walked a few blocks to the site where Blanche and Jim Strother's fatal encounter had taken place. (The small home where the Strothers lived has long since disappeared.) As it turned out, Jim Greene had only recently learned the fate of his grandmother. His father had assiduously avoided discussing this family secret. As we walked, the Greenes mentioned that family members had remembered Jim's father, James C. Greene, leaving Culpeper County soon after the murder. (Blanche's mother, Alice, had received custody of

James's sister, Dorothy, after the murder. Dorothy had worked as a domestic in Alexandria, as her mother had done. She had died by the time I met the Greenes.) Shirley Greene had carefully read Jim Strother's pardon file, too. A detail I had missed, but that she immediately understood, was that young James had inadvertently told Jim Strother of Blanche's visit to another man the evening of the murder. Little wonder that he had held the secret of his mother's fate closely.

James C. Greene, almost sixteen years old at the time of his mother's murder, traveled north. Unable to afford train fare, he hitched a ride on a lumber truck. He arrived unannounced at the home of his aunt, Pearl Greene Lightfoot, in South Orange, New Jersey—another traveler along the highways of the Great Migration. "Boy how did you get here and where did you come from," Pearl exclaimed. "God knows I don't know what to do with you." Still in the grips of the Great Depression, she luckily found the young man a position cleaning a dental office and delivering packages.[19]

The dentist, Charles E. Bowmar, carefully observed his new employee. Although Greene had been disparaged by his teachers in school, Bowmar intuited that he was intelligent, proficient with his hands, and mechanically inclined. He began doing odd jobs around the office, fixing plumbing, repairing windows, and painting. Soon he began assisting the dental technician, and a career was born. James C. Greene would become the go-to technician for Black dentists in the tristate region, providing dental molds, dentures, and other supplies. He became a highly respected member of the African American community. Jim Greene recalled that he could go to any store or restaurant in South Orange as a youth and buy what he wanted. All he had to do was say that he was James C. Greene's son, and the bill was sent to his father.

Jim Greene graciously shared genealogical trees and other documents regarding his family. The most detailed was a biography of his father written by Dr. Bowmar, a touching tribute titled "A Story of James C. Greene." The four-page typescript is a classic tale of American perseverance and redemption. The dentist clearly empathized with Greene's difficult road. Dr. Bowmar might have had advantages that Greene did not, but, like all Black people, he understood the sting of racial discrimination and the difficulties of the Great Migration. Bowmar held an undergraduate degree from Johnson C. Smith College, a historically Black institution in Charlotte, North Carolina, and a graduate degree in dentistry from Meharry Medical College. Yet when he tried to set up a practice in the North, no one would lend him the money for the necessary equipment. The young dentist landed a job as a Pullman porter, one of the only unionized Black professions. Dr. Bowmar eventually earned enough capital to open his practice.

Bowmar documented James C. Greene's rise from confused and dispirited teenager to a successful professional. Greene had been disparaged as a "piece of useless humanity" by a grade-school teacher and was without skills. Bowmar wrote, "If there was ever a man who was predicted to be a failure, here he is." Greene's friend and mentor recorded Greene's Horatio Alger–like rise from a parentless, lost child into a professional man with a fine house and an accomplished family: "The run-away boy . . . has finally come through."

Dr. Bowmar also noted the achievements of Greene's namesake son. He encouraged James Jr. to attend his alma mater, Johnson C. Smith College, where Jim majored in mathematics, led several student organizations, and played football on scholarship. He went on to a distinguished career in technology, working as a systems engineer with IBM Corporation and holding positions with other prominent tech companies. One other life-changing event occurred at Johnson C. Smith—Jim met his wife, Shirley.

The next day, we traveled into the countryside to the Greene family's old home place and the surrounding community in Cedar Grove in the shadow of Mount Pony. Memories came flooding back to Jim Greene as we explored the haunts of his youth. Jim's father, like many people who migrated north, had sent his young son to visit with Culpeper relatives during summers in the early 1950s. As we explored the abandoned Greene home, a rambling, frame farmhouse now obscured by the growth of trees and underbrush, Jim reconstructed a web of family relationships along Woolens Lane. We tramped through high grass and brambles to the well where the family drew their water. Just beyond the spring, his aunt Lucille's home still stood, and further down the street was the place of his uncle Clifton Taliaferro. He recalled playing baseball in the fields near Clifton's house. Jim was moved—as was I—as we retraced his childhood steps across the landscape.

The Culpeper that Jim Greene remembered primarily centered on the family farm, the Free Union Baptist Church, and rides into the town of Culpeper in the back of a pickup truck. Some memories were pleasant, but others remind us that the dangerous world Strother described in some of his songs was not a thing of the past in the 1950s—and in many ways is still with us. One particularly chilling episode stands out. Jim Greene and a few young friends had come to town and innocently bantered with a group of young white girls. His uncle Cliff Taliaferro received a threatening phone call that evening warning him that behavior like that wasn't tolerated in the South. This occurred at a time when the media had brought to a national audience the story of the lynching of Emmett Till. Jim's father never again sent him back to Culpeper for the summer.

The insights that Jim and Shirley Greene shared with me brought some closure to the story of Blanche Greene and James Lee Strother. While I could not fully give voice to Blanche as I had hoped, I felt that our visit had given me a rare window onto her family and legacy. Most important, I hope that it helped the Greenes gain a better understanding of James C. Greene's difficult experience as a young man. For me, that is as important as the musical legacy of James Lee Strother.

We will never know exactly what happened in the house on Barbour Alley on April 2, 1935, except that a man fatally shot his wife. We will also never know if lawyers for the defendant could have convinced an all-white jury of a reduced sentence or acquittal, although the chances seem slim. But we can see, in retrospect, how Strother's lyrics of cheating women and unfaithful spouses were not merely stock blues expressions but personal complaints of perceived injustices.

14

The Virginia State Prison Farm

Ain't no hammer in this mountain,
Ring like mine, ring like mine.
—JAMES LEE STROTHER, "This Old Hammer," recorded 1936

John Lomax and Harold Spivacke both spoke glowingly of the "beautiful rolling country" they saw as they motored down the road to the Virginia State Prison Farm. I couldn't agree more. Once clear of the capital's west-end sprawl, the rider passes along the undulating hills of the Virginia Piedmont. Moving west along the two-lane road, the farmland and small settlements are now disrupted only occasionally by the entrances to tony subdivisions with faux-colonial names. To the left, the traveler catches brief glimpses of the James River, the original highway for commerce and travel in this bucolic environment. Just as when Jim Strother made this journey, it is still an overwhelmingly rural landscape. The state prison farm sits comfortably within the countryside, with its large agricultural fields falling back to the bottomland of the James.

I made several visits to the farm over the years before its closure in 2015. In 1989 and 1990, I made two forays in order to collect artifacts for an exhibition from the abandoned brickmaking operation that hugged the river and where prisoners performed backbreaking labor in terrible conditions in Strother's time. While there, I experienced a small reminder of the dangers inmates faced: a copperhead rose out of a brick mold to greet me in a small shed along the river. A wizened, no-nonsense guard's tour of the prison is another vivid memory. He told fascinating stories, some right out of the popular film *O Brother, Where Art Thou?* He claimed that prisoners watched movies along with local residents during his early days at the prison. This account was a slight embellishment, but not by much. It turns out that the State Farm's chapel doubled as a movie theater. The inmates watched B- or C-grade moving pictures each Saturday at 1:30 p.m., with another show at 8:00 p.m. "for the officers, their families and friends in the surrounding community." Several locals later validated this remarkable account.[1]

Around 2003, I returned to research the musicians who were recorded there in 1936. While I gained little in the way of new information, it did inspire me to dig deeper and eventually commemorate the event. In partnership with Jan Ramsey, then president of the James River Blues Society, I wrote and sponsored a state historical marker in honor of the men who made these recordings, one of six markers memorializing Virginia's blues and music heritage. Luckily, the documentary record yielded more than I could have imagined regarding the circumstances of the session and the fate of Jim Strother after his brief turn in the sun as a recording artist.

Before he would make the journey to the State Farm in Goochland County, Strother first passed behind the walls of the Virginia State Penitentiary in Richmond. Driver and guard W. H. Miller traveled a wide swath of Northern and Piedmont Virginia on May 21, 1935, gathering prisoners. He picked up four men—two "colored" and two "white"—from the Culpeper jail that day, including Jim Strother. Miller delivered the men to one of the oldest state penitentiaries in the United States. Following bureaucratic procedure, the penitentiary clerks and physicians assigned Strother an inmate number, recorded his general physical appearance—"tall and slender"—and duly noted his blindness in both eyes. Strother sat for his "mug shot," an image that strikingly revealed the damage to his eyes. The blind musician probably seemed relatively useless to Warden Rice M. Youell and the guards at the penitentiary—not fit to work in the shoe shops or other work sections. In the eyes of the state and his incarcerators, James Lee Strother was now prisoner #33927.[2]

Despite the seriousness of his offense, officials transferred Strother to the Virginia State Prison Farm in Goochland County, Virginia, only a month later. Hardly a flight risk and unable to provide most types of labor, it was an easy decision. Strother's blindness and occupation set him apart from most of his fellow inmates, but he had one thing in common with a majority of the prisoners at the prison farm—he was Black. Grinding poverty, vagrancy laws, and other elements of the Jim Crow system kept a steady

Jim Strother entered the Virginia State Prison Farm in 1935. The imposing bell tower and cellblock greeted new prisoners to the farm. The chapel, just out of sight beyond the main building, not only held religious services but also served as a movie theater for inmates and the local population. (Photograph, ca. 1940, Virginia Chamber of Commerce Collection, Library of Virginia, Richmond)

stream of African Americans flowing into Virginia's legal and penal system. In 1935, Jim Strother joined more than a thousand African Americans who walked through the gates of the Virginia State Penitentiary. Black men made up about 60 percent of the prisoners admitted that year, but the true racial disparity only becomes clear when one considers Virginia's population. In 1930, white Virginians outnumbered Black Virginians nearly two to one as the Great Migration drained Virginia and other Southern states of their Black populations.[3]

The history of Virginia's penal system reflected its movement in and out of the mainstream of American culture. The state built one of the earliest penitentiaries in the United States. Famed architect Benjamin Henry Latrobe designed the horseshoe-shaped edifice in harmony with Enlightenment ideals of penal reform championed by no less a light than Thomas Jefferson. Harsh corporal punishment gave way somewhat to enforced penitence and surveillance. Virginia stood at the forefront of an international movement for penal reform, although the law of slavery always challenged the commonwealth's attempts at change. By the late antebellum period, many realized that the Revolutionary generation's Enlightenment zeal had not fundamentally changed the reality of crime or the prisons. Harsh physical conditions and forced labor still characterized these dismal places.

After the Civil War, Virginia instituted the model that dominated corrections across the American South—the notorious convict lease system. Private industries leased prisoners from the state to perform the most dangerous and labor-intensive work imaginable, including lumbering, coal mining, and canal and railroad construction. This form of forced peonage sidestepped Black rights through a loophole in the Thirteenth Amendment, which had abolished slavery. It invalidated involuntary servitude "except as a punishment for crime whereof the party shall have been duly convicted." White authorities used their power to criminalize innocent behavior—as today. Standing, walking, or just existing while Black became, for the police and courts, vagrancy, idling, and any number of other arbitrary statutes. With an essentially inexhaustible supply of labor provided by the arbitrary enforcement of Black Codes and later Jim Crow laws, employers and the state had almost no incentive to concern themselves with the safety or health of convicts. As the chilling old saying went, "One dies, get another." In a perverse way, these men (and some women) were expendable in ways that enslaved laborers had not been.[4]

A recent study of the myth of John Henry comes to the conclusion that the legendary "steel driving man" was himself a Virginia convict leased to work on railroad tunnels during the Reconstruction period. According to this account, the real John Henry's labors killed him, mirroring the fate of the folk song's protagonist, and he was laid to rest at the "White House," the Virginia State Penitentiary, "in the sand." The archeological discovery of an extensive, but long forgotten, burying ground just outside the prison's walls adds some plausibility to this theory. Whether this account definitively connects the legend with the real-life prisoner is probably beside the point. John Henry continued to live on in the folk songs and legends of almost every community across the South and especially in its prisons. An inmate named Jimmie Owens performed the song for John Lomax in 1936 at the Virginia State Penitentiary just weeks before he encountered Jim Strother at the prison farm. Owens employed a classic East Coast approach to the song, fretting the high E string of his guitar with a metal slide or knife.[5]

In a somewhat surprising turnaround, a set of unique circumstances led Virginia to phase out the convict lease system in the 1890s—one of the few states of the former Confederacy to do so. Issues of profitability, increased revenues from the workshops at the existing state penitentiary, and the rise of political opposition by way of the biracial Readjuster Party in the 1880s all played a role. Virginia politicians had long prided themselves on their supposedly more paternalistic form of white supremacy and anti-democratic one-party rule, congratulating themselves that their system was more "civilized" and less corrupt than that of the Deep South states of Mississippi, Alabama, and Georgia. Yet prisoners at the penitentiary in Richmond and the Virginia State Prison Farm still did hard industrial and agricultural labor—they simply did it within the prison's walls or in the farm's fields. Corrections officials also sent inmates to work camps scattered across the state to maintain roads under the newly formed State Highway Commission beginning in 1906. Convict roadwork became the last vestige of the lease system in Virginia and one of the most enduring images of Southern "justice" in American popular culture.[6]

Jim Strother's Virginia State Prison Farm hugged both banks of the James River west of Richmond in Goochland and Powhatan Counties. Vast expanses of rolling fields in cultivation greeted each prisoner who entered the farm. Inmates planted, hoed, and reaped more than 11,000 acres of oats, wheat, corn, potatoes, rye, and other cash crops. A 1934 report counted 189 head of dairy stock, 56 of beef stock, and 469 swine. The northside operations, where Jim Strother resided, had all of the dairy stock; southside, the beef. Prisoners also worked the 48 mules stabled on the farm and bred horses; the farm recorded colts and mares in its inventory. Five saddle horses were conspicuously listed. These mounts were no doubt ridden by the armed guards who controlled the men as they labored.[7]

Officials in Richmond anxiously looked for new industries to employ the incarcerated. Strother's time in the State Farm corresponded with the construction of the prison's brickworks. Located near the James River amid substantial clay deposits, the works featured little of the current technology used for making bricks, such as automated mixers and extruders to form them. The works had much more in common with nineteenth-century processes—man and mule mixed clay and sand in traditional ring pits while other inmates produced hand-thrown bricks in open-air casting sheds. All of this work took place exposed to the soul-sapping heat of Virginia's summers and the unpredictable winters. The only nod to industrial progress in the complex was a beehive kiln; in June 1937, superintendent R. R. Penn wrote to the State Prison Board proudly reporting the successful test-firing of bricks in the new kiln.[8]

We don't know what type of labor Strother performed at the prison farm. He would not have done agricultural labor and certainly not the heavy work of throwing bricks in the casting sheds of the sprawling prison brickyard. Yet the institution's strict regimen demanded some form of employment. Strother fell into the general class of "inmates who are disabled, in ill health or for some other reason unfit for manual labor," many of whom were "kept reasonably well occupied at knitting, rig weaving or some other form of light work." Possibly he did minor tasks in the prisoner barracks or administrative offices. As we shall see, Warden Penn definitely knew of his talents as an entertainer. A good musicianer could come in handy, performing for fellow inmates.[9]

Strother joined about two hundred other convicts at the State Farm when he arrived in June 1935. By the time Strother stepped in front of the microphone to record for the Library of Congress, the incarcerated population had grown to around three hundred. Why this rapid growth occurred in a single year is not clear, but the constant complaints of the penitentiary superintendent about overcrowding in Richmond is one possibility. Transfers were periodically made from one institution to the other.[10]

Strother entered a penal institution that had seen its share of controversy. A probe by the State Board of Charities and Corrections in 1919 charged that the leadership of the State Prison Farm was "not abreast with the times." The board's report to Governor Westmoreland Davis excoriated the administration for allowing idleness to run rampant at the farm. They reported a "lack of occupation or entertainment for the men, particularly on Sunday, which permits them to engage in gambling and other disobediences." Poor recordkeeping hindered parts of the investigation, in itself a black mark on the prison. The board declared that State Farm superintendent H. T. Parrish had "neither the temperamental nor sociological training which fits one for the office of warden."[11]

The 1919 investigation resulted in Parrish's dismissal and the appointment of R. R. Penn, the man Jim Strother would know as the warden. His appointment hardly seemed to meet the expectations of the Board of Charities and Corrections. Roland Reid Penn only had an eighth-grade education; it seems unlikely that he had any "sociological training." Penn rose through the ranks along the usual path of experience and seniority—first as a guard at the state penitentiary, then as a captain, and finally as super-intendent of the Prison Farm. He was an insider and certainly not a re-former. Predictably, he was soon under fire himself. In 1922, Earl E. Dud-ding, a rather eccentric fellow and founder of the Prisoners' Relief Society, charged Penn and his administration with various abuses. Ultimately, the accusations didn't stick.[12]

Penn may have lacked the kind of training that Progressive reformers thought proper, but he did have some redeeming qualities—solving the problem of idleness, for one. The son of a Bedford County farmer, Penn knew the practicalities of raising crops and tending livestock, and the farm ran well under his stewardship. Penn also advocated for improvements in conditions at the farm under the tutelage of the penitentiary superinten-dent, Rice M. Youell, known as a moderate reformer within the world of prison management. While certainly less foreboding than the state peni-tentiary, the State Farm remained a dangerous place for inmates and guards alike. In an echo of Strother's experience in his early years in Baltimore, the farm featured a ward strictly for tubercular patients. Penn routinely re-ported the deaths of inmates consigned to their last days imprisoned in the ward. Their seclusion ostensibly prevented the spread of their disease, but other dangers threatened the farm's general population.

In early 1935, William R. McCraw, the secretary of the State Prison Board, wrote anxiously to Dr. I. C. Riggin, the commissioner of Virginia's Department of Health. McCraw expressed the board's dismay at a recent outbreak of spinal meningitis at the State Farm. The board's heightened alarm was justified by McCraw: "Since this is the third outbreak at the State Farm within the last three years the prison board is deeply concerned." He asked Riggin's help with providing the "fullest cooperation and assistance" from his department in order to find the causes of the outbreak. Appar-ently, they were unsuccessful.[13] Yet another outbreak of the deadly disease swept through the farm during the second year of Jim Strother's sentence. Superintendent Penn had the unenviable task of notifying family members when their loved ones passed away and making arrangements to transfer the bodies. Adding to the misery, an outbreak of influenza had also struck the farm. Penn noted that "a large number of inmates and employees were confined to their beds." No wonder Jim Strother sang "If I live to see De-cember, / I'm going home, I'm going home" during his recording session.[14]

This was the context of Jim Strother's life in the Virginia State Prison Farm. He may have been unable to see the surrounding fields, stables, barracks, brickworks, and other elements of the landscape, but he could strongly sense them—and those sense impressions would have been largely familiar. He knew well the smell of sweat and the bray of a mule; the morning dew and the aroma it produced on fields of wheat; and the smell of freshly cut hay. He also knew the songs—songs to regulate work, songs to pass the time, songs of powerful men, songs to holler at the world.

In his 1936 recording session, Strother performed one of the defining songs of Black labor, life, and imprisonment—the venerable "Take This Hammer," or, as the Library of Congress catalogers titled it, "This Old Hammer." Later commercial recordings often used the title "Nine-Pound Hammer." In his reworking of this classic work song, Strother's performance not only speaks to his immediate plight at the Virginia State Prison Farm but also echoes the fate of many thousands of other Black people unfairly forced into convict lease and other kinds of exploitative labor and incarceration. Strother, like his musical peers, learned the song outside the walls of the prison, but it continued to be shaped inside.

Jim Strother had heard such songs his entire life from the ubiquitous gangs of railroad laborers who traveled through the northern Piedmont. The old Virginia Midland line became part of the Southern Railroad during Strother's youth, and the steel tracks bisected Culpeper County from north to south, extending through the major northern Piedmont towns— Warrenton, Gordonsville, Orange—and connecting Virginia's countryside with Alexandria, Washington, DC, and beyond. Members of his extended family had worked the railroad lines as far north as Pennsylvania. As a young man he lived through the end of the age of convict lease in Virginia, but prisoners continued to work the roads. Just a county away from Jim Strother's childhood home, John Jackson, one of Virginia's finest and best-documented traditional musicians, recalled learning to play a slide version of "John Henry" from a prison worker near his home in Rappahannock County—one of the first tunes he was taught. John performed it just as the prisoner, "Happy," had shown him, holding a knife between the fingers of his fretting hand to slide along the high E string to produce the song's melody.[15]

"John Henry," "Take This Hammer," and related railroad and hammer tunes were ubiquitous among Southern songsters. Likewise, the songs became fodder for street musicians at a very early time. J. D. Johnson Jr., of Durham, North Carolina, reported a version of "Take This Hammer" to Newman White in 1919, noting that it was heard "sung by an old Negro, who accompanied himself on the banjo, in a small town in eastern North Carolina." Dorothy Scarborough documented several versions by Virginia singers, including those collected in Lynchburg by Lucy Dickinson Urquhart and another heard by Evelyn Cary Williams "from the singing of Charles Calloway, of Bedford County, Virginia, a Negro worker on the road." Calloway's version, like Strother's, includes the ominous "If I live to see December / I'm going home" couplet. It is the last stanza of Strother's song.[16]

This striking verse certainly reflected Strother's situation at the Virginia State Prison Farm, but its roots are found in the desperate conditions of convict lease workers who lived and died doing some of the most danger-ous jobs on earth—tunneling, mining, lumbering, and building infrastruc-ture. In the context of the Piedmont and Blue Ridge region, the work often involved tunneling through mountains to make way for railroad lines. Take the dark origins of "Swannanoa Tunnel," a related tune from the Asheville region of North Carolina. Largely sanitized by later interpreters, includ-ing the influential North Carolina performer and collector Bascom Lamar Lunsford, the song's earliest lyrics express the hopelessness of men worked to death in dangerous circumstances. Falling rocks, black powder mishaps, and long days of grinding labor all took their toll.[17]

Black men caught up in the Jim Crow carceral system brought these songs to their tasks. Prisoners sang versions of "Take This Hammer" in almost every Southern prison visited by John Lomax and his associates. Clifton Wright and a group of convicts sang it at the Virginia State Pen-itentiary on May 31, 1936, just a few weeks before Strother recorded his version. Wright and his associates performed the call-and-response classic as a work song, providing a rhythmic pulse to coordinate the movements of the chorus of workers. Wright and his team also performed the tradi-tional track liner's chant "Can't You Line 'Em" for Lomax. I well recall the Buckingham Track Liners, retired Black railroad men of the Chesapeake and Ohio line, intoning such songs in the early twenty-first century at the Richmond Folk Festival long after the living work tradition had given way to mechanization on America's railroads. Strother's Taylor relatives lived this tradition on the same railroad line.[18]

In the prison environment, the song took on an even deeper meaning as a plea for escape and solace. Strother transformed the highly regulated beat of the work song into a more rhythmically loose and melancholy feel with his banjo. Strother opens the tune with a John Henry–esque boast:

Ain't no hammer in this mountain
Ain't no hammer in this mountain;
Ain't no hammer in this mountain,
Ring like mine, ring like mine.

The blind singer then articulates a classic formulation from the prison and work crew tradition—the escapist wish to run, to lay down the hammer, to rest:

Take this hammer, carry it to the walker,
Tell him I'm gone, tell him I'm gone.

This old hammer git too heavy
This old hammer git too heavy;
This old hammer git too heavy,
Go lie down, go lie down.

The melody and feel of Strother's version of the old song are substantially different from both the traditional work song and the later commercially recorded versions. No doubt he perfected his approach long before the song became enshrined in a slew of popular commercial recordings in the 1920s. Al Hopkins and His Buckle Busters, the band also known as the "Hill Billies," performed on the first commercial 78-rpm record of the song as "The Nine Pound Hammer" for the Brunswick label in New York City in 1927. Their version fuses elements of several folk song streams, notably the "Roll on Buddy" refrain. Charlie Bowman, the band's fiddler on the recording, told folklorist and musician Archie Green that when he was a teenager, the Black railroad crews came through his town and he spent a lot of time hanging around them to listen to their music. He learned the song at that time and then remembered it twenty-two years later in the New York studio. In Green's words, "Nine-Pound Hammer stemmed directly from locutions and a melody used by black railroad-construction laborers early in the century."[19]

The song lived on primarily through the commercial recordings of white country artists, especially Merle Travis's popular reworking of the tune, although Mississippi John Hurt recorded an elegantly simple but powerful version in 1930 for OKeh Records as "Spike Driver Blues." Strother's lyrics, drawn from the deep well of folk tradition, appear again and again in commercial works. "Ain't no hammer in this mountain, / Ring like mine, ring like mine," sang Strother, just a few years before Charlie and Bill Monroe waxed a version for Bluebird Records. Bill's unmistakable staccato mandolin, the rock-solid rhythm, and the brothers' harmonies presaged Bill's instrumental role in the birth of bluegrass music.[20]

Strother added some lines that, while not completely original, seem to speak to a more personal, philosophical place. Near the end of his song, he turns his mind to truisms of the world and thoughts of home:

> Everything that you see shining,
> Ain't no gold, baby, ain't gold.
>
> Everything that you see shining,
> Everything that you see shining;
> Everything that you see shining,
> Ain't no gold, baby, ain't no gold.
>
> Tell little Hattie she better be quilting,
> Gonna be cold, gonna be cold,
> Tell little Hattie she better be quilting
> Gonna be cold, lovin' babe, gonna be cold.
>
> Oh little Hattie keeps on writing
> Oh little Hattie keeps on writing;
> Oh little Hattie keeps on writing,
> I'm going home, baby, I'm going home.

In Strother's hands, "This Old Hammer" becomes plaintive and melancholy, a plea full of lamentation and resignation backed by a light, delicate banjo accompaniment that eschews the driving pulse of other versions. Strother's rendition uses simple rolls that somewhat echo his singing. While Strother was certainly skilled enough to perform instrumental showpieces, it was compelling vocal tunes—whether humorous, contemplative, or intense—that constituted the street musician's stock in trade. Although the final stanza could easily be dismissed as a stock expression typical of other versions of this ubiquitous song, we should at least inquire about what it meant for a blind Black man to sing these words. It certainly fits into Strother's jaded worldview, especially after he became incarcerated, but it is difficult not to imagine a deeper meaning—that the world of the sighted is just as illusory as that of those who rely on their other senses. Such an introspective worldview might have been useful in maintaining one's sanity while "bound in jail" like Paul and Silas.

15

Recording the Folk

*[W]e got a lot of beautiful records which have given many people much
pleasure ever since. . . . [I]t was probably one of the most successful trips
ever undertaken by the Archive.*
—Harold Spivacke to John A. Lomax, 1936

Strother had barely served a year of his sentence when Warden R. R.
Penn summoned him to his residence at the State Farm. Such a request might have been concerning. What did he want? Had there
been a violation of prison rules? Strother arrived at the warden's house to
find two white strangers: Harold Spivacke, assistant chief of the Division
of Music of the Library of Congress, and famed musicologist John Lomax,
honorary curator of the Archive of American Folk Song. The two white
men noticed him, too. Spivacke recalled Strother sitting on the steps of the
warden's house with a "battered banjo." Warden Penn obviously knew of
Strother's talents and likely had employed him as an entertainer for guests,
employees, and fellow inmates on occasion. Soon Strother would have the
opportunity to again ply his trade.

Spivacke later recounted his memories of the State Farm session in a letter to Lomax. He recalled the scene that greeted them after driving from the
state capital to the State Prison Farm on Saturday, June 13, 1936:

> The Warden had expected us and prepared for us a reception in typi-
> cal Hollywood fashion. He and his family were sitting on the veranda
> of his house while on the lawn in front he had a Negro quartet which
> burst into song the moment we appeared. On the steps of the house

John Lomax first noticed Jim Strother strumming a "battered banjo" on the steps of the superintendent's house at the Virginia State Prison Farm. Lomax interviewed Strother and obviously thought highly of him. The next day, Strother recorded thirteen songs with Harold Spivacke in charge of the recorder. The farm has shut down, but the building looks much the same today. (Photograph, 1954, Goochland County Historical Society)

was sitting a blind Negro strumming a battered banjo. On hearing the quartet you said something to me about "trouble ahead" which I did not understand but which became perfectly clear to me later. For the next two hours, you sat on the steps with the blind Negro, whom you soon recognized as a real talent for folk singing, and did nothing but get acquainted. Your reference to "trouble" was caused by the fact that the Warden's quartet was very poor; and I admired your tact in getting rid of them after half an hour or an hour and at the same time obtaining from the Warden permission to roam the yard at will. But it was when you sat for two hours with the blind Negro, just getting acquainted, that I realized what a consummate artist you are. You encouraged him to tell you his life's history, you swapped songs with him, and did everything but make records. Being a novice at the game, I several times suggested to you by whispered hints that we might start making records because time was short, only to have you wave me away.[1]

The confused Spivacke retired with Lomax to Richmond for the night. The next day, they returned and set up their recording machine outside the prison's cellblock. Lomax casually brought in Jim Strother and told Spivacke to "go ahead and make records" while he scouted another camp and the prison yard. Spivacke thought he had been dealt a "dirty trick" and "felt pretty much like the boy who was being taught to swim by being thrown in the water." He soon came to realize the real work had been done the day before. Spivacke marveled that "all I had to do was ask him to sing one song after another and turn over the records and set the needles, etc."[2] The sum total of Strother's recordings on Sunday, June 14, 1936, included twelve songs in which he accompanied himself on banjo and guitar and one in collaboration with fellow inmate Joe Lynn Lee. (There are alternate takes of two songs.) Spivacke later reminisced that "it was probably one of the most successful trips ever undertaken by the Archive."[3]

His tribute to Lomax's skills as Strother's interlocutor plays on his confessed ignorance of the ways of the folklore collector to humorous effect, but the entire trip must have been profoundly disorienting for the thirty-two-year-old New York City native. A PhD in musicology from the University of Berlin could hardly prepare him for the rough-and-ready musical world of the rural South. Lomax, either for dramatic effect or simply because the opportunity presented itself, stopped along the roadside in Virginia to acquire some moonshine on their trip to the State Farm. The urbane, classically trained Spivacke—by his own admission an "uppity city fellow"—had never been in a prison before, and he confessed that he "was scared stiff."[4]

Spivacke's fawning description of Lomax's prowess at extracting "authentic" music from Strother was rooted in their personal relationship and his unfamiliarity with what they were experiencing. Spivacke had come to know Lomax through his position at the Library of Congress and at social gatherings. (Spivacke would later become chief of the Music Division at the Library of Congress.) The fact that John Lomax reproduced Spivacke's letter in a book about himself—*Adventures of a Ballad Hunter*—is also significant. John and his son Alan Lomax both made a habit of overdramatizing their importance as interpreters of folk culture vis-à-vis the artists they recorded. John Lomax's self-promotional works followed a predictable pattern as he cast himself as a heroic adventurer in the mold of a Livingstone, reporting back to the civilized world the exotic practices of America's underclass and its misunderstood music. Of course, such a strategy also sold books.[5]

Alan Lomax's partial erasure of his Black collaborators in his book *Land Where the Blues Began* also reflected this "heroic folklorist" mindset.

The Fisk–Library of Congress Coahoma County Study in Mississippi in 1941 and 1942 had been the brainchild of John Wesley Work III, a third-generation educator and music scholar at Fisk University, a historically Black college. Work envisioned the comprehensive study and solicited the Library of Congress's participation. Plus, Work, aided by Black colleagues Lewis Jones and Samuel C. Adams Jr., was a full participant in the project. Yet when Lomax's book appeared in 1993, it barely mentioned Work and made little use of the Fisk team's deep statistical and survey data. Work and his colleagues would not get their due until the 2005 publication of their prodigious research. Centering themselves in their accounts of fieldwork wasn't the only active intervention the Lomaxes practiced. John especially felt comfortable suggesting and sometimes demanding certain kinds of materials from his subjects.[6]

Spivacke's admiration for John Lomax's skill in preparing Strother ignored the obvious—Lomax was curating Strother's repertoire and, in doing so, attempting to assert his own artistic and folkloric vision of Black authenticity. His dismissal of Warden Penn's "poor" quartet is characteristic of his approach. Lomax likely associated most quartet singing with the successful groups that made hundreds of commercial recordings in the 1920s and 1930s. Their barber-shopped chords, ragtime rhythms, and jazz inflections would certainly have had Lomax smelling the "corrupting" influence of commercial records and radio. Unfortunately for us, this group might actually have been quite exciting to hear. Virginia's Hampton Roads region produced many of the greatest quartets of the era, and Alan Lomax would work extensively with one of the best—the legendary Golden Gate Quartet, which would later record Strother's "Blood-Stained Banders."[7]

John Lomax had no qualms about imposing his ideas of authentic Black folk music on the musicians with whom he dealt. In some situations, he paid a small sum to his informants. Sometimes he employed more subtle forms of coercion. He unblushingly reported that he allowed inmates to believe that their participation might have an effect on their sentence, although, even in the case of Lead Belly, Lomax had nothing to do with the prisoner's release, despite persistent myths to the contrary. At the very least, he pushed for the kinds of songs and styles that fit his conception of certain Black archetypes and psychologies.

Lomax's focus was not on the individual musician but on the archetypical "Negro" as expressed through song. As scholar Erich Nunn put it, to Lomax, the "lyrics of 'negro' folk songs represent less the specific feelings of individuals than they do evidence of a generalized negro character." The infamous recording session with Georgia songster Blind Willie McTell is the most obvious case—and the most widely reported—of Lomax's single-minded search for certain types of songs that represented the Black experience writ large, as he understood it. The Texan asked McTell whether he knew any "complaining songs." McTell evasively dances around the question but Lomax pushes on, giving McTell an example of such a tune: "It's Hard to Be a Nigger." McTell's palpable discomfort leaps off the audio as he loses his composure and deflects the question. His further assertion—an obvious white lie—that "the white people's mighty good to the Southern people, as far as I know" clearly demonstrates the limits to which a Black informant was willing to explore racial themes in such an interview.[8]

In Strother's case, the Lomaxes reduced him to the stereotypical character of the blind "itinerant street singer." This inattention to the individual may also be a factor in their lack of historical accuracy relating Strother's life story. Whether through Lomax's own carelessness or conscious distortions, or Strother's caginess in not letting Lomax know too much about him, Lomax got several aspects of Strother's life story spectacularly wrong. Lomax claimed that Strother killed his wife with an axe and that he was blinded in a mining accident, both errors that are still being repeated by contemporary folklorists and researchers.[9]

John Lomax sometimes went much further than prodding interviewees or offering small inducements to get the songs he wanted. Coercion was especially at play in the case of the incarcerated. John and Alan confronted one recalcitrant inmate who refused to sing a levee camp song. The prisoner, only identified as "Black Sampson," rejected the "sinful" number based on his religious convictions. Even the intercession of the prison chaplain, who promised to make it right with the Lord, could not convince him. He boldly asserted, "I got my own 'ligion." The Lomaxes then enlisted the full coercive power of the state: the warden intervened and forced the man to sing the requested song. The prayer he said before he sang the tune revealed that he might have done so because the warden might "turn him out."[10]

John Lomax had no such trouble with Jim Strother. The session captured Strother's wide-ranging abilities in folksong, though clearly not the full range of his musical knowledge. All in all, Lomax got what he wanted from Strother. He certainly overdelivered on a "sinful tune" with "Poontang Little, Poontang Small." He also satisfied Lomax's predilection for "com-

James Lee Strother and Joe Lynn Lee performing "Do Lord, Remember Me" at the Virginia State Prison Farm on June 14, 1936. Lee used straws or wires to beat on the bass strings of Strother's guitar as he played. (Library of Congress, Prints and Photographs Division, Washington, DC)

plaining songs" when he sang of the abuses of harsh boss Mike Hardy, the subject of Strother's scorn in "I Used to Work on a 'Tractor." "Thought I Heard My Banjo Say" spoke to the older dance tunes. It was probably the only song by a Black performer from the old fiddle and banjo tradition that Lomax recorded. Strother also delivered numerous spirituals—which Lomax clearly valued as the singer's strongest material—with unquestioned pedigree in the Black experience of enslavement. "Fighting On" (called "We Are Almost Down to the Shore" by Strother), "Run Down, Eli," "Do Lord, Remember Me," and "Blood-Stained Banders" are all rooted in the antebellum experience. Making his living on the streets and in traveling shows made Strother a master of gauging his audience. Such a seasoned veteran could quickly and easily adapt to a listener's expectations; Strother thus produced a catalog of old-time "complaining songs" and gospel material for the recording machine that met Lomax's requirements.

But the blind musician also went beyond the scope of Lomax's limited imagination. Perhaps we're lucky that Spivacke was at the controls of the recorder as Strother laid down a healthy dose of the medicine show and minstrel stage. His inexperienced but open ears allowed him to capture "Tennessee Dog" ("Oh his head is long, his ears is flat / He never stops eatin' 'til he balls that jack") and "Jaybird." These songs reveal the influence of minstrelsy and the traveling-show stage. Lomax, like folklorist Benjamin Botkin, might well have looked askance at such material. Also buried in the grooves beyond the intent of both Lomax and Spivacke were unmistakable moments of imagination and originality. Strother's lyrics to "Blood-Stained Banders" stand apart from traditional versions, as does his excoriation of Mike Hardy.

A savvy performer, Strother also integrated blues, a relatively new musical form, into his repertoire. "Going to Richmond," an eight-bar blues, reveals Strother's adaptation to current musical styles and the preferred instrument of the bluesman, the guitar. Superior production methods and the introduction of steel strings had brought the guitar to the attention of Black performers in the late nineteenth century. Louder, full of sustain, and able to deliver bass lines for "ragging" a tune, the instrument took its place in tent shows, house parties, and other entertainments. Later, catalog retailers Sears and Roebuck and Montgomery Ward played a key role in the dissemination of inexpensive models of the instrument to rural America, but there is ample evidence that Black performers had begun picking the instrument up several decades earlier. Ohio newspaper editor Wendell Phillips Dabney, the son of antebellum Virginia's most prosperous Black caterer, taught and performed on the banjo and mandolin but excelled on the guitar. He authored and published an instruction manual for the instrument. Born near Richmond, Virginia, in 1865, Dabney describes a rich musical culture in his home state ranging from creating diddley-bows as a youth—in this case, a piece of wire strung across a fence—to performing in minstrel shows. Before moving to Cincinnati, Dabney taught in the segregated Richmond schools and gave concerts with the Richmond Banjo and Guitar Club.[11]

Black people in urbanized areas on the East Coast had more disposable income than their peers in the Delta and the Cotton South. Even farm families in Virginia had access to greater resources, as evidenced by their much higher rates of land ownership. It stands to reason that even Culpeper County's Jim Strother could acquire a secondhand instrument of reasonable quality. Accounts from newspapers and sightings of musicians confirm that the guitar had become fairly ubiquitous by the turn of the century, when Strother came of age.[12]

"Going to Richmond" follows a chord progression typical of standards such as "Crow Jane" and "Key to the Highway." Songsters from almost every regional blues tradition performed this eight-bar tune type; some songs, such as "Red River Blues," were especially common in the East Coast and Virginia tradition. (I well recall cutting my musical teeth on this classic early in my own blues guitar apprenticeship.) Interestingly, Strother's version uses neither the syncopated, alternating bass figures favored by Virginia musicians nor the driving, monotonic bass heard in later versions. Strother's picking pattern produces a hypnotic, circular arpeggio on each chord, with a less "raggy" feel. It sounds, in fact, much like the banjo approach that he employs on several of his songs.[13]

As always, Strother's own lived experience can be found nestled in his blues recordings. Two songs in particular speak to Strother's situation at the State Farm and his pleas to Governor James H. Price for a conditional pardon. Both denounce conniving, unfaithful women in the language of the blues. In "Going to Richmond," a strophic eight-bar blues, Strother rails against "that woman that sure gone and wrecked my life."

> Yes, I'm going to Richmond
> Baby, I'm back from paradise,
> Going to see that woman that sure gone and wrecked my life. . . .

> Yes, I'm leaving ol' *Perry*
> And I'm headed for Tennessee,
> Going to see that brownskin that sure made a fool of me.

It would be easy to dismiss Strother's complaints about women as a stock litany of blues lyrics about bad women and infidelity, but against the backdrop of Blanche's murder the words are immediate and visceral. Many of the lyrics in "Going to Richmond" closely parallel Strother's letters to Governor Price seeking his pardon. Strother accused his wife of stepping out to see another man the very night of her murder, and he alleged long-term infidelity on her part. His eight-bar blues echoed these accusations:

> Yes, your fair brown will tell you
> That she'll love you all her life [*spoken:* "poor boy"],
> Meet another dude 'round the corner and retell that same lie twice.

Strother gave further evidence of his song's autobiographical intent by expressing his regret at marrying a younger woman. When Strother married Blanche Greene in 1923, he was at least twenty years her senior. Here he counsels a younger man on such folly:

Yes, that old false teachin'
And I believe my soul 'tis so [*spoken:* "poor boy"],
Son, don't you trust no young woman, no where on earth you go.

The most direct reference to his situation—one that clearly establishes the target of his hatred in "Going to Richmond"—is a specific reference to Blanche's place of residence at the time of their marriage:

Alexandria women,
I sure, God, do so despise,
Got a hand full of gimme and a mouthful of much obliged.

Near the end of his broadside against his second wife, Strother reprises his lament to Governor Price about his mistreatment at the hands of an abusive spouse while integrating a classic blues trope:

I've got the blues, babe,
And can't be satisfied,
Going down by the river and hang down my head and cry.

'Cause I've been mistreated,
And I can't be satisfied,
I've been mistreated and I can't be satisfied.

"Going to Richmond" clocks in at almost six minutes, a relatively long piece even for a field recording. Stretching out songs to keep the interest of attentive onlookers was an essential skill for street buskers, but anyone who has played guitar on the streets of the cities of the Chesapeake region knows that the combination of humid conditions, sweat, and steel strings can wreak havoc with even well-developed calluses. Accordingly, Strother matter-of-factly tells his audience that if cash contributions are not forthcoming, he will bring his song to a close:

I done played this piece, babe,
'Til my fingers got sore;
Now, if it ain't nothin' doin',
I ain't gonna play no more.

Taken in its entirety, there is little doubt at whom Jim Strother aimed his musical barbs. Strother identifies Blanche's place of residence, her status as a younger woman, and her duplicitousness. On that fateful April evening, Blanche literally "met another dude 'round the corner," according to Strother's telling of the events that led up to her death. Even the title of the song has a personal meaning. Strother definitely went to Richmond as a result of his impetuous and violent act.

"Going to Richmond" wasn't the only song that Strother recorded at the Virginia State Prison Farm with a cynical message about women. "Daddy, Where You Been So Long" is an even more blunt and cutting commentary on the evils of women:

> She calls me honey when I comes in town,
> Big black nigger when I'm gone,
> But as soon as I return with a ten-dollar bill,
> It's Daddy, where you been so long?

> *Chorus:* Oh, it's Daddy, where you been,
> Daddy where you been,
> Daddy where you been so long?

Strother's use of the racial epithet in conjunction with his Blackness suggests the many ways the term could be used. Strother's other uses of the same term occurred in pieces derived from the time of slavery, when, as in the former slave narratives, it is generally not loaded with as much vitriol. Here the usage he places in Blanche's mouth is clearly derogatory and is coupled with colorism. In "Going to Richmond" he speaks of his "fair brown" and her betrayal; now she emphasizes Strother's blackness behind his back. Given the images of Strother's and Blanche's family background, it is quite possible that they were in fact considerably different in skin tone.

Strother's lyrics here are especially harsh, although references to skin color are common in Black folk songs. The very title of another Virginia blues recording telegraphs its message. Stephen Tarter and Harry Gay recorded "Brownie Blues" for Victor Records in the follow-up to the famed Bristol Sessions in 1928. Propelled by a beautifully synchronized ragtime guitar duet, Steve Tarter sings:

Jet black is evil, so is yellow, too
Jet black is evil, so is yellow, too,
So glad I'm brown skinned, don't know what to do.

The attribution of color traits to both African American men and women was an enduring feature of blues lyricism and revealed distinct cultural preferences. Self-hatred of Blackness is perhaps most common, but celebrations of the same are not unknown. A group recorded by the Lomaxes in Atlanta, Georgia, sang one of the more common expressions of a Black woman's desirability, proclaiming that a "brown-skinned woman make a preacher lay his Bible down" but "a jet-black woman make a jack rabbit hug a hound." Strother's channeling of Blanche's backstabbing denunciation of her husband obviously conveys a less positive meaning.[14]

Two early commercial recordings provide aural examples of similar lyrics to Strother's "Daddy, Where You Been So Long," but with a different melody. One is by the mysterious guitarist and singer Bayless Rose and the second by white West Virginia singer and slide guitarist Dick Justice. Justice's release on the Brunswick label contains this refrain:

Old black dog when I'm gone, lord, lord.
Old black dog when I'm gone.
When I come back with a ten-dollar bill,
And it's, "Honey, where you been so long?"[15]

The second two lines of this stanza are a well-known formula in early songster material. The formulation appears in both blues songs and in modal mountain ballads such as "I Wish I Was a Mole in the Ground." That these lines flowed from a common stock into both Black and white musical traditions mirrors the confusion about the identity of Bayless Rose, who sang essentially the same lines as Dick Justice on his 78-rpm recording of "Black Dog Blues," recorded in 1930 for Gennett Records. Collectors, historians, discographers, and record producers have never quite known what to do with Rose. His recordings have been issued on compilations of both white hillbilly and Black songster material, and there are competing accounts of his racial identity. The standard discography of early African American blues and gospel music claims him, but not the definitive county music discography.[16]

Record producer, 78-rpm record collector, and researcher Chris King speculated that Rose may have been Melungeon, based on interviews with Dick Justice's widow. According to her, Justice learned this tune from a white man named Bailey Rose who had oddly dark features. Possible Melungeon identity makes the story even more intriguing, given the song's racial theme. The identity has been claimed by certain Appalachian families who tended to be "darker" than the average person of European heritage and lived within tight-knit communities defined by kinship. The darkness of their skin has typically been explained away by resort to murky stories about descent from Indigenous people, Portuguese migrants, or even Sephardic Jews. Recent DNA analysis points to a much less exotic but far more obvious answer: descent from European and sub-Saharan African people. Especially in the twentieth century, people in Appalachia claiming this heritage had every reason to emphasize their Europeanness, as Virginia and other states imposed the "one drop" rule. For someone like Bayless Rose, being white would be a significant advantage in Jim Strother's America.[17]

Backed by his sprightly ragtime guitar, Bayless Rose sang:[18]

> Call me old dog when I'm gone, gone, gone,
> Yes, you call me old dog when I'm gone;
> When I come back with a ten dollar bill
> Honey, where you been so long?

In a subsequent use of this central theme, Rose adds "black" to the verse—"Old black dog when I'm gone"—as in the Justice version.

The song's appearance on early commercial country recordings is not surprising. According to Robert Gordon, the first curator of the Library of Congress's folk song collection, mountain songsters, especially "banjo-pickers," performed the song widely. Gordon's 1938 collection of American folksong includes a ten-stanza rendition that includes a number of verses that connect to Strother's version—including the use of the same racial epithet.[19]

> Oh you call me a nigger when I'm gone,
> You call me a nigger when I'm gone
> But when you see me comin'
> With my pockets full of gold,
> It's Honey where you been so long?

The informants for Gordon's rendition, which is undoubtedly a composite of several versions, were mountain whites. Even if the folklorist didn't tell us so in his introduction to the song, this verse would certainly give it away:

> I don't like a nigger nohow
> I don't like a nigger nohow!
> You may rub him an' scrub him
> An' rub him up an' down
> But a nigger'll be a nigger till he dies!

The blatant racism of this stanza demonstrates how context and intent are crucial to understanding folksong. The previous "Oh you call me a nigger when I'm gone" stanza tracks with Strother's version, and it's quite likely the song migrated from Black musicians to whites in Appalachia. Coming out of the mouths of mountain whites—people who posted the sundown-town signs referred to in Strother's "Thought I Heard My Banjo Say"—it had a very different meaning. In Strother's song, we see an angry conflict between a man and woman with strong overtones of colorism. In the version from mountain whites, the use of the racial pejorative is deeply negative and overtly racist. Who sings the song matters.

Jim Strother displayed his hard-earned skills as an itinerant Black bard on June 14, 1936. While we can rightly credit John Lomax for capturing Strother's music for posterity, Strother's thirteen songs confounded many of Lomax's assumptions about Black folk music. Strother went beyond the bounds of the folklorist's conception of "uncorrupted" folk traditions with his minstrel and medicine-show material, uneasily teetering on the edge of the commercial stage and tent show. Likewise, Lomax no doubt heard Strother's barbs aimed at the "Alexandria woman"—his wife Blanche—as formulaic blues expressions, not as the bitter and deeply personal statements that they were. Harold Spivacke imagined that Lomax's two-hour interrogation of Strother confirmed the folklorist as a "consummate artist," yet Strother was never going to reveal himself fully to the white Texan with the recording machine. More importantly, Strother clearly understood that Lomax and the Library of Congress would be of no help in gaining the thing he desired most—his freedom.

16

The Pardon

If I live to see December,
I'm going home, I'm going home.
—JAMES LEE STROTHER, "This Old Hammer," recorded 1936

Jim Strother would not go home for another two Decembers and three months after he sang these lines at the Virginia State Prison Farm on June 14, 1936, but his campaign for a conditional pardon began less than two years after John Lomax and Harold Spivacke encountered him at the prison. Nearing the third anniversary of his conviction in Culpeper County, Strother dictated the first of five letters to Governor James H. Price pleading for a pardon. His entreaty met a swift rebuke. Price's secretary curtly observed that Strother had only served about three years of a twenty-year sentence. "Unusual reasons would have to be given Governor Price before he would feel justified in extending clemency in your case, at this time," the letter concluded. Apparently three years was simply too little punishment for a second-degree murder charge. Despite this setback, Strother renewed his efforts later that year. The governor's clemency apparatus began examining Strother's case in earnest in June 1939, sending inquiries to prison officials and members of the justice system in Culpeper County.[1]

Strother knew he had to do something else to curry Price's support. He had to this point shown very little contrition for the murder. In 1939, he changed course, writing to the governor, "I have served a long [sentence] for the unintentional slaying of my philandering wife who consorted with other men in my own house. Even so I am truly sorry & repentant for the act." As he had in previous pleas to the governor, Strother confidently pointed to his ability to make a living performing music.[2]

Paging through Strother's pardon file is mainly an exercise in understanding the cold-blooded bureaucratic calculations of the carceral state. Yet, ironically, the yellowing files also hold something deeply personal—family connections—and the one relationship that Jim Strother had with another person based on deep affection and trust. That person was William Taylor. Alternately described in the files as a second cousin or nephew of Strother's, Taylor championed his freedom and diligently campaigned on his behalf. Taylor clearly felt a deep familial affection for the musician and looked up to him.

In one of his earliest letters to Governor Price on Strother's behalf, Taylor begged the commonwealth's chief executive, "Please give him another chance for you know that he is blind and I will take good care of him for he is just as same as a father to me. . . . [Y]ou know that I love him and you can put him in my care if you only let him go free." It seems that Strother had mentored Taylor during his years in Baltimore. Strother provided Taylor with a strong link to Taylor's past and his paternal family. "I need him up here with me for he is the older one on my father's side that is living and he can tell me a lot in life yet that I don't know," Taylor explained to Governor Price as he begged for Strother's release. We know that Strother was always connected to this side of his family while in Baltimore. Sarah Truman, William's aunt, had lived with Strother and his first wife, Mary, when they resided in the Biddle Alley District during their early years in the city.[3]

Taylor also took concrete steps to secure Strother's release. In a letter to the blind musician, he apologized for failing to reply to a previous communication due to trouble at his home and having to move to another residence suddenly. He also recounted his efforts to save enough money to hire a lawyer to argue for Strother's freedom. Aware that his conditional pardon might soon be granted, Strother enclosed Taylor's letter in his own communication to Governor Price, informing the chief executive, "I am writing them not to do so, for I am sure your Excellency will give my case the same fair consideration as well without a lawyer as with one, and I don't want my cousins to spend their money for me."[4]

The deep emotional connection between William Taylor and Jim Strother intrigued me. I spent many hours trying to establish the nature of their relationship, but the solution eluded me for years. Why would a young man born in Maryland doggedly fight for the release of a much older second cousin/uncle and also take the former convict into his home? The answer would be found in kinship ties, the forces of the Great Migration, and the terrible death toll of the urban ghetto.

Strother's pardon file provided the first clue. In 1939, the musician listed Susan Taylor of Culpeper County as his second cousin. Likewise, Alan Lomax wrote her in 1942 in a vain attempt to find Jim Strother. Surely finding her might establish a family connection to William Taylor, and luckily, she wasn't hard to locate. Born in the wake of the Civil War to Washington and Martha Toms around 1867, Susan married Charles William Taylor on March 3, 1887; both were natives of Culpeper County. Her husband, Charles, was a relatively prosperous farmer, and his death certificate revealed the likely connection between them and the Strother family. Charles's mother, Mary, had been born enslaved in the 1840s and her maiden name was Strother. Given their respective ages, Susan Taylor's mother-in-law, Mary Strother Taylor, and Jim Strother's mother, Susan, might have been sisters, but they might also have been more distantly related.

Just as Strother had made his way to Maryland by 1900, so too had Charles and Susan Taylor and their families migrated northward to find work. The couple decided on yet another major terminus of the Great Migration out of Virginia—the Philadelphia region. With their extended family in tow, by 1900 the couple had settled in Montgomery County, Pennsylvania, where the patriarch worked as a "railroad repairman." Three of Susan's brothers accompanied the family north and boarded with them. Two worked with Charles on the railroad gangs and another labored in a brickyard. Charles Taylor and the Toms brothers worked on the railroad section gangs that replaced the ties, fishplate, and rails along the line. The chants and songs that such workers used to coordinate their movements echoed in Jim Strother's later recordings, especially his version of "This Old Hammer." By 1910 the Taylor family had returned to Culpeper, and Charles settled down to the life of a farmer. His son George Washington Taylor returned north periodically to find work. Charles Taylor died in 1936, leaving his wife, Susan Taylor, alone.

At this point, I was convinced that William Taylor, who had been born in Maryland, was connected to Charles Taylor. As it turned out, I had the right family, but the wrong Taylor. Charles Taylor's brother, Andrew, was the missing link between Jim Strother and William Taylor. The older son of Mary Strother and William Taylor, Andrew had also migrated northward in the early 1900s. He married Hannah Johnson's daughter Fannie Jane in

1894. At the same time as Strother's travels to Sparrows Point, the Johnsons lived in Howard County, Maryland, close to Ellicott City, one of the first major railroad towns in the country and an early hub of the Baltimore and Ohio Railroad. William Taylor, born in 1907, appears to have been their first child. Tragically, Fannie died within months of giving birth. Andrew Taylor disappears from the record. By 1910, Hannah Johnson, now a sixty-eight-year-old widow, was raising her grandson as a laundress "working out" in Baltimore City.

The closeness of the families is revealed by their households in Baltimore. Jim Strother and his first wife, Mary, counted William's aunt, Sarah Johnson Truman, and her young son Walter among the members of their Baltimore household on Walnut Street in 1910. Meanwhile, Sarah's mother, Hannah, took care of her daughter Lillie and her nephew—three-year-old William Taylor. Hannah Johnson, Taylor, and Strother all lived on Ware Street at various times and later occupied houses next door to each other on nearby Mace Street in the period from 1915 to 1920. William Taylor and Strother obviously became close during their time living in that neighborhood in the Twelfth Ward near the Baltimore and Ohio Railroad yards and the Jones Falls area. Sarah Johnson Truman was also a member of her nephew William's Baltimore household when they greeted Jim Strother on his return to Baltimore after his incarceration.[5]

William Taylor had another unusual and sadly ironic connection to Jim Strother and his experience. Hannah's son, Gillis Eli Johnson, also lived in their household in 1910. William's uncle Gillis, in a strange but not unprecedented turn of fate, also lost his sight at roughly the same time as Jim Strother. His World War I draft card declared him "totally blind" and gave his employment as a chair caner at the Maryland Workshop for the Blind. In fact, he had begun working there around 1911, plying the same craft that Strother would resort to during several periods of his life.[6]

While William Taylor was putting pen to paper to write the governor of Virginia, the bureaucratic wheels of the state were already in motion. While some aspects of America's carceral state could be rather informal—and those who ran the system probably wanted it that way—releasing a prisoner was not. Although the commonwealth's chief executive had sole discretion to commute a sentence or pardon a prisoner under the state constitution, certain steps had to be taken. The Virginia governor's office had already initiated an investigation into Strother's request to return to Baltimore with the Maryland Division of Parole and Probation. The Maryland authorities duly dispatched a parole officer to Taylor's last known address but found that he no longer lived there. In a flurry of memos, Price's secretary sought his residence. She also wrote to Penitentiary Superintendent Youell, who went straight to the source—Jim Strother—to secure William Taylor's current whereabouts.[7]

Virginia's governor valued efficiency. A staunch Progressive and supporter of President Franklin D. Roosevelt's New Deal efforts, Price surprised Senator Harry Flood Byrd's political machine by declaring early for the Democratic primary. Price's popularity gave him the Democratic nomination, essentially ensuring his election in one-party Virginia in 1937. During his first year in office, Price championed and signed numerous Progressive measures, including an Old Age Assistance Plan that allowed Virginians to secure Social Security benefits. He soon found himself in conflict with the conservative Democratic establishment, and Byrd and his allies thwarted his plans to reorganize state government—including the corrections system. The rejection of Price's reforms meant that Strother's only hope for freedom rested with the governor.[8]

Virginia had no parole system established by law. The governor alone wielded that authority under his constitutional power of executive clemency. Price's record revealed some hope for Strother; the governor pardoned 325 inmates in his first year in office, a significant increase from the 238 pardons issued in 1937. Still, only 7.3 percent of the total prison population received a pardon in 1938. All bets were off within such a capricious system. A federal study issued the year of Strother's release, 1939, and commissioned by the governor himself criticized the informal Virginia system because it "favors those who are well-to-do, who 'know the ropes' or who have influential backing." Strother had none of those things, but he did have the persistence of William Taylor.[9]

Virginia and Maryland officials carefully vetted Strother's Baltimore relatives, sending investigators to look into their circumstances. The parole supervisor John H. McFaul Jr. visited the Taylors at their new home at 1029 Rice Street, a "five room brick house in a small street in a colored neighborhood," dismissively reporting that the "house is not very well furnished nor very neat." More to the point of his visit, McFaul learned that William Taylor made a salary of $18.00 per week as an automobile mechanic and that his wife, Sadie, earned $8.00 a week as a domestic. No doubt this satisfied the Maryland authorities that Strother would not become a ward of the state. McFaul further reported that Taylor "would be glad to keep his uncle

and thought he might get him some work in a blind institution for the colored." (Reflecting the frequency with which working people moved abodes,
the Taylors had moved to yet another address by the time of Strother's
release!)[10]

By now we know how Commonwealth's Attorney R. A. Bickers reacted
to Strother's pending release. Bickers questioned the blind musician's claims
of self-defense, based on reports of jealousy and abuse. Despite these reser-
vations about the facts of Strother's crime, Bickers counseled the governor:
"I further note that he states that if pardoned he would go to some relatives
in Baltimore, Maryland. I feel inclined to recommend a conditional pardon
to him provided he would return to Baltimore, which was the original place
of residence before he came to Culpeper." In Bickers's version of Southern
justice, the expediency of removing a bad element from the state overrode
any qualms about actual guilt or innocence. That the crime was perpetrated
on a Black woman, the most vulnerable and least protected member of
American society, surely informed Bickers and the governor. Price also calculated that there would be few (or no) political consequences for ridding
the state of a blind Black felon.[11]

Strother himself invoked his disability in a canny act of self-preservation
in his several letters to the governor of Virginia arguing for his release. Ironically, he both downplayed its significance and used it to exculpate himself
for his crime. Countering Bicker's insinuations, he claimed abuse by a wife
who took advantage of his inability to see. He also sought to mitigate his
act of murder by claiming that he only shot in self-defense. He subtly noted
his blindness while arguing that the killing was an accident. Yet in another
letter, Strother asserted his ability to travel freely and make a living as he
had previously done—in other words, he would not be a burden on the
state. Jim Strother clearly understood the culture's tropes of blindness and
deployed them skillfully to a man in power just as he might solicit pity or
admiration on the streets to passersby.

The efforts of Strother and his Maryland relatives, especially William
Taylor, finally paid off. Governor Price signed Strother's conditional pardon in September 1939, sending him to live with William Taylor and his
wife, Sadie, in Baltimore. Back in the city where he had performed for more
than twenty-five years, Strother boarded with the Taylors, his cousin by
marriage Sarah Truman, and others at 1214 ½ Pennsylvania Avenue, just
a few blocks from the heart of Baltimore's Seventeenth Ward, where he had
arrived as a Southern migrant around thirty years before.[12]

~ LEGACIES ~

17

Do Lord, Remember Me

When I was in trouble, Lord, remember me
—JAMES LEE STROTHER and JOE LYNN LEE, "Do Lord, Remember Me,"
recorded 1936

James Lee Strother invoked an old spiritual of hope for John Lomax in 1936. His cry for deliverance was powerful and direct. No matter his state of belief after his many trials, he sounded optimistic that the Lord would indeed remember him. He probably had little faith that the world would do so. The editor of Culpeper's *Virginia Star* certainly didn't think so, declaring Strother's murder conviction the "last chapter" in his "tragic story." Folklorist John Lomax and his Library of Congress recording machine exploded that prediction. Indeed, James Lee "Jim" Strother's legacy has proved far more enduring than the small-town newspaperman who closed the book on him in 1935 could have ever imagined.[1]

While Strother lived in obscurity in Baltimore, his music first reached a wider public in the now-classic 1941 volume *Our Singing Country*. Edited by John Lomax and his son Alan and published by Macmillan, the volume brought together in print many of the field recordings that the Lomaxes and others had committed to disc in the 1930s. The Lomaxes chose to include one of Strother's most enigmatic songs in *Our Singing County*: "Blood-Stained Banders." In the introduction to the song, they portrayed Strother as the archetypical blind street singer.[2]

Alan Lomax clearly valued the originality and power of Strother's performance on "Blood-Stained Banders." He next selected the song for the third release in the American Folklife Series, *Afro-American Spirituals, Work*

Songs, and Ballads, released in 1942 by the Library of Congress. Made up of five 78-rpm records, the set brought together recordings from six Southern states, songs primarily performed by penitentiary inmates. Lomax wrote to the warden of the Virginia State Penitentiary and enclosed a letter to Strother asking for permission to use "Blood-Stained Banders" for a small fee. The letter, dated March 18, 1942, reads:

Dear Jimmy Strothers [*sic*]:

The Archive of American Folk Song is planning to make up a group of the best representative American folk songs to be distributed in Latin America. Among the records we hope to use are your performance of "Blood-stained Banders" which you recorded for Mr. John A. Lomax several years ago. We will pay you $5.00 for the use of this record which occupies part of one record and will send you two copies of the record.[3]

Penitentiary superintendent Rice M. Youell replied a few days later that the man Lomax sought had been granted a conditional pardon and his whereabouts were unknown. Youell's response was somewhat surprising. He had been privy to Governor James H. Price's consultations with state officials and had been well aware that Strother's appeal for pardon was premised on Strother's return to Baltimore. Then again, Youell daily held the fates of hundreds of prisoners in his hands; those who had left his fiefdom weren't his highest priority. The superintendent did inform Lomax of a few other possible informants in his search for Strother. But Lomax's subsequent letters to the Culpeper County sheriff and postmaster, as well as several of Strother's family members in Virginia, also failed to locate him. The blind street musician had again become largely invisible to history except through his songs. Importantly, Lomax's attempts to contact Strother also belie another long-held belief—that the Lomaxes cared little about crediting and compensating folk artists.[4]

A year later, fellow folklorist Benjamin Botkin wrote to Strother's relative Susan Taylor to find the elusive songster to offer him $13.75 for permission to use two of his songs on the Library of Congress's album set *Negro Religious Songs and Services*. His letter met the same fate as Lomax's—sent back and marked "returned to writer." Botkin wrote to yet another relative whose "name has been given to us as one who might know where he [Strother] is located." Unfortunately, Blanche Strother was the intended recipient of the correspondence. Botkin obviously had no idea that she was Strother's murdered wife, long dead and buried in the cemetery at Free Union Baptist Church.[5]

While the 78-rpm record sets released by the Library of Congress likely reached only a limited audience—and certainly not Jim Strother—a more ambitious project sent his voice out over the airwaves. In 1941 the Library of Congress established the Radio Research Project in order to investigate "the possible uses of radio as a medium by which pertinent parts of the record of American culture maintained in the Library of Congress may be made available to the general public." Philip H. Cohen, former production editor at the US Department of Education, headed the project, which was initially funded by the Rockefeller Foundation. The specter of World War II loomed over the program's earliest projects, with the Books in the News series focused on key American national defense industries and on "hot spots" around the world.[6]

The Library of Congress believed that culture could provide patriotic support for the mobilization effort by reinforcing ideas of American exceptionalism and national character. *The Ballad Hunter* featured John Lomax introducing a series of ten fifteen-minute programs "explaining and illustrating the folk songs of the American people as they are sung by the people themselves." The series was innovative in that it used actual field recordings from the Archive of American Folk Song along with Lomax's comments, a technique compared at the time to "that used in the motion picture industry, each recording being edited and reedited until the exact portions wanted from the field recordings had been extracted." Jim Strother's "Blood-Stained Banders" appeared on the seventh program, which featured the religious music of "Southern Negroes." Inquiries about the set steadily came in from across the country; by the end of January 1942, about nine months after its release, *The Ballad Hunter* had sold more than two hundred copies, with many others distributed for free.[7]

To further the reach of *The Ballad Hunter*, the project duplicated the five sixteen-inch transcription discs for wider distribution under a grant from the Carnegie Corporation of New York. "For radio stations, for schools, for libraries, the BALLAD HUNTER programs offer an unequalled opportunity to hear the everyday music of the people—the simple, human stuff—the roots of democracy," proclaimed an advertising sheet produced and distributed as Americans mobilized for World War II. To endorse the set, the Library of Congress used no less a nationalist and expansionist than Teddy Roosevelt, quoting his 1910 letter to John Lomax that exclaimed, "It is

The image on this advertisement for John A Lomax's recording *The Ballad Hunter* exemplifies the persona of Lomax as the consummate collector—at ease and in charge of his subject. (John A. Lomax and Alan Lomax Papers, Archive of Folk Culture, American Folklife Center, Library of Congress, Washington, DC)

a work of real importance to preserve permanently this unwritten ballad literature of the back-country and the frontier."[8]

The Library of Congress emphasized folk music as essential to the country's democratic values and national character. Carl H. Milam, executive secretary of the American Library Association, endorsed the set as "an aid to appreciation of America's cultural heritage, which libraries, along with other agencies for democratic education, will welcome." Likewise, the head of the Music Educators National Conference declared *The Ballad Hunter* "a vast storehouse of strong robust music which is inseparably linked with our national growth." The compilers of *The Ballad Hunter* celebrated America's musical traditions, but, as the name of the series makes clear, John Lomax himself was the central figure—the arbiter of authenticity and the meaning of America's folkloric traditions. One advertisement called him "the man who has spent a lifetime searching for the stirring and melodious songs that belong to the American people."[9]

The cover of an advertising brochure for *The Ballad Hunter* shows Lomax perched backward on a chair in front of an African American singer playing a guitar. The microphone sits between them as Lomax directs the activity and oversees the session, relaxed but clearly in charge. The image is the embodiment of Harold Spivacke's praise for Lomax as "a consummate artist" in charge of his subjects, such as Jim Strother. Indeed, much of the ad copy focuses on Lomax. The songs are, of course, vital and important, but the overarching master narrative is Lomax's as he "tells the story of his song-hunting travels, and presents for the first time America's folk music sung by authentic singers, along with eloquent and authoritative explanation of its background." Lomax stands as the indispensable interlocutor of American traditional culture without whom the recordings would not even exist. The copywriter asserted Lomax's intellectual and cultural authority while at the same time seeking to diminish the social, class, and racial distance between Lomax and his subjects. In a bid to buttress Lomax's democratic bona fides and, perhaps more important, the authenticity of the music and project, the brochure's author claimed that the "people like to sing for John Lomax, and on these records there's a feeling of naturalness, ease, and sociability."[10]

Lomax's spoken introduction to Strother's "Blood-Stained Banders" on *The Ballad Hunter* captures these seemingly contradictory impulses. Slowly telling his story in his deliberate, distinctive Texas drawl, Lomax strikes the pose of a Southern man of the people, yet his narrative unfolds with a sophisticated sense of poetic flair and dramatic pathos. The Strother whom Lomax defines on *The Ballad Hunter* is a tragic figure, his sight cruelly taken by fate, unable to see the beauty of his physical surroundings. In blindness he resorts to life as a street musician and finally turns to religion as a salve. This is the familiar story of the blind musician as a victim of Providence — just as William F. Stone, Benjamin Botkin, and the many people who observed him on the street had seen him. Lomax, not Strother, is the master of Strother's story. It also establishes the Southern white as the interpreter of the Black experience. Lomax intones:

> Overlooking the beautiful valley of the James River about 30 miles above Richmond, Virginia, Big Jimmie Strothers sits every day and strums his banjo and sings; but Jimmie Strothers does not see the beautiful valley—he is blind. Years ago an explosion in the mines destroyed his sight. Afterwards, he earned his living as a street-corner entertainer. Now grown old, his favorite songs are spirituals. He says, "If you want to go to heaven over on the other shore, keep out of the way of the blood-stained banders, oh, good shepherd, feed my sheep. Some for Paul, some for Silas, some for to make my heart rejoice. Can't you hear the lambs a-crying, oh good shepherd, feed my sheep."

One of the five 78-rpm records from the 1943 Library of Congress compilation *Negro Religious Songs and Services*. Recordings by both Strother and Joe Lynn Lee featured on this early set. Library of Congress, Washington, DC, 1943. (Courtesy of the author)

It is likely that Strother's decision to perform four sacred songs among his thirteen recordings was influenced by Lomax's ideas about authenticity. Lomax's colleagues at the Library of Congress seemed to agree that Strother's sacred material stood out from the rest of his repertoire. In 1943, the songster's music was again prominently featured on the collection *Negro Religious Songs and Services*. His collaboration with inmate Joe Lynn Lee, "Do Lord, Remember Me," leads off the 78-rpm record set, which also includes Strother's "We Are Almost Down to the Shore." These songs brought Strother's life and music full circle back to his rural Virginia beginnings. Both reflected traditional spiritual songs common at the time of slavery and deeply rooted in Virginia's sacred music tradition.

Botkin, a pioneering folklorist in his own right and assistant in charge of the Archive of American Folk Song, edited the album set. His comments in the liner notes seem to contradict John Lomax's assessment of Strother as a truly authentic folk performer. He opined that "BLIND Jimmie Strother learned his hearty minstrel style of gospel singing while traveling with

a medicine show," a statement that might call into question the blind singer's bona fides to sing authentic spiritual material. In contrast, Botkin stated
that Strother's musical partner on "Do Lord," Joe Lee, "sings jubilee songs
in truly spiritual fashion." Unironically, he concluded that both displayed
"considerable showmanship." Botkin seemed untroubled by this supposed
merging of minstrel stagecraft and folk religiosity, perhaps recognizing the
complicated roots of folk performance in a commercialized society. Yet
I think Lomax was closer to the mark in this instance.[11]

"Do Lord, Remember Me" is one of the most venerable spirituals in the
African American tradition. It first appeared in written form in the 1867
seminal work *Slave Songs of the United States*. Compiled by Northerners
who worked among the freedmen and women in Union-occupied areas
of the American South, it is a rare glimpse into the antebellum songs of
the enslaved. Tidewater Virginia was an especially fertile ground for these
collectors. Federal forces occupied Norfolk and the surrounding Hampton
Roads area early in the Civil War, and large numbers of enslaved Virginians from the surrounding countryside liberated themselves by escaping
to the Union lines. Federal commanders, caught flat-footed by this rush to
freedom, struggled to deal with the migration, which began well before the
Emancipation Proclamation. General Benjamin Butler solved the problem
for the army by declaring the formerly enslaved as "contraband of war" and
employing the freedmen and -women in a variety of capacities in support
of the Union Army. (It would be another six months before the United
States would begin enlisting African Americans into the Union Army.)
Some of the earliest transcriptions of the songs of the enslaved were drawn
from the men and women huddled in these camps. The Confederates' loss
of human property and their labor proved not only the Union's gain but
a boon to later musicologists.[12]

The version in *Slave Songs of the United States*, however, is significantly
different from the version widely known in the early twentieth century and
still commonly heard today. "Do Lord, Remember Me" has a two-verse
opening stanza with its own melody line and then concludes with a variant
of the well-known refrain:

Oh, Lord, remember me
Do, Lord, remember me,
Remember me as de year roll round;
Lord, remember me.

The hand of the transcriber seems obvious in the melody of the song, which is a good bit more complicated than the versions typically heard. The famed African American musicologist John Wesley Work III, of Fisk University, produced a transcription of the song that captured the spiritual in its more traditional form—an example that comports with the recording from the Virginia State Prison Farm by Strother and Lee and other early recorded versions of the song. At least three groups sang the tune before the microphones of commercial companies before 1930.[13]

The Fisk professor's reading highlights the song's strophic structure, internal refrains, and use of the pentatonic scale, all hallmarks of traditional spirituals. Strother and Lee sing in unison an octave apart in the same direct, straight-ahead manner that characterized the early rural church and brush arbor. As Work himself noted of the spirituals:[14]

> Although the spirituals usually lend themselves readily to four-part harmony, and concert singers have sung them with varied tempos and dynamics quite effectively, nevertheless, in the rural churches from where they mostly spring they are sung with a minimum of such modifications. There are few contrasting passages such as loud and soft; no notes are held for effect longer than the pulse indicates; and strangest of all, there are no retards to anticipate the closing cadence. The leader establishes his tempo and maintains it throughout the song. Harmony occasionally is in two parts, rarely three. I have never encountered four-part harmony.[15]

Work's comments on the nature of the early spirituals are supported by aural evidence from the federal Works Progress Administration project to record the memories of formerly enslaved Americans. Based out of Hampton Institute, the Virginia project was especially robust and employed a large number of African American interviewers—in fact, the majority. One especially enterprising worker, Susie R. C. Byrd, built a strong connection to the Petersburg community where she lived, holding monthly sessions with older African Americans. As part of her work, she recorded groups of formerly enslaved Virginians singing traditional songs. Poor recording equipment and the condition of the discs make most of these recordings virtually unlistenable, but a few are of enough clarity to give us a rare hint of the African American church under slavery. One song, "Slavery Chain Done Broke at Last," reflects Work's description of Black hymnody quite well. Strother and Lee took a similarly simple but compelling approach to "Do Lord."[16]

Strother's guitar accompaniment to the old folk spiritual is direct and effective. Its strong, rhythmic pulse undergirds the intertwined vocals of Strother and Lee. Strother's strong baritone rolls along below Lee's urgent and keening tenor voice. The feeling and spirit of the song would not have been out of place in a rural Southern church during Strother's childhood—or even earlier—if Baptist congregations had allowed such instruments.

The vocal approach and overall execution of "Do Lord" by Strother and Lee are not the only elements of their performance that hark back to older folk practices. Botkin noted that on "Do Lord," "Joe Lee beats two pieces of wire on the finger-board of the banjo, deftly avoiding the fingers of the player." In fact, Strother plays guitar on the song, easily apprehended from both the aural evidence and the only image of Strother and Lee from the Virginia State Prison Farm sessions. The recording captures not only guitar and voice but also a percussive sound driving the song's rhythmic pulse. The often-reproduced image of the two inmates seated before the Library of Congress's microphone reveals the source of this buoyant sound—Joe Lee is "beating straws" on Strother's guitar. Striking the instrument's bass strings in time with the blind musician's insistent bass lines, Lee creates a polyrhythmic bounce to the song's straightforward drive.[17]

Using straws or sticks to accentuate the rhythmic pulse is an old folk technique common to American fiddling and may well have originated in Black folk practice. A fascinating glimpse of its use in the antebellum era comes from Sam Forge, born enslaved around 1850 in East Texas. Interviewed in the 1930s as part of the federal Works Progress Administration's life histories project, he recounted: "W'en de contest start each man plays his best . . . an' most of de time he had someone to accompany him, sometimes wid a straw lookin' piece he put across de strings of de fiddle, den he bounce hit up an' down on de strings an' beat out his accompanyin' de fiddler, de faster de fiddler plays de faster de boy jig his accompanyin' for him."[18] Famed bandleader W. C. Handy, the self-proclaimed "Father of the Blues," recounted the technique as part of the passing world of the plantation dance and fiddler. "A boy would stand behind the fiddler with a pair of knitting needles in his hands," he observed, and "from this position the youngster would reach around the fiddler's left shoulder and beat on the strings in the manner of a snare drummer." The buoyant bouncing of the needles, the intricate stomping of the fiddler's feet, and the movements and calls of the dancers created a truly ecstatic release from a harsh and difficult existence.[19]

Examples of "fiddlesticks" or "beating straw" on the violin can be found on American field recordings in the Southern old-time and Cajun traditions in the twentieth century. The technique worked especially well when the fiddler "discorded," or cross-tuned, his or her fiddle, for example tuning the strings to the notes AEAE. These tunings produced a distinctive droning sound when double stops (bowing two strings at once) were employed. The straw beater bounced his implements against the two lowest strings while the fiddler played the higher ones. Yet this technique appears infrequently on commercial recordings, with perhaps the only example recorded by a white hillbilly band, Reaves White County Ramblers, that hailed from Arkansas. Remarkably, the field recording of Lee and Strother seems to be the only example of straw beating on a guitar; accounts of the technique in Virginia, even on fiddles, are elusive.[20]

Joe Lynn Lee (spelled Lea in many archival records) stands out on this duet with Strother and is even more compelling on his solo a cappella recordings for Lomax. Lee's background and performances reinforce his grounding in deep folk traditions. Slightly older than Strother, Lee sings in a high, penetrating voice full of conviction and intensity. His voice gains added urgency when matched with the frightening lyrics of his "Rise, Run Along, Mourner":

> People in the land of Georgia
> The little they cared about God;
> But when the news got in the land,
> The man was burnin' on the log.
> He was settin' down gamblin'
> His friends 'came frightened and scared;
> The flames of fire came out of his mouth,
> Came through his nostrils and ears.
>
> *Chorus:* Let me tell you 'bout the man were burning
> 'Way down yonder in the land of Georgia;
> That man were burning,
> For blaspheming the name of God.[21]

Joe Lynn Lee entered the prison system on a conviction for "malicious wounding." A local "conjure doctor" in the Danville, Virginia, area, Lee performed powerful and sometimes
haunting religious songs for John A. Lomax and accompanied Strother on "Do Lord, Remember Me." (Prisoner photograph of Joe Lynn Lee, Records of the Virginia State Penitentiary, State Records Collection, Library of Virginia, Richmond)

Lee's apocalyptic vision of immolation as divine retribution was not
out of character. People in the Dan River region called on Lee for proph-
ecy, spells, potions, and remedies as a well-known local "conjure doctor"
and herbal healer. Lee and his wife, Kittie, alternately lived in Pittsylvania
County, Virginia, and Caswell County, North Carolina, with Joe working
as a railroad laborer and farmhand. Lee's path to the Virginia State Prison
Farm began in jail in Danville, Virginia. One Ike Carter had received treatment from Lee but refused to pay. Lee then reputedly used an iron bar
to inflict a wound on his patient's head that required thirty-five stitches to
close. Convicted of "malicious wounding," he joined Jim Strother and the
other inmates at the farm who recorded for Lomax and Spivacke in 1936.
Lee's repertoire was entirely Christian sacred songs, which might seem
incongruous for a conjurer and root doctor, but, like Strother's mixing of
the spiritual and secular, Lee easily joined the supernatural and the sacred
within the cosmology of Black spirituality and practice.[22]

Lee's intense spiritual expressions thoroughly spooked the urbane but
inexperienced Harold Spivacke. Lomax played one of Lee's songs back to

him, inspiring Lee to "[get] to shouting . . . and preached eloquently to us for five minutes or more frightening poor Spivacke terribly who thought he had gone crazy." Lee proclaimed, "My soul is wrapped up in the care of the Lord and nothing in this world can harm me." Such a powerful, spirit-possessed declamation on God's (and the spirit's) active protection in the world is easily reconciled with Black conjure and religious practices. Lee's inspired performances featured prominently on the early Library of Congress albums alongside those of Strother.[23]

As the songs and recordings of Jim Strother went out into the world, he was himself "almost down to the shore"; he was in poor health, struggling to make his way financially, and living with his younger relatives in Baltimore. He almost certainly had no idea that his music had gone out over the airwaves and had been heard in libraries, classrooms, and a few homes since his release from the Virginia State Prison Farm just a few years before. His songs, despite his own relative isolation, were now becoming part of America's public folk legacy, and these musical messages from an earlier era would continue to ripple outward after his death.

18

The Folk Process

I had never heard anything so cool and in a most profound way, this moment of musical synchronicity would change my musical life! I was enthralled with this tune on so many levels.

—JORMA KAUKONEN on hearing the Roger Perkins and Larry Hanks version of "Blood-Stained Banders"

In 1969, Jefferson Airplane released its sixth album, *Volunteers*, to critical and popular acclaim. Sales were brisk; the album soon reached gold status. On it, Jorma Kaukonen, the band's guitar player, sings a song titled "Good Shepherd." The lyrics of the song, if not the exact melody or spirit, are clearly derived from Strother's "Blood-Stained Banders." This led to the obvious question: How did a West Coast psychedelic rock band come to perform a relatively obscure field recording by a Virginia prison inmate? The answer is an excellent example of the ebbs and flows of the "folk process" celebrated by participants in the folk revival of the late 1950s and early 1960s. (It's worth mentioning here that Strother had only been dead for twenty-one years when this version was recorded.)[1]

Kaukonen steeped himself in traditional music in his early years, as did many young artists who would go on to fame in the rock era. His subsequent and current band, Hot Tuna, plays a wide variety of music from folk sources. Many aficionados of traditional fingerstyle blues attend his music camps at the Fur Peace Ranch in Ohio. Like most musicians of that era, Kaukonen acquired some songs from reissue recordings but more commonly from other musicians. On his website, Kaukonen explained his introduction to Strother's "Blood-Stained Banders":

> You know one thinks of life's little intersections . . . happenstance oc-
> currences that change one's life. In 1963 or thereabouts I was hang-
> ing out at the Offstage in San Jose and playing there as much as they
> would allow. I was known as Jerry Kaukonen back then . . . I hadn't
> yet shed the nickname and returned to Jorma . . . but that is another
> story. Anyway, a pair of folksingers Roger Perkins, and Larry Hanks
> were booked into the place and of course, I wouldn't have missed it for
> the world. This was a simpler time when the enjoyment of folk music
> in all its guises was the quintessential form of entertainment. Roger
> tuned his guitar to drop D and played Good Shepherd. I flipped when
> I heard it and had Roger show it to me. I found out later that the au-
> thor of the tune is Jimmy Struthers [sic] and the original title is Blood
> Strained Banders [sic].[2]

Located at 970 South First Street in San Jose, the Off Stage hosted aspiring artists who would later become important figures in the development
of several strands of folk and rock music. Janis Joplin, David Crosby, and
Mother McCree's Uptown Jug Champions—including future Grateful Dead
members Jerry Garcia, Bob Weir, and Ron "Pigpen" McKernan—all performed at the Off Stage. Kaukonen and his Jefferson Airplane bandmate
Paul Kantner, both one-time students at Santa Clara University, also made
a habit of frequenting the place. Here they heard not only seminal folk
groups, such as the New Lost City Ramblers, but also many local folk performers like Roger Perkins and Larry Hanks, who would go on to varying degrees of musical success. Perkins and Hanks also backed up many of
these artists.

But where and how did Kaukonen's source, folk singers Roger Perkins
and Larry Hanks, learn "Blood-Stained Banders"? Unfortunately, Roger
Perkins passed away in 2009. Luckily, I was able to contact and speak with
Perkins's musical partner, Larry Hanks, and his wife (and fellow musician)
Deborah Robins, who both still live in the Bay area and enjoyed fulfilling
folk music careers. When I spoke to Deborah Robins on the phone, I was
delighted to find out that she had recently recorded "Blood-Stained Banders." Both were incredibly helpful. Robins even sent me a video recording of Larry Hanks playing the version of "Good Shepherd" that they had
performed in front of Jorma Kaukonen more than sixty years ago. The arrangement tracks quite well with the Jefferson Airplane version, of course.
Perkins added an ascending progression with minor chords, giving the song

a somewhat more ethereal sensibility absent in the original but appropriate to the musical aesthetics of the folk revival. Kaukonen recalled that he "had never heard anything so cool and in a most profound way, this moment of musical synchronicity would change my musical life!"[3]

Hanks remembered that it had been Perkins who brought the song "Good Shepherd" to the duo, but he was unsure of the source. It's possible that Perkins picked up the song from another folk performer through the tried-and-true method of oral transmission. Less likely is that an enterprising individual might have mined the 1941 published transcription from *Our Singing Country* for one of the ephemeral songbooks circulating within the folksong community. Hanks and Perkins lived and performed together from roughly 1962 to 1966, and they both owned significant collections of vinyl records. My money is on the theory that either Perkins or a fellow folk singer heard Strother's song from the 1958 LP reissue of John Lomax's *Ballad Hunter* set.

The original 1941 set, aimed at radio stations, schools, libraries, and similar organizations, consisted of five sixteen-inch transcription discs for limited distribution. In 1958, a grant from the Carnegie Corporation of New York provided funds for the set to be reissued on standard 33⅓ vinyl. Another generation now heard John Lomax's somewhat overdramatic "lectures"—they were actually very short introductions—that contextualized musical excerpts from American folk music that he had collected for the Archive of American Folk Song in the Library of Congress. Ironically, a record set first released during America's war mobilization in 1941 as a way to reinforce American nationalism now provided raw materials for the folk revival—and ultimately the anti–Vietnam War counterculture.[4]

It's difficult to imagine, in an age when almost every obscure musician's output is readily available online, that those of us who came to traditional music in the 1960s faced a landscape of scarcity for original recordings. Some early students and interpreters of American roots music—members of the electric blues band Canned Heat, for example—eagerly hunted for prewar recordings on 78-rpm discs because scarcely anything had been reissued on vinyl. Seminal artists and folk-music tastemakers such as Dave Van Ronk, Bob Dylan, Jerry Garcia, Ralph Rinzler, and John Cohen counted Harry Smith's 1952 *Anthology of American Folk Music* on Moe Asch's Folkways label as a key influence. Likewise, to an avid 1960s folk singer, *The Ballad Hunter* would have been pure gold. Not only did it bring together rare field recordings into thematic groupings but it also provided information on the artists and songs by a widely recognized authority—the collector John Lomax himself. In many ways, the 1960s folk singers and songsters were replicating the complicated paths that many of the songs sung by traditional artists had taken, albeit with the aid of new means of transmission.[5]

While reissue recordings aided the folk singers' search for new material, the "folk process" was still alive and well. The same year that the Library of Congress reissued *The Ballad Hunter*, Folkways Records released an LP album with the song "Blood-Stained Banders"—not by Jim Strother but by a fresh-faced band of white Oberlin College students dubbed The Folksmiths. This eight-person troupe had just completed a tour of the northeastern United States, where they had spread the gospel of folk music at summer camps and resorts. Their mission was not only to perform but also to teach. The group offered workshops and an educational "kit" including a fifty-five-page songbook, game and dance books, a list of folksong publishers, and a roster of contemporary folk singers. Like any good evangelists, the group members were sending forth their acolytes to convert others. Joe Hickerson's membership in the group presaged a long and distinguished career as a music archivist, folklorist, and performer. Pete Seeger's performance at Oberlin during Hickerson's freshman year especially inspired him. "I was hooked!" he exclaimed. He and the other members of the Oberlin folk club attended regional folk festivals, meeting some of the luminaries of the burgeoning folk scene.

The Folksmiths had just spent several weeks in rehearsal at Pete Seeger's house when the group walked into Moe Asch's studio in New York City to record. The album that came out of this session is something of a landmark; it includes the first revivalist recording of the song "Kumbaya." While perusing the liner notes, I was struck by the web of connections in the tight-knit 1950s folk community. The group learned songs from established folk singers such as Tony Saletan and Peggy Seeger, camp counselors, and published songbooks.[6]

Indeed, the group's connections to members of the Seeger family suggested a possible source for Strother's song. In their liner notes, "Blood-Stained Banders" was described as a "spiritual and street-singer's song of the southern mountains." This indicated a knowledge of the song's origins (at least Strother's origins, according to John Lomax). A letter in Joe Hickerson's papers revealed how and why. Sarah Newcomb, a band member from Virginia, wrote Hickerson on August 24, 1957: "As to Library of Congress notes on 'Blood-Strained [*sic*] Banders.' If you mean our wry touch of humor (How Wry I Am) about learning the song therein, I can't tell you anything. Except that the Librarians had a lean and hungry look and made nasty cracks about John Lomax. But if you want Facts, why then I'll trot down to the ol' Bibliotheque first chance I get." Hickerson and his bandmates were in the process of finishing the liner notes for the Folkways release and used their local member to research the song.[7]

Hickerson and his comrades had likely heard the song though the Seegers. Ruth Crawford Seeger, Peggy Seeger's mother, had done the musical transcription of Strother's song for the Lomaxes' book *Our Singing Country* and published her own arrangement in a subsequent songbook, *American Folk Songs for Christmas*, in 1953. Peggy would later record her mother's version with her brother Mike and daughter Penny on a Christmas album—without Strother's most disturbing imagery. When I dropped the needle on the Folksmiths LP, it was immediately obvious that musically, this was the Seeger rearrangement, although they kept Strother's original words. The Seegers reimagined the song by taking it back to another tradition—the shape-note hymn singing of rural white churches. One last ironic note: in 1963 Joe Hickerson became the librarian and director of the Archive of Folk Song at the Library of Congress and thus the custodian of James Lee Strother's recorded legacy.[8]

Before the Library of Congress's reissues, the tour by The Folksmiths, the performances of Hanks and Perkins, and the psychedelic version by Jefferson Airplane, elements of "Blood-Stained Banders" had already wended their way over time and space for at least 150 years. Countless common people in the United States, white and Black, heard Methodist circuit-rider John Adam Granade's gospel song "Let Thy Kingdom, Blessed Savior" in a world on fire with religious fervor at the dawn of the nineteenth century. The passing of such a gospel song through oral tradition in ecstatic performance at tent revivals and brush arbors would have appealed to unlettered white congregants as well as enslaved people. The song's enduring appeal explains its inclusion in African American minister Marshall W. Taylor's seminal 1882 publication, *A Collection of Revival Hymns and Plantation Melodies*, which brought together 170 hymns, camp-meeting songs, and spirituals "intended primarily for use by black congregations of the white Methodist Episcopal Church." The song's chorus is clearly a building block for Strother's song.[9]

There was one more surprise awaiting me regarding Strother's most enduring recording. Completely by chance I encountered another version of the song that reinforced some truisms about interpreting the musical past. I first opened Taylor's *Collection of Revival Hymns and Plantation Melodies* only to analyze Taylor's version of Granade's "Let Thy Kingdom, Blessed Savior." Yet as I flipped through the book, another song jumped off the page—a much closer reading of Strother's performance in both lyrics and melody. Titled "Shouting on the Other Shore," it provided a link between Strother's 1936 recording and its circulation among African American congregations and communities as part of a rich Black folk culture.[10]

"Shouting on the Other Shore" from Taylor's compilation uses the same chorus lyrics as Strother's recording. It obviously had origins in Granade's original formulation, but it clearly had circulated in its new form among enslaved people long before Strother recorded the song. Not surprisingly, the tune for "Shouting" is more in line with Strother's song and African American vocal traditions. The Taylor hymn goes thus:

> My mother died a-shouting
> Over on the other shore;
> Don't you hear the lambs a-crying?
> O good shepherd, feed my sheep.
>
> *Chorus:* Some for Paul, some for Silas
> Some to make my heart rejoice;
> Don't you hear the lambs a-crying?
> O good shepherd, feed my sheep.[11]

So where did the compositions in Taylor's collection come from? Taylor had a long professional and family association with his native region. He held several offices in the Lexington Conference of the Methodist Episcopal Church before becoming the presiding elder for the Ohio Conference and moving to Cincinnati. It was here that he published his remarkable compilation. Taylor paid tribute to those who advanced his work: "Publishers, ministers, members, male and female, have aided me, furnishing songs, and in many other ways too numerous to name, without which my work must have been much less successful than it is."[12]

The introduction to Taylor's compilation stressed the authenticity of the work. This was no secondhand gathering of tunes or a "minstrel" publication:

PLANTATION MELODIES. 245

148. Shouting on the Other Shore.

America Bell.   Heb. 13: 20.

1 My mother died a-shouting
Over on the other shore;
Don't you hear the lambs a-crying?
O good Shepherd feed my sheep.

246   PLANTATION MELODIES.

Chorus.
Some for Paul, some for Silas,
Some to make my heart rejoice;
Don't you hear the lambs a-crying?
O good Shepherd feed my sheep.
2 My father, etc.
3 My brother, etc.
4 My sister, etc.
5 My classmates, etc.
6 My preacher, etc.
7 My leader, etc.
8 My children, etc.
9 My neighbors, etc.

Serendipity often comes into play during research. I stumbled on this version of Strother's song in Marshall Taylor's hymnbook while looking for something else. "Shouting on the Other Shore," in Marshall W. Taylor, *A Collection of Revival Hymns and Plantation Melodies* (Cincinnati: Marshall W. Taylor and W. C. Echols, 1882), 145–46. (Courtesy of Special Collections, University of Virginia Library)

The tunes accompanying these songs were caught by the musical composer as they were sung in her hearing. This composer was once a slave, and is well acquainted with all the characteristics of the music and the songs prevalent in the religious meetings of the colored people. Dr. Taylor's wife, who, as the Preface indicates, has been an efficient assistant, was likewise once a slave. The compiler has enjoyed special advantages. Having been constantly associated from childhood with the people of his race, both in social and Church life, he has had the best of opportunities for perfect familiarity, by observation and practice, with the usages, music, and language of their religious worship under a great variety of circumstances.[13]

Josephine Robinson and Amelia C. Taylor, the clergyman's daughter, received credit for preparing the tunes. Little is known about Josephine Robinson. She lived with Rev. Marshall Taylor and his family in their Cincinnati home in 1880. Only twenty-one years old, she must have proved an able and energetic collaborator. Like Taylor's wife, Nancy, and so many of their Cincinnati neighbors, Robinson had been born in Kentucky.[14]

Luckily for later researchers, Taylor and his assistants recorded the names of those from whom they collected sacred songs. "Shouting on the Other Shore" is credited to America Bell, a name unique enough to be narrowed down to a few possibilities in the area of Taylor's and his collaborators' activities. Two possible sources emerge, both Black women born in the era of slavery in Kentucky who resettled in Ohio. The most likely source for "Shouting on the Other Shore" was America Bell Welsh, the Kentucky-born wife of James Welsh. She and her large family lived in Danville, Kentucky, in the post–Civil War period, migrating to Cincinnati sometime in the 1880s after the death of her husband. Born around 1825, she would have been well versed in her community's sacred music. Although she does not appear in Cincinnati records until 1890, her Kentucky home was well within the region that Taylor traveled for his ministerial duties.[15]

That a formerly enslaved woman from Kentucky born in the antebellum era and a Virginia songster born around 1881 sang essentially the same song melody with the same chorus lyrics ought to caution us to be circumspect about making assumptions about the relative ubiquity of songs based on the written word or later aural recordings. Songs that were in wide circulation among the enslaved may have never appeared in the documentary record or on the recordings of field workers and commercial companies. In this case, a single field recording preserved a song from a much earlier era. And then Jorma Kaukonen's chance encounter with two folk singers perpetuated the song as part of an oral folk-music culture. The trail of "Blood-Stained Banders" stretched from enslaved Kentuckians to West Coast rockers while moving in and out of the folk and commercial stream multiple times. "Blood-Stained Banders" might be Strother's greatest artistic achievement as well as an example *par excellence* of the tangled roots and branches of American music. It embodies the complexity of the so-called folk process, reaching backward and forward with Strother's lived experience as its vital center.

19

Songs of Protest

If religion was the one thing money could buy,
The rich would live and the poor would die,
Don't want to stay here no longer.
—JAMES LEE STROTHER, "Run Down, Eli," recorded 1936

Jefferson Airplane wasn't the first internationally known group to cover Jim Strother's most famous song, "Blood-Stained Banders." During the summer of 1943, Virginia's Golden Gate Quartet had recorded the song on a sixteen-inch radio transcription disc for NBC on its Thesaurus label. The double-sided recording included eleven sacred and topical songs for broadcast. The "Gates" not only reigned as the most famous and successful Black gospel quartet of their era but also became closely associated with the American left and the pre–World War II folk music movement.

Founded in the quartet-singing hotbed of Hampton Roads, Virginia, the group formed at a Norfolk high school in the late 1920s. Building on the Tidewater tradition of earlier groups such as the Silver Leaf Quartette and the Norfolk Jubilee Quartet, the quartet pioneered a lively, heavily syncopated spiritual style, bringing the group to international prominence in the 1930s. The quartet waxed hundreds of 78-rpm commercial recordings and appeared at legendary impresario and producer John Hammond's "Spirituals to Swing" concerts at Carnegie Hall. I recall that during a quartet workshop, I asked the Blind Boys of Alabama's Clarence Fountain about his early influences. He said "the Golden Gate Quartet" without hesitation.

I found his response fascinating, since the style of the Blind Boys is considerably different, yet it spoke to the group's pervasive influence.[1]

The Thesaurus recording that featured "Blood-Stained Banders" also highlighted the quartet's political activism in the 1940s. The disc delivered songs such as "Can't Serve God and Mammon" and "Stalin Wasn't Stallin'," placing the group firmly in the New York City orbit of the political Left. Some of the quartet's commercial recordings of this era also explored political themes of race and class. The group's anti-segregation song "No Restricted Signs (Up in Heaven)" advocated equality not only for Black people but also for all races and classes:

> So they tagged along and what did they see?
> Snow white angels, colored angels,
> Sons of David and some Chinese;
> You don't dress swell, not for that hotel,
> You can check in in your dungarees—
> Welcome! Welcome![2]

The members of the quartet knew and had performed for Alan Lomax, who traveled in the same New York circles. It is almost certain that Lomax introduced the quartet to Strother's recording. The Left's search for folk music that could be employed for political ends was well known.

The Golden Gate Quartet's reworking of "Blood-Stained Banders" presaged an even more radical refashioning of Strother's song by a leading light of American folk and protest music. The same year that Jorma Kaukonen heard "Good Shepherd" at the Off Stage in San Jose, another audience learned the tune via *Broadside* #33, a radical folk revival magazine edited by Agnes "Sis" Cunningham and her husband, Gordon Friesen. It featured a recasting of "Blood-Stained Banders"—by folk icon and Left activist Pete Seeger with his father, Charles—as a full-blown protest anthem. Regular folk had frequently used their traditional music as a form of protest, and there had been a long debate about what type of music was truly appropriate to inspire revolution. Pete and Charles Seeger reframed Strother's song as follows:

> If you want to go to freedom
> Over on the other shore,
> Keep away from the long-tongued liars,
> Hold fast to the freedom cause.

Chorus: Thru the danger we're not turning,
No more shame & misery,
Can't you hear your children cryin',
Don't you want us to be free.[3]

The Seegers' reframing of Strother's song was part of a venerable tradition. Radical movements had often appropriated tunes from popular and folk sources for protest anthems. For example, in the 1880s, the Knights of Labor took the tune and some of the words of the religious song "Hold the Fort" for their main labor anthem. Likewise, Black women laboring in the tobacco stemmeries of Richmond, Virginia, adapted the spiritual "I Shall Not Be Moved" as a rallying cry during a 1930s strike, inserting lines lauding their leaders and castigating the factory owner by name. The song, now employing the collective "we," became a staple of protests during the labor and civil rights movements.[4]

The recasting of "Blood-Stained Banders" seems entirely appropriate, based on Strother's numerous direct comments on racial and class discrimination. The most conventional of Strother's critiques of race and class were passed down from the formerly enslaved. These were the expressions, explored by Black scholars such as Zora Neale Hurston, that emphasized how African American song used techniques such as indirection, irony, and role-reversal—signifying—to provide in-group meaning, to shield their true thoughts from whites, and to simply survive. A classic example is the common and oft-quoted formulation found in many Black secular songs contrasting the situation of the white and Black man:

If you work all the week,
An' work all the time,
White man sho' to bring
Nigger out behin'.[5]

An example from Jim Strother's "Jaybird" echoes songs and expressions from the time of slavery:

White folks in a parlor,
Drink up all that dram,
Darkies in the barnyard,
Eaten up the white folks' ham.

Strother and his ancestors flipped the relationship of enslaver and enslaved and the theft of their labor; ironically, while thought to be in a subordinate situation, they "steal" (of course, how can you steal what your labor has produced?) from the "white folks" and outwit their so-called betters. Yet other expressions of class and race are more direct, as in Strother's "Run Down, Eli":

> If religion was the one thing money could buy,
> The rich would live and the poor would die,
> Don't want to stay here no longer.
>
> Why, I so thank God it is not so,
> All got right to the Heaven's door.
> Don't want to stay here no longer.

Such statements of Black "protest" in song may not seem very heroic or "progressive" to us. Yet such words were not just clever wordplay; they did real work in the Black community. Jim Strother went much further than the opaque references in songs such as "Corn Shucking Time" and "Jaybird." He cogently identified and overtly named the evils of white supremacy and economic subjugation. Strother's overall repertoire evinces a deep sense of righteous grievance. To be sure, it is less the overtly folk-political protest of a Josh White than a dark invocation of a truly dangerous and unfair world. His lyrics evoke not only the perils of encountering racism in the Jim Crow South but also a sense of class struggle and labor exploitation from his own lived experience.

The world of "Blood-Stained Banders," "I Used to Work on a 'Tractor," and "Thought I Heard My Banjo Say" was a place where a soul or a life could be lost; where Mike Hardy and his fellow bosses stole a man's money and his self-worth; and where sundown in the wrong country town could lead to danger and death. Most songsters would avoid such songs before white or mixed audiences, according to scholar Paul Oliver, "except under the cover of a heavy screen of other associations." All the more reason to take Strother's and other songsters' words seriously when they sang such material for white folklorists. Words and even sounds mattered. A whistle aimed at the wrong person could get you killed.

Recall the chilling story that Jim Greene, the grandson of Jim Strother's second wife, Blanche Greene, told me about visiting Culpeper County during the summer in the 1950s. He and several of his young friends had engaged in some back-and-forth bantering with a group of white girls. That evening his uncle received a threatening phone call, and his father never let him return for a summer visit to Culpeper again. Part of Strother's music wasn't simply to confront white power but to teach young people to survive in a white-dominated world. When Strother sang "Don't let sundown catch you here," he did important cultural work that was literally a matter of life and death. If we focus more on the Black musicians and less on their interrogators, we can better appreciate the bravery it took to sing some of these lines.[6]

Some have compared Strother's most forthright critiques, especially "I Used to Work on a 'Tractor," to the folk songs collected by Lawrence Gellert in the same era. Gellert had no particular ideological commitment to radical politics, but he found a ready audience for his materials with his brother Hugo and his Socialist and Communist comrades in New York. The largely white intelligentsia of Left politics intuited in Gellert's "songs of protest" an Indigenous, proletarian music that might engage Black people in the class struggle. Gellert seized on this interest by publishing in Left journals such as New Masses. Eventually it would result in his book, Negro Songs of Protest, which cemented Gellert's reputation among a mostly Northern radical Left audience. Still, Gellert's assessment of such songs was in the eye of the beholder. Much of the material in his collection had already been captured in fieldwork by other researchers but not given the same radical interpretation. For example, Fisk University professor and administrator Thomas W. Talley documented similar material in his pathbreaking Negro Folk Rhymes, but his intent was folkloric rather than polemical.[7]

What compelled Jim Strother to sing such provocative lyrics for his white interrogators? Ironically, the man responsible for recording Strother—John Lomax—had intentionally sought out material that he characterized as "complaining songs," and Jim Strother definitely delivered. A Southern paternalist who did not question the racial hierarchy of his region, Lomax was blind to Strother's most trenchant critiques; he viewed such material as born of Black "self-pity" based in feelings of inferiority.

I have often wondered whether Strother's early experiences in Virginia had some bearing on his willingness to make explicit lyrical comments regarding racism, labor exploitation, and even class. Strother's youth coincided with the rise and fall of the biracial Readjuster coalition in Virginia, a rare moment in the history of the post-Reconstruction South when Black people had a real political voice. His second wife's grandfather had voted as early as 1867, and he certainly knew many other Black people who had participated in politics. Even into the early 1890s there were still Black elected officials in Virginia before the 1902 state constitution severely limited Black voting. He undoubtedly knew prominent citizens, like Henry Lightfoot, who had held public office in Culpeper County in his lifetime. Perhaps some Black Virginians who came of age after Emancipation and before the imposition of full-blown Jim Crow had a more assertive attitude and a more nuanced viewpoint on race than the following generations. Complaints from Culpeper's newspapers and elites about the patrons who attended Henry Lightfoot's establishment and did not show proper deference to white people also applied to Strother.

Strother's commentary on race certainly stands in contrast to most of the Black music recorded by the generation who followed his own. As Paul Oliver concluded, "overt comments on relations between the races were rare" in commercially recorded blues. Even expressions of covert racial discourse in the repertoire of blues artists seem to have waned. This change was coupled with another major transformation: the move from collective expressions of "trouble in mind" to an individual, first-person viewpoint. Pre-blues secular tunes were often rooted in collective community experiences. Strother sang that "we are almost down to the shore" and memorialized the corn shucking, a collective event.

Did Pete and Charles Seeger intuit a radical message in Strother's songs that influenced their selection of "Blood-Stained Banders" as the blueprint for a freedom anthem? We'll never know, but it was an inspired choice. Strother's voice of protest is plainly evident to those who wish to hear it. While Strother's continued influence on contemporary musicians is important, for me, his hard-hitting critiques of America's racial and class order constitute his most enduring legacy.

20

The Songster Tradition

When I heard "We Are Almost Down to the Shore," I was just completely elated. And then of course there's "Do Lord, Remember Me" that starts out with Joe Lee and Jim. I mean it's such a powerful sound.
—DOM FLEMONS

Enthusiasm for American folk music has arisen cyclically, periodically imposing itself onto American popular culture over the last hundred years. The twentieth century has seen the rise and fall (and sometimes resurrection yet again) of fiddle contests, folk festivals, blues revivals, and Hawaiian crazes. These revivals have served different cultural purposes for each generation, some of them not very savory. (Today, old-time musicians lionize the performers who vied for honors at the White Top Mountain Festival, but many are unaware that one of the festival's founders, John Powell, was a virulent racist who specifically used the event to promote the superiority of "Anglo-Saxon" culture.) Having lived through several iterations of these folk revivals as a performer, presenter, and interpreter, I have always found the history of such movements fascinating.

One particular encounter with the generational nature of these revivals stands out in my mind. Appropriately, the event took place near Galax, Virginia, one of the great wellsprings of traditional American folk music. At the Blue Ridge Music Center, nestled along the picturesque Blue Ridge Parkway, I had the welcome task of hosting a discussion of the blues and songster tradition with Dom Flemons, Phil Wiggins, "Boo" Hanks, and Lightnin' Wells. As I pondered how to moderate the session, I realized that the assembled musicians represented a fascinating continuum of the folk process and the songster tradition. Born in 1928, James Arthur "Boo" Hanks resided in the tobacco belt along the Virginia border with North Carolina. A farmer and industrial worker, he played the guitar as an avocation locally until brought to the public's attention by the Music Makers Relief Foundation while in his seventies. He was one of the last living musicians born to the music. Phil Wiggins and Michael "Lightnin'" Wells are both children of the 1960s but come from very different experiences. Wiggins, of course, is a blues harmonica master and elder statesman and a NEA National Heritage Fellow. He came to the music through a circle of older Washington, DC–area Black musicians, most notably his longtime musical partner, John Cephas. Wells's experience echoes my own: a white youth in the 1960s intrigued by a wide range of traditional music, especially early blues, who sought out obscure recordings and older players.[1]

Dom Flemons, born in 1982, added a fascinating perspective to the panel as both a young artist and as a representative of a new generation of folk revivalists. He has avidly taken on the songster mantle and is a leading light in the recent movement of young Black artists seeking to reclaim and reinvigorate the early musical styles that came before the blues. A founding member of the Carolina Chocolate Drops in 2006, musical collaborator with traditional musicians such as John Dee Holman and "Boo" Hanks, and now a highly successful solo artist, he has elevated many obscure artists to public recognition. Equal parts educator, historian, and musician, he also has a clear understanding of the importance of the social context of this music. He revels in his own role as an African American songster, playing a wide variety of styles before people from all walks of life. Just as the street songster was a ubiquitous presence in America before the 1930s, so Flemons and other Black artists now perform this music for people around the world in the global town square. Jim Strother lives on through these musicians, a legacy that he would have never anticipated.[2]

Flemons's connection to Strother is direct and fundamental. As a young student attending Northern Arizona University, he began to delve into early Black musical traditions. Fortuitously, he found a copy of the Library of Congress's *Negro Religious Songs and Services* and recalled its profound impact. Flemons remembered that "when I heard 'We Are Almost Down to the Shore,' I was just completely elated. And then of course there's 'Do Lord, Remember Me' that starts out with Joe Lee and Jim. I mean it's such a powerful sound. And then of course they've got the picture of the two of

"Fighting On" first appears in the 1891 expanded version of the Hampton Institute's songbook and in the subsequent 1901 edition, and it tracks closely with Strother's "We Are Almost Down to the Shore." Thomas P. Fenner, *Cabin and Plantation Songs as Sung by the Hampton Students* (New York: G. P. Putnam's Sons, 1901), 93. (Courtesy of Special Collections, University of Virginia Library)

them as well. And to see the two of them sitting there singing the song in front of the microphone—it's a very iconic image, and an evocative image of a world that no longer exists."[3]

Flemons admired the commercial recordings of legendary songsters such as Henry Thomas, Gus Cannon, and Papa Charlie Jackson, but it was not until he heard the field recordings of musicians such as Strother that he began to appreciate "the songsters as a folk-cultural phenomena." He enthused about Strother's wide repertoire, his ability to code-switch depending on his audience, and the ways he embedded subtle social commentary into his songs that other Black people would understand and appreciate. I interviewed him after I had already researched and even written much of this book. Luckily for me, he echoed many of the points that to me make Strother one of the most fascinating African American musicians of his era.[4]

Inspired by the Library of Congress's *Negro Religious Songs and Services*, Flemons chose Strother's "We Are Almost Down to the Shore" as one of the few covers on his 2023 release, *Traveling Wildfire*. A precedent for Strother's song appears as "Fighting On" in a few late nineteenth-century compilations of spirituals, most notably the expanded 1891 edition of Thomas P. Fenner's *Cabin and Plantation Songs as Sung by the Hampton Students*. Strother's melody closely mirrors the notated version in the Hampton compilation, suggesting a common folk source in the rich spiritual soil of Virginia.[5]

Flemons, in the enduring spirit of the "Folk Process," transforms the song into a lovely, hymnlike invocation of Black spirituality in the face of oppression. His direct and stately vocal floats over his own delicate fingerstyle guitar and the persistent drone of Marc Orrell's pump organ. Lashon Halley's voice joins Flemons's to emphasize the song's urgent chorus:

> Fight on, fight on,
> Children and don't turn back,
> We are almost down to the shore.[6]

In Flemons's own words, the song "is a definitive testament to the resilience of people who have been oppressed, marginalized, and displaced from their homes." James Lee Strother couldn't have said it better.

21

Mount Auburn

I done played this piece, babe,
'til my fingers got sore,
Now if it ain't nothing doin'
I ain't gonna play no more.
—JAMES LEE STROTHER, "Going to Richmond," recorded 1936

James Lee Strother lives on. His music still inspires musicians and reaches new audiences every day in the modern digital soundscape. But in the 1940s, as his songs began to ripple through popular culture, Strother himself was almost certainly unaware that others were hearing his voice for the first time. He could have used the encouragement of knowing that he had unexpectedly left a legacy; he would have also welcomed the few dollars that the Library of Congress had tried to send his way. Instead, Strother's twilight years only brought more hardships.

He left the Virginia State Prison Farm a free man—as free as a blind Black man in America could be in 1940. True to his promise to the Commonwealth of Virginia, he returned to Baltimore and moved into 1214 ½ Pennsylvania Avenue with his nephew William Taylor and Taylor's wife, Sadie. Taylor, in his late thirties, drove for a coal company, while Sadie worked as a domestic for a private family. Strother found himself back in the city he had long called home; in fact, he lived just a few blocks from the notorious alley district where he had started his musical career. Baltimore's residents would not again hear Strother's ringing banjo or deep baritone voice, however. Despite his assurances to Governor James H. Price that he could still make his living performing "string music," that hope (or boast) was chimerical.

Strother's freedom was always compromised, but now other factors came into play. Beyond his blindness, he struggled with other serious physical disabilities. Strother had left the Virginia State Prison Farm a broken man. Superintendent R. R. Penn's report on prisoner #33927 to the governor gave a grim assessment of the physical toll that life as a street musician and incarceration had taken on the sixty-two-year-old musician:

> Weight 188 lbs, a gain of 20 lbs. Lungs normal. Heart: mitral systolic murmur with hypertrophy present. Arteriosclerosis present. Blood pressure high. Wasserman negative. Small left hernia present. Blind in both eyes. General condition poor.[1]

The matter-of-fact medical language of the report clinically describes Strother's serious cardiovascular disease—hardening of the arteries, high blood pressure, and a heart murmur. Years of an uncertain life on the road and in the streets conspired with more than four years of incarceration to reduce Strother to a shadow of his former self and limit his options as he returned to Baltimore. The city he found on his return had also changed in many ways—and in important ways that militated against a return to his former life.

If Strother had walked the few blocks to his former neighborhood in the "Lung Block," he would have found no trace of it—although many Baltimoreans, Black and white, would have considered that a good thing. The African American reformers who railed against the iniquities and evils of the Biddle Alley District in the early 1900s finally found their champion. It was R. Maurice Moss, the secretary of the Baltimore Urban League, who brought about the demise of the Biddle Alley neighborhood. In December 1929, the black journal *Opportunity* celebrated that "the shouts and laughter of little children will soon be heard where death and suffering wrought havoc a few years ago. Unsightly shacks which housed insidious disease and crime will soon be no more. The 'lung block,' which sent its hundreds of Negroes infected with tuberculosis to untimely graves and was a source of infection for the whole city, will soon be demolished." Even before this work for a city playground had begun, the northern edge of the Biddle Alley District had been transformed by the construction of the first elementary school for African Americans by the Baltimore City School Board—ninety-seven years after the establishment of public education in the city. Samuel Coleridge-Taylor Elementary School #122 still stands and is today designated a city historic landmark.[2]

Naming the school after the Afro-British musician and composer was likely inspired by his historic visits to Washington, DC, and Baltimore in 1904 and 1906. Coleridge-Taylor's father, a physician in Sierra Leone, had roots in America as a descendant of enslaved people freed during the American Revolution for their service to the British. Coleridge-Taylor enjoyed worldwide fame for his compositions based in folk sources, especially African and African American music, and he was familiar with many notable American civil rights leaders and musicians. Apparently, he was not a fan of much of the music produced by America's Black entertainers. He saw little value in ragtime tunes and other American popular styles. As to the coon songs, he denounced them as "the worst sort of rot. . . . In the first place there is no melody and in the second place there is no real Negro character or sentiment . . . they are not Negro melodies." Sylvester Russell, the *Indianapolis Freeman's* noted theater critic, fired back that these were indeed "Negro musics," a position that Jim Strother would have certainly appreciated.[3]

Even more dramatic changes would have greeted Strother just northwest of his lodgings with the Taylors at 1214 ½ Pennsylvania Avenue. After a few minutes' walk, Strother would have arrived in the heart of Baltimore's Black entertainment district, which had only begun to fully emerge when he left in the early 1920s. A new generation of artists had made their names on Pennsylvania Avenue in the upscale entertainment palaces that lined the thoroughfare. The Royal Theatre had opened as the Black-owned Douglass Theatre around the time that Strother left Baltimore. It was the jewel in the crown of Black Baltimore's entertainment district, hosting celebrity artists such as native sons Cab Calloway and Eubie Blake as well as Louis Jordan, Ethel Waters, Louis Armstrong, and classic blues shouter Bertha Idaho. The best African American musicians, comedians, and other performers followed a circuit of elite venues that included the Royal, the Howard Theatre in Washington, DC, and, of course, the Apollo in Harlem.

Now Strother heard the sounds of sacred quartets swinging in the jubilee style, the beginnings of jump blues, the big bands of Ellington and Basie, and the pumped-up religion of the Holiness and Pentecostal churches spawned by Thomas A. Dorsey's gospel revolution. Strother must have understood that this musical transformation had made his repertoire of nineteenth-century gospel songs, rural blues, and medicine-show ditties anachronistic and out of touch with the buying public.

The tent and medicine shows of Strother's youth had been done in by the one-two punch of new media of entertainment and advertising—primarily radio—and the birth of drug regulation and medical professionalization. The patent-medicine show reinvented itself on the airwaves, promoted by country and blues artists. The Crazy Water Crystals Company of Mineral Wells, Texas, hawked its laxative elixirs with the aid of the Briarhoppers, Dick Hartman's Tennessee Ramblers, and Mainer's Mountaineers on station WBT out of Charlotte, North Carolina. In Louisiana, Cajun politician Dudley J. LeBlanc engaged hillbilly artists to promote Hadacol, a nostrum reputed to cure diabetes, rheumatism, and any number of other ailments. By the late 1930s the Federal Drug Administration, medical associations, and state and federal lawmakers began to limit the advertising claims of patent medicines and control their distribution. Five years before Jim Strother's return to Maryland, state legislators enacted a law that outlawed "so-called medicine shows and patent medicine shows" in a bid to eliminate quack medicine.[4]

The street scene upon Strother's return to Baltimore had also changed. There were still African American musicians who plied their trade on the streets of America's cities in both the North and South, but their numbers had diminished. Gospel singers predominated, and their style and repertoire spoke to the rise of Holiness and Pentecostal religion. In contrast, Strother's spiritual material probably seemed tame and dated to contemporary listeners. The recordings of street evangelists such as Sister O. M. Terrell, the Two Gospel Keys, and Flora Molton give a sense of the gospel sound heard in Savannah, Charleston, and Washington, DC, and it is not the sound of the older spirituals or gospel songs. Of course, the country people who had arrived with Strother's generation still walked the streets, and they might provide an audience, but, by and large, a new generation of African American consumers crowded the city's sidewalks seeking more modern entertainment. Older white patrons might also respond to Strother through nostalgia, but not many.

Even before he left the Virginia State Prison Farm, Strother realized that any hope that he could return to his former life as a street musician was slim. His pleas to Governor Price for his release vacillate from confidence that he could return to his place on Baltimore's street corners to admission that he was likely to be reconciled to the Maryland Workshop for the Blind. He understood that the state bureaucracy would view him either as an economic liability or as an "unproductive" citizen. Strother reminded the governor that he was currently "an absolute expense" to the commonwealth of Virginia. His release also required the acquiescence of the Maryland authorities, who would need assurances that he would not be a drain on the public treasury. Accordingly, he hedged his bets.

In a June 1939 letter, Strother assured Governor Price that he "formerly worked and supported [himself] at the Maryland Workshop for the Blind in Baltimore, Md. I have relatives in Baltimore who want me with them; and where I would be enabled to work again." The next month he wrote again, further elaborating how he would earn his keep in Baltimore. He argued that his relative William Taylor "can give me a good home & I can help take care of myself in the manner & by the means heretofore related to you. In addition, I can earn some money from the playing of string music in which I am considered to be proficient & accomplished." That view, however, was unduly optimistic.[5]

Officious reformers had once stood in the way of his musical livelihood and pushed him toward the Maryland Workshop for the Blind. Now his declining health dictated more sedentary work versus life on the streets. When the census taker arrived at his dwelling in 1940, he duly noted Strother's occupation as "blind chair cainer" [sic] with his own shop. Caning was one of several professions taught at the Maryland Workshop for the Blind, along with piano tuning and broom making.

James Lee Strother's end came less than nine years after his return to Baltimore. Committed to the Good Samaritan Hospital on June 23, 1948, he endured for five days until his death on June 28. The coroner noted his cause of death as "senility," with the additional condition "Decubitus Ulcers"—bedsores. The Baltimore Afro-American included his name on a list of deaths in its July 3, 1948, issue. The undertakers laid the blind songster to rest at Mount Auburn, one of Baltimore's oldest African American cemeteries.

I uncovered the story of Strother's death by emailing my old friend and colleague Kevin Swanson at the Maryland State Archives, and he quickly located the death certificate. I made an appointment to see the cemetery records at Enoch Pratt Free Library and to visit the site. I soon discovered that Mount Auburn Cemetery had been in decline for years. The burying ground's fate wasn't a surprise to me. Richmond's African American cemeteries have been similarly neglected for years, plagued by absentee owners, inattention from the city, and their locations in older African American

I visited Baltimore's Mount Auburn Cemetery in 2015 searching for Jim Strother's grave. Like so many physical landmarks of his life, his grave marker could not be found—if one was ever erected at all. Mount Auburn Cemetery, Baltimore, Maryland. (Photograph by Corlis Kimball Chamberlain)

neighborhoods—out of sight and out of mind to most of the city's residents. Only in the last few years has committed work by local activists led to improvements and the beginnings of restoration.[6]

One of the final ironies of the story of Jim Strother emerged as I searched for information on Mount Auburn online. One of the first headlines to jump onto my computer screen proclaimed: "Baltimore's Oldest Black Cemetery Finally Restored, With Help of Inmates." Somehow it seemed like a perverse kind of poetic justice that fellow prisoners had cleared Strother's final resting place. Luckily for me, it happened just as I discovered Strother's place of burial. Yet my visit to the cemetery—one of my last trips to map the life of the blind musician—ended much like the rest of my research. While I walked among the graves of his fellow Black Baltimoreans and observed Black Baltimore in its ways of death, Strother, as always, remained elusive. No headstone marks the final resting place of a man who, but for a brief moment, entered the larger stage of American culture but just as quickly fell back into the shadows. Yet we still hear his words, his voice, and his banjo and guitar.[7]

APPENDIX A

JAMES LEE STROTHER AND RELATIVES

Government Documents

This table provides entries for James Lee Strother's relatives, primarily the Greene, Taylor, and Strother families, in US census population schedules, vital records such as marriages and deaths, and military records. Similar records for incidental figures in the story are found in the endnotes. Unless otherwise noted, these documents are online in Ancestry.com or FamilySearch.com.

JAMES LEE STROTHER AND FAMILY

NAME	DOCUMENT TYPE	RELEVANT DOCUMENTS
Thornton & Alsie Strother (grandparents)	US Census	**1870:** Cedar Mountain Township, Culpeper County, VA, p. 10. **1880:** Locust Dale Magisterial District, Madison County, VA, enumeration district 109, p. 29.
Susan Strother Stanton (mother)	US Census	**1880:** Cedar Mountain Township, Culpeper County, VA, population schedule, enumeration district 33, p. 22. **1900:** Town of Culpeper, Catalpa District, Culpeper County, VA, enumeration district 5, sheet 9. **1910** (possible): Precinct 3, Washington, DC, enumeration district 36, sheet 2A. **1930:** Town of Culpeper, Culpeper County, VA, enumeration district 1, sheet 21B.
	Marriage Certificate	Marriage of Robert Stanton and Susan Strother, Oct. 10, 1922, Register of Marriages, Culpeper County, VA.
	Death Certificate	Death certificate of Susan Stanton, Town of Culpeper, Culpeper County, VA, Jan. 5, 1931.
James Lee Strother	US Census	**1900:** As "James L. Strather," 15th District, Precinct 1, Sparrows Point, Baltimore County, MD, enumeration district 61, sheet 11. **1910:** 17th Ward, Baltimore City, MD, enumeration district 287, sheet 9B. **1930:** Town of Culpeper, Culpeper County, VA, enumeration district 1, sheet 21B. **1940:** 17th Ward, Baltimore City, MD, enumeration district 4–532, sheet 9B.
	Birth	Register of Births, June 4, 1881, Culpeper County, VA, Library of Virginia, Richmond.

JAMES LEE STROTHER AND FAMILY

NAME	DOCUMENT TYPE	RELEVANT DOCUMENTS
	Draft Registration	World War I Draft Registration Card for James Lee Strother, Culpeper County, VA, Sept. 12, 1918.
	Marriage Register	Marriage to Blanche Greene, Register of Marriages, Nov. 19, 1923, Alexandria, VA, Library of Virginia, Richmond.
	Death Certificate	Death certificate of James Strother, June 28, 1948, Baltimore City, MD, Maryland State Archives, Annapolis.

BLANCHE GREENE AND FAMILY

NAME	DOCUMENT TYPE	RELEVANT DOCUMENTS
Noah and Martha (Champ) Greene (grandparents)	US Census	**1870:** Locust Dale Township, Madison County, VA, p. 10. **1880:** Locust Dale Magisterial District, Madison County, VA, enumeration district 109, p. 27.
Robert and Lucy (Hawkins) Deane (grandparents)	US Census	**1850** (Lucy): Culpeper County, VA, p. 447. **1880:** Cedar Mountain Township, Culpeper County, VA, enumeration district 33, p. 23. **1900:** Cedar Mountain District—Eastern Div., Culpeper County, VA, enumeration district 7, sheet 8.
	Marriage Register	"Marriages (Colored) Under Act of Assembly of Virginia, February 27, 1866," Culpeper County, p. 5. Cohabitation Registers Digital Collection, Library of Virginia, Richmond.
Robert Lee and Alice (Deane) Greene (parents)	US Census	**1880** (Alice): Cedar Mountain Township, Culpeper County, VA, enumeration district 33, p. 23. **1880** (Robert L.): Locust Dale Magisterial District, Madison County, VA, enumeration district 109, p. 27. **1900:** Cedar Mountain District—Eastern Div., Culpeper County, VA, enumeration district 7, sheet 9. **1910:** Cedar Mountain District, Culpeper County, VA, enumeration district 18, sheet 9A. **1920:** Cedar Mountain Township, Culpeper County, VA, enumeration district 19, sheet 12A. **1940:** Cedar Mountain Magisterial District, Culpeper County, VA, enumeration district 24-3, sheet 3A.
	Marriage Certificate	Robert Lee Greene marriage to Alice Deane, March 6, 1890, Culpeper County, Culpeper County Courthouse, Culpeper, VA.
	Death Certificate	Robert L. Green, Cedar Mountain Magisterial District, Culpeper County, VA, June 5, 1946. Alice H. Green, Cedar Mountain Magisterial District, Culpeper County, VA, July 17, 1954.

BLANCHE GREENE AND FAMILY

NAME	DOCUMENT TYPE	RELEVANT DOCUMENTS
Blanche (Greene) Strother	US Census	**1910:** Cedar Mountain District, Culpeper County, VA, enumeration district 18, sheet 9A. **1920:** Cedar Mountain Township, Culpeper County, VA, enumeration district 19, sheet 12A. **1930:** Town of Culpeper, Culpeper County, VA, enumeration district 1, sheet 21B.
	Marriage Register	Marriage to James Strother, Register of Marriages, Nov. 19, 1923, Alexandria, VA. Library of Virginia, Richmond.
	Death Certificate	Blanche Strother, Albemarle County, VA, April 8, 1935.
Unnamed (son)	Death Certificate	Unnamed son, Catalpa District, Culpeper County, VA, Jan. 7, 1924.
James C. Greene (son)	US Census	**1920:** Cedar Mountain Township, Culpeper County, VA, enumeration district 19, sheet 12A.

ELIZABETH VIRGINIA "LIZZIE" GREEN AND FAMILY

NAME	DOCUMENT TYPE	RELEVANT DOCUMENTS
Thornton and Alsie Strother (grandparents)	US Census	**1870:** Cedar Mountain Township, Culpeper County, VA, p. 10. **1880:** Locust Dale Magisterial District, Madison County, VA, enumeration district 109, p. 29.
Lewis & Caroline (Strother) Green (parents and Strother's aunt)	US Census	**1880:** Cedar Mountain Township, Culpeper County, VA, enumeration district 33, p. 15. **1900:** Cedar Mountain District, Culpeper County, VA, enumeration district 6, sheet 15. **1910:** Cedar Mountain District, Culpeper County, VA, enumeration district 17, sheet 2B. **1920:** Cedar Mountain District "west of [Southern Railroad]," enumeration district 18, sheet 3A.
	Death Certificate	Caroline Green, Cedar Mountain Magisterial District, Culpeper County, VA, Nov. 18, 1924. Lewis Green, Cedar Mountain Magisterial District, Culpeper County, VA, Feb. 7, 1929.
Elizabeth Virginia "Lizzie" Green	US Census	**1910:** Cedar Mountain District, Culpeper County, VA, enumeration district 17, sheet 2B. **1920:** As Elizabeth Gaines, Cedar Mountain District "west of [Southern Railroad]," enumeration district 18, sheet 3A. **1940:** Salem District, Culpeper County, VA, enumeration district 24-7, sheet 5A.
	Marriage Certificate	Marriage to Charles P. Gaines, Sept. 14, 1912, Culpeper County, VA.

WILLIAM TAYLOR AND FAMILY

NAME	DOCUMENT TYPE	RELEVANT DOCUMENTS
William and Mary (Strother) Taylor (grandparents)	US Census	**1880:** Salem Township, Culpeper County, VA, enumeration district 36, p. 9. **1910:** Salem District, Culpeper County, VA, enumeration district 22, sheet 2A.
Andrew and Francis Jane (Johnson) Taylor (parents)	US Census	**1880** (Andrew): Salem Township, Culpeper County, VA, enumeration district 36, p. 9. **1900:** Precinct 2, District 2, Howard County, MD, enumeration district 81, sheet 8.
	Marriage Register	Andrew Taylor marriage to Frances J. Johnson, Feb. 15, 1894, Howard County Circuit Court, Volume 1886–1900, pp. 284–85, Maryland State Archives, Annapolis.
	Death Certificate	Frances Jane Taylor, April 10, 1908, Baltimore City, MD, certificate no. C11271, Maryland State Archives, Annapolis.
Charles W. and Susan (Toms) Taylor (aunt and uncle)	US Census	**1880** (Charles): Salem Township, Culpeper County, VA, enumeration district 36, p. 9. **1880** (Susan): Salem Township, Culpeper County, VA, enumeration district 36, p. 32. **1900:** Upper Providence Township—Lower District, Montgomery County, PA, enumeration district 266, sheet 9. **1910:** Salem District, Culpeper County, VA, enumeration district 22, sheet 2A. **1920:** Salem Township, Culpeper County, VA, enumeration district 23, sheet 2B. **1930:** Salem Magisterial District, Culpeper County, VA, enumeration district 24-7, sheet 9A. **1940** (Susan): Salem District, Culpeper County, VA, enumeration district 24–7, sheet 11B.
	Marriage Register	Charles W. Taylor marriage to Susan Toms, March 13, 1887, vol. 3, p. 52, Library of Virginia, Richmond.
	Death Certificate	Charles William Taylor, Salem District, Culpeper County, VA, April 30, 1936.
William and Sarah "Sadie" Taylor	US Census	**1910** (William): 12th Ward, Baltimore City, MD, enumeration district 188, sheet 13B. **1940:** 17th Ward, Baltimore City, MD, enumeration district 4–532, sheet 9B.
Johnson Family (in-laws)	US Census (Basil and Hannah)	**1870:** 3rd Election Dist., Howard County, MD, p. 19. **1880** (Basil, Hannah, and Sarah): 3rd Election Dist., Howard County, MD, enumeration district 103, p. 34. **1900** (Hannah and Gillis): Howard County, MD, enumeration district 83, sheet 5. **1910** (Hannah): 12th Ward, Baltimore City, MD, enumeration district 188, sheet 13B. **1920** (Hannah and Sarah Truman): Baltimore City, MD, enumeration district 192, sheet 12B. **1930** (Gillis): Baltimore City, MD, enumeration district 4–292, sheet 2A. **1880** (Basil, Hannah, and Sarah): 3rd Election Dist., Howard County, MD, enumeration district 103, p. 34.

WILLIAM TAYLOR AND FAMILY

NAME	DOCUMENT TYPE	RELEVANT DOCUMENTS
Sarah Truman and Family (aunt)	US Census	**1880:** 3rd Election Dist., Howard County, MD, enumeration district 103, p. 34. **1900** (James, Sarah, and Lillie): Howard County, MD, enumeration district 82, sheet 4. (Sarah and son Walter with Strothers) **1910:** 17th Ward, Baltimore City, MD, enumeration district 287, sheet 9B. **1920:** Baltimore City, MD, enumeration district 192, sheet 12B. **1930:** 11th Ward, Baltimore City, MD, enumeration district 4–157, sheet 11B. **1940** (Sarah with Taylors and Strother): 17th Ward, Baltimore City, MD, enumeration district 4–532, sheet 9B.

APPENDIX B

THE SONGS

All songs recorded at the Virginia State Prison Farm, Goochland County, by John A. Lomax and Harold Spivacke, June 14, 1936. Lyrics in italics indicate that I am unsure of the exact words.

The following is a list of compact disc reissues of the songs that are still in print as of this publication. Most songs are also available on various internet music sites.

Deep River of Song: Black Appalachia, String Bands, Songsters and Hoedowns. Rounder Records 1823, 1999. Includes "Thought I Heard My Banjo Say" and "Poontang Little, Poontang Small," Take 1.

Deep River of Song: Virginia and the Piedmont, Minstrelsy, Work Songs, and Blues. Rounder Records 11661-1827-2, 2000. Includes "Corn Shucking Time," "Jaybird," "I Used to Work on a 'Tractor," "We Are Almost Down to the Shore," "This Old Hammer," and "Going to Richmond."

Field Recordings, Vol. 1: Virginia 1936–1941. Document Records DOCD-5575, 1997. Includes all songs except "Poontang Little, Poontang Small" and "Going to Richmond."

A Treasury of Library of Congress Field Recordings. Edited by Stephen Wade. Rounder Records 1500, 1997. Includes "Blood-Stained Banders."

Virginia Traditions: Non-Blues Secular Black Music. Blue Ridge Institute, Ferrum, Virginia, BRI 00001, n.d. Includes "I Used to Work on a 'Tractor" and "Tennessee Dog."

"I Used to Work on a 'Tractor" (AFS 744 A1)

James Lee Strother, vocal and banjo

Used to work on a 'tractor,
Mike Hardy was his name;
Wanted me to make four loads a day,
Doggone mule was lame.

Went out early in the morning,
Got stalled and stayed all day.
When I returned in the evening,
These are the words he'd say.

"Where in the world is you been all day,
Here's your money, get away.
With that mule and that *boy's* bushel corn."

Old Mike Hardy, he was mad,
Give my money and he got bad.
With that mule and that *boy's* bushel corn.

Used to work [for a] contractor,
Mike Hardy was his name.
Wanted me to make four loads a day,
And doggone mule was lame.

Went out early in the morning,
Got stalled and stayed all day.
I returned in the evening,
These are the words he'd say.

"Where in the world have you been all day,
Here's your money, get away.
With that mule and that *boy's* bushel corn."

Worked for his brother,
He was same doggone way.

Went out early in the morning,
Got stalled and stayed all day.
I returned in the evening,
These are the words he'd say.

"Where in the world is you been all day,
Here's your money, get away.
With that mule and that *boy's* bushel corn."

"Tennessee Dog" (AFS 744 B2)

James Lee Strother, vocal and banjo

Anybody here want to buy a little dog?
Come right here I'll sell you.
Ain't no catfish, ain't no hog,
And I'm right here to tell you.

Chorus: That dog, that Tennessee dog,
Oh, his head is long, ears is flat,
He never stops eating 'til he balls that jack.
That dog, talkin' about that dog,
He's the meanest dog that come from Tennessee.

Now he can eat more meat than any butcher dog,
Eats steaks, pork chop, and liver.
He catch more rats than any other cat,
On this side the Mississippi River.

Chorus: That dog, that dog, that . . . talking about that dog.
[*Spoken:* "What about him?"]
Oh his head is long, ears is flat,
He never stops eating 'til he balls that jack.
That dog [*spoken:* "Lay down there, son"]. That mean little dog
[*Spoken:* "I said, lay down."]
He's the meanest dog that come from Tennessee.

Does anybody here want to buy a little dog?
I'm right here to sell you.
Ain't no catfish, ain't no hog,
And I'm right here to tell you.

Chorus: That dog, talking about that dog.
Oh his head is long, his ears is flat,
He never stops eatin' 'til he balls that jack.
That dog [*spoken:* "Lay down there, I tell you"], mean little dog,
He's the meanest dog that come from Tennessee.

I say come here to me Tabby
Balls right up and shivers,
He catch more rats than any other cat,
On this side the Mississippi River.

Chorus: That dog, that dog, that dog,
That mean little dog,
Oh yeah, his head is long, ears is flat,
He never stops eating 'til he balls that jack.
That dog, talking about that dog.
He's the meanest dog that comes from Tennessee,
I mean.

"This Old Hammer" (AFS 745 B1)

James Lee Strother, vocal and banjo

Ain't no hammer in this mountain
Ain't no hammer in this mountain;
Ain't no hammer in this mountain,
Ring like mine, ring like mine.

Take this hammer, carry it to the walker,
Tell him I'm gone, tell him I'm gone.

This old hammer git too heavy
This old hammer git too heavy;
This old hammer git too heavy,
Go lie down, go lie down.

This old hammer gets too heavy,
Go lie down, go lie down.

Rocks in the mountain shine like diamonds
Rocks in the mountain shine like diamonds;
Rocks in the mountain shine like diamonds,
I'm going home, I'm going home.

Everything that you see shining,
Ain't no gold, baby, ain't gold.

Everything that you see shining,
Everything that you see shining;
Everything that you see shining,
Ain't no gold, baby, ain't no gold.

Tell little Hattie she better be quilting,
Gonna be cold, gonna be cold,
Tell little Hattie she better be quilting
Gonna be cold, lovin' babe, gonna be cold.

Oh little Hattie keeps on writing
Oh little Hattie keeps on writing;
Oh little Hattie keeps on writing,
I'm going home, baby, I'm going home.

If I live to see December,
I'm going home, I'm going home.
If I live to see December,
I'm going home, I'm going home.

"Thought I Heard My Banjo Say" (AFS 744 A2)

James Lee Strother, vocal and banjo

Thought I heard my banjo sound,
Thought I heard my banjo sound,
Goin' to Cripple Creek, goin' to town,
Leave Cripple Creek, goin' to roam.
Leave Cripple Creek . . .
Going up Cripple Creek, shootin' off heads,
Don't eat nothin' but *piece of* bread.
Don't eat . . .

. . . banjo sound
Thought I heard my banjo . . .
Thought I heard my banjo sound,
Goin' to Cripple Creek, goin' to town,
Leave Cripple Creek, goin' to roam.

Goin' up Cripple Creek when I please,
Haul my britches up to my knees,
I'm goin' to Cripple Creek when I . . .

Thought I heard my banjo say
. . . my banjo say
Leave ol' Cripple Creek,
Hey man with the common sense,
Throw them *fosters* over the fence.

. . . my banjo say
. . . my banjo sound,
Thought I heard my banjo say
Leave ol' Cripple Creek,
Nickel worth of cabbage, dime worth of lard;
Gonna leave this town for times gettin' hard.

Thought I heard my banjo say . . .
Going up Cripple Creek, shootin' off heads,
Don't eat nothin' but fish and bread.

Thought I heard my banjo say
. . . my banjo sound
Goin' to Cripple Creek,
Leaving Cripple Creek.
Read and run, nigger, read and run.
Drinking whiskey, drinking beer,
Don't let sundown catch you here.

"Going to Richmond" (AFS 749 B)

James Lee Strother, vocal and guitar

Yes, I'm going to Richmond
Baby, I'm back from paradise,
Going to see that woman that sure gone and wrecked my life.

Yes, I'm going to Richmond
And I'm leaving for paradise,
Going to see that woman that sure done wrecked my life.

Yes, I'm leaving ol' *Perry*
And I'm headed for Tennessee,
Going to see that brownskin that sure made a fool of me.

Yes, I'm leaving the *Perry*
Babe, I'm headed for Tennessee,
Going to see that fair brown that sure made a fool of me.

Yes, that old false teachin'
And I believe my soul 'tis so [*spoken:* "poor boy"],
Son, don't you trust no young woman, no where on earth you go.

Yes, that old false teachin'
And I believe my soul 'tis so,
Son don't trust no young woman, no where on earth you go.

Yes, your fair brown will tell you
That she'll love you all her life [*spoken:* "poor boy"],
Meet another dude 'round the corner and retell that same lie twice.

Yes, your fair brown will tell you
That she'll love you all her life,
Meet another dude 'round the corner and retell that same lie twice.

Alexandria women,
I sure, God, do so despise,
Got a hand full of gimme and a mouthful of much obliged.

Alexandria women,
I sure, God, do this despise,
Got a hand full of gimme and a mouthful of much obliged.

I got one old bull dog,
And, baby, a long-leg hound,
I got one high yellow, and two, three browns.

I got one high yellow
Two, three browns,
I got one high yellow, really, and two, three browns.

Train come round the mountain
This morning in a solid moan,
If I live to see tomorrow, gonna roll in my fair brown arms.

Train come round the mountain
In a solid moan,
If I live to see tomorrow, gonna roll in my fair brown arms.

Hmmmm . . .
Got the blues and I can't be satisfied.

I've got the blues, babe,
And can't be satisfied,
Going down by the river and hang down my head and cry.

'Cause I've been mistreated,
And I can't be satisfied,
I've been mistreated and I can't be satisfied.

Yes, I'm going away to leave,
To get you off of my mind,
Babe, I'm going 'way to leave you, get you off my mind.

Yes, I'm going away to leave you,
Babe, to worry you off my mind,
And I won't be worried, honey, 'bout you all the time.

I done played this piece, babe,
'Til my fingers got sore,
Now if it ain't nothing doin',
I ain't gonna play no more.

"Blood-Stained Banders" (AFS 744 B1)

James Lee Strother, vocal and banjo

There are several variations of this title on recordings, manuscripts, and print, including "Blood-Strained Banders," "Blood-Stained Banders," and "Blood-Stained Bandits."

If you want to go to heaven, over on the other shore
Keep out the way of the blood-stained banders,
Lord, good shepherd, feed my sheep.

Chorus: Some for Paul, some for Silas
Some for to make a-my heart rejoice;
Don't you hear lambs a-cryin'
Lord, good shepherd, feed my sheep.

If you want to go to heaven just over on the other shore
Keep out the way of the gun-shot devils,
Lord, good shepherd, feed my sheep.

Chorus: Some for Paul, some for Silas
Some for to make a-my heart rejoice;
Don't you hear lambs a-cryin'
Lord, good shepherd, feed my sheep.

If you want to go to heaven just over on the other shore
Keep out the way of the long-tongued liars
Lord, good shepherd, feed my sheep.

Chorus: Some for Paul, some for Silas
Some for to make a-my heart rejoice;
Don't you hear lambs a-cryin'
Lord, good shepherd, feed my sheep.

"Run Down, Eli" (AFS 747 A1)

James Lee Strother, vocal and banjo

Run down, Eli,
Run down, send down the road,
Don't want to stay here no longer.

Chorus: Won't you run down, Eli,
Run down, send down the road,
Don't want to stay here no longer.

If religion was the one thing money could buy,
The rich would live and the poor would die,
Don't want to stay here no longer.

Why, I so thank God it is not so,
All got right to the Heaven's door.
Don't want to stay here no longer.

Chorus: Won't you run down, Eli,
Run down, send down the road,
Don't want to stay here no longer.

Look way in the East, way in the West
My Lord burned out the wilderness,
Don't want to stay here no longer.

Chorus: Won't you run down, Eli,
Run down, send down the road,
Don't want to stay here no longer.

Lord, I'm sometimes up, sometimes down,
Sometimes level with the ground,
Don't want to stay here no longer.

Chorus: Won't you run down, Eli,
Run down, send down the road,
Don't want to stay here no longer.

This is the way my mother have gone,
Left me here to follow on,
Don't want to stay here no longer.

Chorus: Won't you run down, now, Eli,
Run down, send down the road,
Don't want to stay here no longer.

"We Are Almost Down to the Shore" (AFS 744 A2)

James Lee Strother, vocal and banjo

Chorus: Fight on, fight on
Children and don't turn back,
We are almost down to the shore. [*2x at beginning*]

Fishing, Peter on the sea
Drop your nets and follow me,
We are almost down to the shore.

Chorus: Fight on, fight on
Children and don't turn back,
We are almost down to the shore.

Moses died in the days of old
Where he was buried never been told,
We are almost down to the shore.

Chorus: Fight on, fight on
Children and don't turn back,
We are almost down to the shore.

God called Moses on the mountain top
Placed his laws in Moses's heart,
We are almost down to the shore.

His commandments in Moses's mind,
Said "Moses, don't leave my children behind,"
We are almost down to the shore.

Chorus: Fight on, fight on
Children and don't turn back,
We are almost down to the shore.

"Daddy, Where You Been So Long" (AFS 747 B4)

James Lee Strother, vocal and banjo

She calls me honey when I comes in town,
Big black nigger when I'm gone,
But as soon as I return with a ten-dollar bill,
It's Daddy, where you been so long?

Chorus: Oh, it's Daddy, where you been,
Daddy where you been,
Daddy where you been so long?

Oh, a train ran north and killed a man,
A mile and a half from town,
Yes, his head was found in a driving wheel,
And his body's never been found.

Train ran north one rainy day,
Mile and a half from town,
Killed a man, an innocent man,
Lived so far from home.

"Corn Shucking Time" (AFS 747 B3)

James Lee Strother, vocal and banjo

[*Spoken:* "Go, man"]

Corn shuckin' time, that corn shuckin' time
Ain't gonna bake that possum,
Tell you, friends of mine;
'Til that corn shuckin' time
Won't be having fun,
Ain't gonna bake that possum 'til that corn, corn shuckin' time.

Oh, Annie wanna go to heaven
But she says she is not gwine,
She says she is not going, 'til that corn shuckin' time;
For she knows she's gonna bake that possum,
And then get tipsy on wine,
She says she's ready to go to heaven after that corn, corn shuckin' time.

That corn shuckin' time, corn shuckin' time
Ain't gonna bake that possum,
'Til corn shuckin' time;
Corn shuckin' time, my brother
And we'll all be having fun,
Ain't gonna bake that possum 'til that corn, corn shuckin' time.

"Jaybird," Take 1 (AFS 747 B1)

James Lee Strother, vocal and banjo

[*Spoken:* "Go ahead, Jim. Sing."]

White folks in a parlor,
Drink up all that dram,
Darkies in the barnyard,
Eaten up the white folks' ham.

Jaybird trying to scratch back
Sparrow trying to crow,
Young girls hop in the summertime,
Blind man trying to sew.

Jaybird died with the whooping cough,
Sparrow died with the colic,
I met a bullfrog with a banjo on his back,
Said he's going on down to the frolic.

Squirrel on the fence,
Yelling at a log,
Bullfrogs in the pond,
They are barking like a dog.

Nigger on the woodpile
Can't count to seven,
Put him in a feather bed,
He thinks he's gone to heaven.

"Jaybird," Take 2 (AFS 747 B2)

James Lee Strother, vocal and banjo

White folks in a parlor,
Drink up all that dram,
Darkies in the barnyard
Is eaten up the white folks' ham.

Jaybird trying to scratch back
Sparrow trying to crow,
Young girls hop in the summertime,
Blind man trying to sew.

Jaybird died with the whooping cough,
Sparrow died with the colic,
I met a bullfrog with a banjo on his back,
Said he's going on down to the frolic.

Squirrel on the fence,
He's yelling at a log,
Bullfrogs in a pond,
They are barking like a dog.

Nigger on the woodpile
Can't count seven,
You put him in a feather bed,
He thinking going to heaven.

"Poontang Little, Poontang Small," Take 1 (AFS 749 A1)

James Lee Strother, vocal and guitar

As noted above, some transcribers render the phrase "somebody sold this thing" as "took my salty thing."

Poontang a-little and poontang small
Poontang stretches like a rubber ball
Oh my babe, *somebody sold this thing.*

Well, I hung my poontang from the wire
Rush come down just as hot as fire
Oh my babe, somebody sold this thing

Gonna hang my poontang upon the fence
So the man come and get it ain't got no sense,
Oh my babe, somebody sold this thing.

Boys, done it once, I'm gonna do my best,
I'm gonna tell a little something, 'bout the women out west.
Oh my babe, somebody sold this thing.

Got a humpback livers and kidney feet
—*his shackles* on a streetcar seat,
Oh my babe, somebody sold this thing.

Oh, I b'lieve to my soul she had a lucky hand
'Cause she said to give her *thanks* to the streetcar man,
Oh my babe, somebody sold this thing.

Poontang a-little and-a poontang small
Poontang stretches like a rubber ball,
Oh my babe, somebody sold this thing.

Oh wire, brier, limber, lock
How many geese is in our flock?
Oh, my baby, somebody sold this thing.

Oh, one flew east and a-one flew west
One flew over in the cuckoo's nest,
Oh my babe, somebody sold this thing.

Hung my poontang from a wire
Come down, to the hottest fire
Oh my baby, somebody sold this thing.

My dress up 'bove my knees,
I'm gonna give my poontang, who I please,
It's oh my babe, somebody sold this thing.

Oh, poon I want, tang I crave
Tang's gonna carry me to my lovin' grave,
Oh my baby, somebody sold this thing.

My man has gone, couldn't do me once,
I'm gonna *dup* my husband 'til my man comes,
Oh my babe, somebody sold this thing.

"Poontang Little, Poontang Small," Take 2 (AFS 750 B)

James Lee Strother, vocal and guitar

Poontang little, poontang small
Poontang stretches like a rubber ball,
Oh my babe, *somebody sold this thing.*

Like my poontang against the fence
Man don't like it ain't got no sense,
Oh my babe, somebody sold this thing.

I hung my poontang from the wire
Went and got it down to the hottest fire,
Oh my babe, somebody sold this thing.

Gonna pull my dress up to my thighs
I'm gonna give my poontang exercise,
Oh my babe, somebody sold this thing

Gentlemen, I'm gonna do my best,
I'm gonna tell you little somethin' 'bout the women out west,
Oh my babe, somebody sold this thing.

Had a humpback livers and kidney feet
Then the little poontang on the streetcar seat,
Oh my babe, somebody sold this thing.

And I believe to my soul she had a lucky hand,
Said she'd give her tang to the streetcar man,
Oh my babe, somebody sold this thing.

[*Spoken:* "Rock steady, children"]

Gentlemen, I'm gonna do my best
I'm gonna tell you little somethin' 'bout the women out west,
Oh my babe, somebody sold this thing.

Humpback livers and kidney feet,
Pay no attention to who they beat,
Oh my babe, somebody sold this thing.

Gonna back my poontang against the fence,
You don't come and get it, ain't got no sense,
Oh my babe, somebody sold this thing.

Oh poontang a-little and poontang small
Poontang stretches like a rubber ball,
Oh my babe, somebody sold this thing.

Going out west, going all day,
Ain't comin' back 'til Christmas day,
Oh my babe, somebody sold this thing.

Poontang little, poontang small
Poontang stretches like a rubber ball,
Oh my babe, somebody sold this thing.

Gonna back my poontang against the fence,
Don't come and get it, ain't got no sense,
Oh my babe, somebody sold this thing.

Gonna pull my dress up 'bove my knees
Gonna give my poontang, who I please,
Oh my baby, somebody sold this thing.

Gonna pull my dress up to my thighs
I'm gonna give my poontang exercise,
Oh my babe, somebody sold this thing.

Oh poontang little, poontang small
Poontang stretches like a rubber ball,
Oh my baby, somebody sold this thing.

I hung my poontang from the wire
Went on down through the hottest fire,
Oh my babe, somebody sold this thing.

I hung my poontang upon the fence,
Ain't seen nothing of poontang since,
Oh my babe, somebody sold this thing.

Oh gentlemen, I'm gonna do my best
Tell you little somethin' 'bout the women out west,
Oh my babe, somebody sold this thing.

Gotta humpback livers and kidney feet,
Poontang is on the streetcar seat,
Oh my babe, somebody sold this thing.

[Spoken: "Rock steady, children"]

I believe my soul she had lucky hand,
But the jacket for the streetcar man,
Oh my babe, somebody sold this thing.

My man is gone, Virginia bound,
I'm gone lay on back 'til my man comes,
Oh my babe, somebody sold this thing.

"Do Lord, Remember Me" (AFS 746 B2)

James Lee Strother, vocal and guitar; Joe Lynn Lee, vocal and beating straws

Do Lord, do Lord, Lord, remember me
Do lord, do Lord, oh, Lord, remember me (Hallelujah!)
Do Lord, do Lord, Lord, remember me;
Oh, do Lord, remember me.

Oh, when I'm in trouble, down on my knees
When I was in trouble, Lord, remember me
Oh, when I was in trouble, Lord, remember me
Oh, do Lord, remember me.

Do Lord, do Lord, Lord, remember me.
Do Lord, do Lord, Lord, remember me,
Hallelujah, do Lord, do Lord, do remember me
Oh, do Lord, remember me.

Oh, when I am tired, Lord, remember me
Oh, when I am tired, Lord, remember me
Oh, when I am tired, Lord, remember me
Oh, do Lord, remember me.

I am going to take a little journey, Lord, remember me;
I am going to take a little journey, Lord, remember me;
I am going to take a little journey, Lord, remember me.
Oh, do Lord, remember me.

Oh, do Lord, do Lord, Lord, remember me (Hallelujah!)
Do Lord, do Lord, Lord, remember me (Hallelujah!),
Do Lord, do Lord, Lord, remember me
Oh, do Lord, remember me.

NOTES

Frequently referenced census and vital statics documents for Strother and his extended family can be found in Appendix A. Citations for Strother's songs and reissues of his recordings are compiled in Appendix B, along with lyrics.

The Library of Virginia, Richmond, is abbreviated LVA below. James Lee Strother's pardon file is held in RG 13, Secretary of the Commonwealth, Executive Papers, 1939 Sept. 12–20, accession 24938, box 1113, Library of Virginia, Richmond. It is abbreviated below as "Strother pardon file."

Introduction

1. The exhibition was held at the Valentine Museum in Richmond, Virginia, and included a catalog and essay: Marie Tyler-McGraw and Gregg D. Kimball, *In Bondage and Freedom: Antebellum Black Life in Richmond, Virginia* (Chapel Hill: University of North Carolina Press for the Valentine Museum, 1988).

2. Kip Lornell, liner notes to *Virginia Traditions: Non-Blues Black Secular Music*, Blue Ridge Institute BRI 001, n.d., compact disc. Adam Gussow reviews the works, filling in the early history of the blues in "W. C. Handy and the 'Birth' of the Blues," *Southern Cultures* 24, no. 4 (2018): 42–68. Important recent works documenting the late nineteenth-century evolution of Black music include Sandra Jean Graham, *Spirituals and the Birth of a Black Entertainment Industry* (Urbana: University of Illinois Press, 2018); Lynn Abbott and Doug Seroff, *The Original Blues: The Emergence of the Blues in African American Vaudeville* (Jackson: University Press of Mississippi, 2017); and Peter C. Muir, *Long Lost Blues: Popular Blues in America, 1850–1920* (Urbana: University of Illinois Press, 2010). Paul Oliver charts the transition from the broad songster repertoire to the rise of the country bluesmen and -women. He notes the varied repertoires of those of Strother's generation. See Oliver, *Songsters and Saints: Vocal Traditions on Race Records* (Cambridge: Cambridge University Press, 1984), 259–60. For "string music," see James Strother #33927, State Farm, Virginia, to Governor James H. Price, Richmond, June 12, 1939, RG 13, Secretary of the

Commonwealth, Executive Papers, 1939, Sept. 12–20, accession 24938, box 1113, LVA.

3. Paul A. Cimbala, "Black Musicians from Slavery to Freedom: An Exploration of an African-American Folk Elite and Cultural Continuity in the Nineteenth-Century Rural South," *Journal of Negro History* 80, no. 1 (1995): 15–29.

4. Howard W. Odum, "Folk-Song and Folk-Poetry as Found in the Secular Songs of the Southern Negroes," *Journal of American Folk-Lore* 24, no. 93 (1911): 258–59. For further discussion of the terms, see Oliver, *Songsters and Saints*, 20–22. For "songster," see, for example, "A Colored Songster, with a Happy Face, Used to Sing, 'I've Got a White Man Working for Me,'" *Washington Times*, June 27, 1919; "Henry Payne, the Local Well Known Negro Songster, Led the Quartet," *Wheeling Intelligencer*, Dec. 30, 1915. Richard Carlin and Ken Bloom, *Eubie Blake: Rags, Rhythm, and Race* (New York: Oxford University Press, 2020), 11. Sidney Bechet, *Treat It Gentle* (New York: Hill and Wang, 1960), 202. The word retained currency among rural Southern whites as well. Ralph Stanley recalled that A. P. Carter, the patriarch of the legendary Carter family, used the term to describe himself. Dr. Ralph Stanley with Eddie Dean, *Man of Constant Sorrow: My Life and Times* (New York: Gotham Books, 2009), 124–25. Despite some debate in the nineteenth century, it seems clear that the term originated in the British Isles. "Americanisms," *Atlantic Monthly*, Nov. 1878, 624. Philotheos Physiologus [Thomas Tryon], *The Way to Health, Long Life, and Happiness, or, a Discourse of Temperance* (London: Andrew Sowle, 1683), 13.

5. Elijah Wald explores the Johnson myth, race records, and blues as commercial music in *Escaping the Delta: Robert Johnson and the Invention of the Blues* (New York: HarperCollins, 2004). Interview with Dom Flemons, May 12, 2021, video recording in the author's possession.

6. I endorse the notion that African American song is a form of collective oral history. For the application of this concept to the blues, see Robert Springer, ed., *Nobody Knows Where the Blues Come From: Lyrics and History* (Jackson: University Press of Mississippi, 2007).

7. Robert R. Moton, "Note to New Edition," in Hampton Normal and Agricultural Institute, *Religious Folk Songs of the Negro as Sung on the Plantations* (Hampton, VA: The Institute Press, 1909), vi. James H. Cone, *The Spirituals and the Blues: An Interpretation* (New York: Seabury Press, 1972), 32, 111.

8. Charley Patton, "I'm Going to Move to Alabama," Paramount 13014, recorded in Grafton, WI, 1930, 78-rpm record. Bessie Smith, "Gulf Coast Blues," Columbia A3844, recorded in New York City, 1923, 78-rpm record.

1. Family

1. This stanza from Strother's "Daddy, Where You Been So Long" is echoed in other folk songs, most notably the song alternately titled "Black Gal" or "In the Pines."

2. Kellee Blake, "'First in the Path of the Firemen': The Fate of the 1890 Population Census," *Prologue Magazine* 28, no. 1 (1996): 64–81.
3. I refer to Blanche as James Strother's second wife because the Baltimore census lists Mary Strother as his wife in 1910, and William Stone's open letter in the *Baltimore Sun* does the same. I have not found an official marriage document for James and Mary. The 1930 census states that this is both Blanche's and James's first marriage. James City is documented on the Virginia Department of Historic Resources website here: https://www.dhr.virginia.gov/VLR_to _transfer/PDFNoms/056-5011_James_City_Historic_District_2001_Final _Nomination.pdf. Also see Army Corps of Topographical Engineers, "Map of Culpeper County with Parts of Madison, Rappahannock, and Fauquier Counties, Virginia, United States" (Washington, DC [?]: US Bureau of Topographical Engineers, 1863 [?]), Library of Congress, Washington DC, https://lccn.loc .gov/99439135.
4. Strother's place of birth is given as James City on the Alexandria City marriage register for his marriage to his second wife, Blanche, and on a prisoner register from the Virginia State Penitentiary records. While James City is just across the line in Madison County, there are several records placing his birth in Culpeper County, including his birth record and the death certificate for his and Blanche's unnamed child, who was born prematurely and died on Jan. 7, 1924. See Prisoner Registers–Rough Drafts, vol. 75, 24 November 1934 to 30 June 1936 (Inmates #33031 to 35993), Series II.A.II.5, Virginia State Penitentiary Records, LVA.
5. Caroline Strother is listed in the 1870 census with parents Thornton and Allison (later called Alsie or Elsie). Her death certificate lists the same parents. "Relatives Who Will Take Care of Him," Aug. 9, 1939, Strother pardon file. Teacher Registers, 1928–1932, Culpeper County, VA, private collection, copies in the possession of the author. On The Forest, see Eugene M. Scheel, *Culpeper: A Virginia County's History Through 1920* (Culpeper, VA: Culpeper Historical Society, 1982), 219, 300. T. O. Madden Jr. with Ann L. Miller, *We Were Always Free: The Maddens of Culpeper County, Virginia, a 200-Year Family History* (Charlottesville: University of Virginia Press, 2005), 148. The Crooked Run Baptist Church mentioned here is the Black church built in 1908 on route 657 now used by Abundant Life Baptist Church.

2. String Music

1. Kip Lornell, "Old-Time Country Music in North Carolina and Virginia: The 1970s and 1980s," in *Hidden in the Mix: The African American Presence in Country Music,* ed. Diane Pecknold (Durham, NC: Duke University Press, 2013), 183.
2. James Strother #33927, State Farm, Virginia, to Governor James H. Price, Richmond, June 12, 1939, RG 13, Secretary of the Commonwealth, Executive Papers, 1939 Sept. 12–20, accession 24938, box 1113, LVA. For the history of

the banjo preceding Strother's time and in a pan-Atlantic context, see Kristina R. Gaddy, *Well of Souls: Uncovering the Banjo's Hidden History* (New York: W. W. Norton, 2022).

3. Liner notes for *Deep River of Song: Black Appalachia, String Bands, Songsters and Hoedowns,* Rounder Records 1823, 1999, compact disc.

4. Chris Goertzen, *George P. Knauff's Virginia Reels and the History of American Fiddling* (Jackson: University Press of Mississippi, 2017). "Zip Coon, a Favorite Comic Song" (New York: J. L. Hewitt, ca. 1834). Robert B. Winans, "Black Instrumental Music Traditions in the Ex-Slave Narratives," *Black Music Research Journal* 10, no. 1 (1990): 43–53.

5. Interview with Uncle John Haney, Charles Perdue Duplication Project, 1969–1971 (AFC 1970/046), Archive of Folk Culture, American Folklife Center, Library of Congress, Washington, DC. John Haney in the 1900 US census, Hawthorne Township, Rappahannock County, VA, population schedule, enumeration district 50, sheet 6.

6. Lewis Grigsby and family in the 1880 US census, Locust Dale Magisterial District, Madison County, VA, population schedule, enumeration district 109, p. 41. Obituary of Elicia Grigsby, *Virginia Star* (Culpeper), June 16, 1921.

7. "Mr. Stone Flays Charity Methods," *Baltimore American,* Jan. 27, 1915, 14.

8. Robert B. Winans, "Black Musicians in Eighteenth-Century America: Evidence from Runaway Slave Advertisements," in *Banjo Roots and Branches,* ed. Robert B. Winans, Music in American Life (Urbana: University of Illinois Press, 2018), 194–213. Robert B. Winans, "Black Instrumental Music Traditions in the Ex-Slave Narratives," *Black Music Research Journal* 10, no. 1 (1990): 43–53. Jacqueline Cogdell Djedje, "The (Mis)Representation of African American Music: The Role of the Fiddle," *Journal of the Society for American Music* 10, no. 1 (2016): 1–32, https://doi.org/10.1017/S1752196315000528.

9. Singer-songwriter Steve Goodman celebrated Martin in his song "You Better Get It While You Can (the Ballad of Carl Martin)." Kip Lornell, liner notes to *Virginia Traditions: Tidewater Blues,* BRI Records (Blue Ridge Institute, Ferrum, VA), BRI 006, 1982, LP, p. 9. Interview with Carl Martin, *Cadence—The American Review of Jazz & Blues* 3, no. 1/2 (1977): 17–20. Karl Hagstrom Miller, *Segregating Sound: Inventing Folk and Pop Music in the Age of Jim Crow* (Durham, NC: Duke University Press, 2010).

10. Stephen Wade erroneously attributes the guitar backup on Doc Robert's "Cripple Creek" to Jim Booker rather than his brother John. Doc Roberts, "Cripple Creek," Gennett 6336, recorded in Richmond, IN, Aug. 26, 1927. Booker Orchestra, "Camp Nelson Blues," Gennett 6375, recorded in Richmond, IN, Sept. 7, 1927. For Jim and John Booker's further recordings, see Tony Russell, *Country Music Records: A Discography, 1921–1942* (Oxford: Oxford University Press, 2004), 894–95. On the Booker Orchestra, see Nathan Salzburg's liner notes to "Camp Nelson Blues" in "The Music of Kentucky," annual music issue, *Oxford American* 99 (Winter 2017).

11. "Daddy Stovepipe No. 1" chapter in Steven C. Tracy, *Going to Cincinnati: A His-*

tory of Blues in the Queen City (Urbana: University of Illinois Press, 1993), 8–33. Paul Oliver, *Songsters and Saints: Vocal Traditions on Race Records* (Cambridge: Cambridge University Press, 1984), 26–28. Stove Pipe No. 1 [Sam Jones], "Cripple Creek" and "Sourwood Mountain" / "Turkey in the Straw," Columbia 201-D, recorded in New York City, Aug. 20, 1924. Sam Jones is listed in the 1940 census in Cincinnati as being born around 1890 in Kentucky.

12. Robert B. Winans, "Black Banjo Tradition in Virginia and West Virginia," *Folklore and Folklife in Virginia: Journal of the Virginia Folklore Society* 1 (1979): 7–30.

13. Brownie McGhee and Happy Traum, *Guitar Styles of Brownie McGhee* (London: Oak Publications, 1971), 8.

14. Interview with Edsel Moore, William Moore's son, Camden, NJ, in the writer's possession. Also see Gregg Kimball, entry for William "Bill" Moore, in *Encyclopedia of the Blues*, vol. 2, *K–Z*, ed. Ed Komara (New York: Routledge, 2005), 706–7.

3. Spiritual Songs

1. As Jocelyn Neal has shown, the introduction of instrumentation based on relatively simple chordal structures and rhythmic pulses can significantly change a tune from its a cappella form. Jocelyn Neal, "Ernest Stoneman's 1927 Session: Hillbilly Recordings of Gospel Hymns," in *The Bristol Sessions: Writings about the Big Bang of Country Music*, ed. Charles K. Wolfe and Ted Olson (Jefferson, NC: McFarland, 2005), 187–213.

2. "Fighting On" appears in the 1891 expanded version of Thomas P. Fenner, *Cabin and Plantation Songs as Sung by the Hampton Students* (New York: G. P. Putnam's Sons, 1891), 93, and as "Fighting On! Hallelujah!" in *Jubilee and Plantation Songs: As Sung by the Hampton Students, Jubilee Singers, Fisk Students, and Other Concert Companies* (Boston: Oliver Ditson, 1887), 53.

3. Sandra Jean Graham, *Spirituals and the Birth of a Black Entertainment Industry* (Urbana: University of Illinois Press, 2018).

4. Interview with Nancy Williams in *Weevils in the Wheat: Interviews with Virginia Ex-Slaves*, ed. Charles L. Perdue, Thomas E. Barden, and Robert K. Phillips (Charlottesville: University of Virginia Press, 1976), 322.

5. Interviews with Charles Grandy and Arthur Greene in Perdue, Barden, and Phillips, *Weevils in the Wheat*, 119, 124–25.

6. For examples of the song "Run, Nigger, Run" as used in slave culture in Virginia, see interviews with Robert Williams, May 8, 1937, and George White, April 20, 1937, transcribed in Perdue, Barden, and Phillips, *Weevils in the Wheat*, 309–10, 323–26.

7. See Marie Tyler McGraw, *An African Republic: Black and White Virginians in the Making of Liberia* (Chapel Hill: University of North Carolina Press, 2014). Eugene M. Scheel, *Culpeper: A Virginia County's History Through 1920* (Culpeper, VA: Culpeper Historical Society, 1982), 161–63.

8. Scheel, *Culpeper,* 253–57. There is no grave marker for Blanche Green at Free Union, but her mother and several sisters were buried there.

9. Scheel, *Culpeper,* 253–57. "Relatives Who Will Take Care of Him," Aug. 9, 1939, James Lee Strother pardon file.

10. Scheel, *Culpeper,* 255. I have standardized the spelling of Blanche's surname as "Greene" when discussing her family. This is the spelling used by her son and daughter as well as her grandson. "Green" is the usual spelling in historical documents, but "Greene" appears as well. Other Green families discussed in the book use the standard spelling.

11. *Culpeper Exponent,* March 17, 1882. William Yager Life History, ca. 1940, interview by Margaret Jeffries, Culpeper, VA, Life Histories Digital Collection, LVA.

12. *Culpeper Exponent,* Oct. 8, 1897; July 22, 1898.

13. See news on Holiness meetings and congregations in the *Culpeper Exponent,* June 30, 1899; July 27, 1900; March 25, 1910; July 21, 1911.

14. Howard W. Odum, *Religious Folk-Songs of the Southern Negroes,* reprinted from *American Journal of Religious Psychology and Education* 2 (July 1909): 265–365.

15. Jane Boswell Moore, "Scenes and Songs in the 'House of Bondage,'" *Advocate and Family Guardian* 31 (1865): 87–89. The *Advocate and Family Guardian* was published in New York by the American Female Guardian Society.

16. Edward King, *The Southern States of North America* (London: Blackie and Son, 1875), 615; see also *Hampton and Its Students by Two of Its Teachers, Mrs. M. F. Armstrong and Helen W. Ludlow, with Fifty Cabin and Plantation Songs, Arranged by Thomas P. Fenner* (New York: G. P. Putnam, 1874), 183.

17. R. Nathaniel Dett, ed., *Religious Folk-Songs of the Negro: As Sung at Hampton Institute* (Hampton, VA: Hampton Institute Press, 1927).

18. Robert R. Moton, "Note to New Edition," Hampton Normal and Agricultural Institute, *Religious Folk Songs of the Negro as Sung on the Plantations* (Hampton, VA: The Institute Press, 1909), vi. Jocelyn Neal noted the differences in songs commercially recorded by Appalachia's Stoneman family in the 1920s when compared to the written notation of their shape-note songbooks. See Neal, "Ernest Stoneman's 1927 Session."

19. Eileen Southern, "Hymnals of the Black Church," *Black Perspective in Music* 17, no. 1/2 (1989): 58; see 63 for the quotation from the "white church father."

20. For example, see E. K. Love, *History of the First African Baptist Church* (Savannah: Morning News Print, 1888), 152; John R. Clements, "The Blood-Stained Banner," in *Heart Songs: For Sunday Schools,* comp. Fred A. Fillmore (Cincinnati: Fillmore Bros., 1893), 142–43. Susan Jonusas, *Hell's Half-Acre: The Untold Story of the Benders, a Serial Killer Family on the American Frontier* (New York: Viking, 2022).

21. John and Alan Lomax, *Our Singing Country: A Second Volume of American Ballads and Folk Songs,* ed. Ruth Crawford Seeger (New York: Macmillan, 1941).

22. Richard Hylan, "John Adam Granade: The 'Wild Man' of Goose Creek," *Western Folklore* 33, no. 1 (1974): 77–87. It was only with the rise of the modern

West that "music" became defined by formal compositions meant to be written and read. As musicologist Anne Dhu McLucas asserts, much of the world's music-making is still rooted in various forms of face-to-face transmission. See McLucas, *The Musical Ear: Oral Tradition in the USA* (Burlington, VT: Ashgate, 2010), 1–2.

23. Acts 16:16–40.

24. William Francis Allen, Charles Pickard Ware, and Lucy McKim Garrison, eds., *Slave Songs of the United States* (New York: A. Simpson, 1867) xi, 3.

25. Strother's song is sometimes confused with (or seen as a version of) another old spiritual: "Hear de Lambs A-Cryin." First published in the earliest compilation of spirituals (1874) sung by Hampton Institute students, it is clearly a very different composition, both lyrically and musically. The only apparent connection to "Blood-Stained Banders" is the refrain "Hear the lambs a-cryin' / Oh, Good Shepherd, feed my sheep." This spiritual became a staple of the many university-sponsored singing groups that sprang up after the Civil War. The most celebrated of the university groups, the Fisk University Jubilee Singers, graced the Columbia recording studios in 1920 to wax a version of the song; Fisk University Jubilee Singers, "You Hear the Lambs A-Cryin," Columbia A3596, recorded in New York City, Dec. 28, 1920, 78-rpm record. The spiritual became a favorite of composers and singers in the era of spirituals as art song. Paul Robeson and Lawrence Brown performed a stately version in concert and for the Victor record label in 1927: Paul Robeson and Lawrence Brown, "Hear, de Lam's A-Cryin," Victor 20604, recorded in New York City, March 30, 1927, 78-rpm record.

4. Land and Labor

1. E. Hergesheimer, mapmaker, and C. B. Graham, lithographer, "Map of Virginia Showing the Distribution of Its Slave Population from the Census of 1860" (Washington, DC: United States Coast Survey, 1861), LVA. Eugene M. Scheel, *Culpeper: A Virginia County's History Through 1920* (Culpeper, VA: Culpeper Historical Society, 1982), 163. On the dominance of grain and diversified agriculture in Culpeper, see US Department of the Interior, Census Office, *Report of the Statistics of Agriculture of the United States at the Eleventh Census, 1890* (Washington, DC: Government Printing Office, 1895), 388, table 14, and 455, table 20. On Saunders, see Joshua D. Rothman, *The Ledger and the Chain: How Domestic Slave Traders Shaped America* (New York: Basic Books, 2021), 142–47.

2. Scheel, *Culpeper,* 215–26. *Consolidated List of Persons Registered as Voters in the State of Virginia,* Dec. 12, 1867, printed as doc. 5 in *Documents of the Constitutional Convention of the State of Virginia* (1867), 51–52.

3. The list of the twenty-one farmers with more than one thousand acres is from Scheel, *Culpeper,* 246. I compared this list with the 1860 census slave schedules.

4. Labor contract between Harriet Strother and Charles L. Graves, Dec. 29, 1865,

Records of the Freedmen's Bureau, Gordonsville District, VA, National Archives and Records Administration.

5. Harriet Strother and family, 1870 US census, Ruckersville District, Greene County, VA, population schedule, p. 82. The oldest child, Catherine, is listed as fifteen years old and "without occupation," and most of the other children were "at home." Harriet's son Addison, only ten, helped support them as a hired farm laborer for a white family elsewhere in the county. Addison Strother, listed as a "farm laborer" in the 1870 US census, Stanardsville, Greene County, VA, population schedule, p. 77.

6. On Sweeney, see Bob Carlin, *The Birth of the Banjo: Joel Walker Sweeney and Early Minstrelsy* (Jefferson, NC: McFarland, 2007). The literature on minstrelsy is voluminous. Here are a few basic books: Robert C. Toll, *Blacking Up: The Minstrel Show in Nineteenth-Century America* (Oxford: Oxford University Press, 1974); Eric Lott, *Love and Theft: Blackface Minstrelsy and the American Working Class* (Oxford: Oxford University Press, 1993); William J. Mahar, *Behind the Burnt Cork Mask: Early Blackface Minstrelsy and Antebellum American Popular Culture* (Urbana: University of Illinois Press, 1999); and W. T. Lhamon, *Raising Cain: Blackface Performance from Jim Crow to Hip Hop* (Cambridge, MA: Harvard University Press, 1998).

7. Sandra Jean Graham, "Composing in Black and White: Code-Switching in the Songs of Sam Lucas," in *The Oxford Handbook of Music Censorship,* ed. Patricia Hall (Oxford: Oxford University Press, 2017), 559–92. Also see "Don't You Hear the Baby Crying" on the Songs of Sam Lucas website, https://popmusic .mtsu.edu/lucas/lucassongs.html#baby. Macon's corpus of songs closely mirrored that of Strother's, including folk material, songs from the medicine-show stage, and adaptations of gospel material. While Macon was a white Tennessean, the comparison is apt. Born in 1870, he delivered furniture across central Tennessee and absorbed a great trove of native material from both Blacks and whites. By the time he became one of the most celebrated members of the Grand Ole Opry radio broadcast on WSL in Nashville, he was already fifty-seven years old. Strother and Macon both developed their repertoires in a rich but sometimes confusing musical world. See Michael D. Doubler, *Dixie Dewdrop: The Uncle Dave Macon Story,* Music in American Life (Urbana: University of Illinois Press, 2018).

8. For a comprehensive account of the corn-shucking festival, see Roger D. Abrahams, *Singing the Master: The Emergence of African American Culture in the Plantation South* (New York: Pantheon Books, 1992). Abrahams also includes transcriptions of period accounts.

9. One of the best descriptions of a corn shucking in Virginia is recounted by Booker T. Washington, a native of Franklin County, in "Christmas Days in Old Virginia," *Tuskegee Student* 19 (Dec. 21, 1907): 1. John Spencer, who had been enslaved in King George County, Virginia, recalled the chant of the corn-song leader in *Weevils in the Wheat: Interviews with Virginia Ex-Slaves,* ed. Charles L.

Perdue, Thomas E. Barden, and Robert K. Phillips (Charlottesville: University of Virginia Press, 1976), 219.

10. Shane White and Graham White, *The Sounds of Slavery: Discovering African American History Through Songs, Sermons, and Speech* (Boston: Beacon Press, 1995), 49.

11. William Wells Brown, *My Southern Home; or the South and Its People* (Boston: A. G. Brown, 1880), 91–95.

12. Abrahams, *Singing the Master,* 107–30.

13. Jane Dailey, *Before Jim Crow: The Politics of Race in Postemancipation Virginia* (Chapel Hill: University of North Carolina Press, 2000).

14. Edward R. Ayers, *The Promise of the New South: Life After Reconstruction* (Oxford: Oxford University Press, 1992), for statistics on black land ownership, 208–10 and chart on 514; Crandall A. Shifflet, *Patronage and Poverty in the Tobacco South: Louisa County, Virginia, 1860–1900* (Knoxville: University of Tennessee Press, 1982), 16–22; Scheel, *Culpeper,* 224; Samuel T. Bitting, *Rural Land Ownership Among the Negroes of Virginia* (Charlottesville: Publications of the University of Virginia Phelps-Stokes Fellowship Papers, 1915). In the nearby Piedmont county of Louisa, the number of Black landowners increased from 22 in 1870 to 1,314 in 1900.

15. On 1902 land ownership, see Scheel, *Culpeper,* 224. "Delinquent Tax List for the Year 1902," *Culpeper Exponent,* Sept. 18, 1903. "Delinquent Real Estate in Culpeper County for 1931," *Virginia Star* (Culpeper), Nov. 30, 1933.

5. The Wharf

1. Daniel E. Sutherland, *Seasons of War: The Ordeal of a Confederate Community, 1861–1865* (New York: Free Press, 1995), chap. 1.

2. *Piedmont Advance* (Culpeper, VA), Sept. 30, 1886; March 17, 1887.

3. *Culpeper Exponent,* Aug. 6, 1897.

4. Eugene M. Scheel, *Culpeper: A Virginia County's History Through 1920* (Culpeper, VA: Culpeper Historical Society, 1982), 300.

5. For nineteenth-century documentation of "Snow-bird on the Ash-Bank" in Virginia, see "An Old Virginian," *Scribner's Monthly,* May–Oct. 1881, 434; "A Death Dance," *Wheeling Register,* March 16, 1881. John Esten Cooke, *Henry St. John, Gentleman . . . a Tale of 1774–'75* (New York: Harper and Brothers, 1860), 79.

6. The 1846 imprint seems to be *The Negro Singer's Own Book: Containing Every Negro Song That Has Ever Been Sung or Printed* (Philadelphia: Turner & Fisher, 1846). Robert Duncan Bass, "Negro Songs from Pedee Country," *Journal of American Folklore* 44, no. 174 (1931): 425. E. C. Perrow, "Songs and Rhymes from the South, II: Songs in Which Animals Figure," *Journal of American Folklore* 26, no. 100 (1913): 133. "Jaybird Died with the Whooping Cough" in Thomas W. Talley's *Negro Folk Rhymes,* ed. Charles K. Wolfe (Knoxville: University of Tennessee Press, 1991), 32–33. Thomas W. Talley, *Negro Folk*

Rhymes: Wise and Otherwise (New York: Macmillan, 1922); Uncle Dave Macon, "Country Ham and Red Gravy," Bluebird 7951, 1938; Dr. Humphrey Bate & His Possum Hunters, Vocalion 5238, 1928. A few of the better recent works that attempt to resolve these complexities of authenticity, folk styles, and commercialism are Diane Pecknold, *The Selling Sound: The Rise of the Country Music Industry*, Refiguring American Music (Durham, NC: Duke University Press, 2007); Karl Hagstrom Miller, *Segregating Sound: Inventing Folk and Pop Music in the Age of Jim Crow* (Durham, NC: Duke University Press, 2010). Erich Nunn, "Country Music and the Souls of White Folk," *Criticism* 51, no. 4 (2009): 623–49.

7. "Ol' Massa in the Parlor," in E. C. Perrow, "Songs and Rhymes from the South, VI: Songs Connected with Drinking and Gambling," *Journal of American Folklore* 28, no. 108 (1915): 141.

8. *Culpeper Exponent*, May 12, 1899. Scheel, *Culpeper*, 312.

9. Jane Dailey, *Before Jim Crow: The Politics of Race in Postemancipation Virginia* (Chapel Hill: University of North Carolina Press, 2000), 22–27.

10. Scheel, *Culpeper*, 219–20, 253, 256. *Culpeper Exponent*, Aug. 30, 1901.

11. *Culpeper Exponent*, Aug. 30, 1901.

12. *Culpeper Exponent*, Aug. 30, 1901.

6. Sparrows Point

1. Prisoner photographs of James Strother, inmate number 33297, Records of the Virginia State Penitentiary, Series II: Prisoner Records, 1865–1990; Subseries B, Photographs and Negatives, 1906–61, 1965–66, State Records Collection, LVA.

2. John A. Lomax, spoken introduction to Strother's "Blood-Strained Banders" on *The Ballad Hunter, Part 7*, Library of Congress, AFS L52, 1958, LP record.

3. In addition to the census entry and the draft registration card, a 1915 *Baltimore Sun* article lists him as blind. The accident that took his sight likely occurred between 1900 and 1910. Despite this evidence, one of Strother's letters to Governor Price states: "I have been totally blind for the past twenty one years," placing the accident about 1917.

4. World War I draft card for James Lee Strother, Culpeper County, Virginia, Sept. 12, 1918. John Lomax, spoken introduction to Strother's "Blood-Strained Banders" on *Ballad Hunter*.

5. "Mr. Stone Flays Charity Methods," *Baltimore American*, Jan. 27, 1915, 14.

6. "Rush of Flame Kills 5," *Baltimore Sun*, Oct. 4, 1906.

7. Bureau of Statistics and Information of Maryland, *Thirteenth Annual Report* (Baltimore: Kohn and Pollock, 1904), 253 ("Negroes at Sparrow's Point").

8. Mark Reutter, *Making Steel: Sparrows Point and the Rise and Ruin of American Industrial Might* (New York: Summit Books, 1988), 49–54.

9. On the design of the town, see Reutter, *Making Steel*, 55–65.

10. The description of Shantytown and quotes from the US Bureau of Labor report are in Reutter, *Making Steel,* 64–65.

11. Sparrows Point resident Florence Parks quoted in Reutter, *Making Steel,* 64; see also 59–65.

12. Bureau of Statistics and Information of Maryland, *Thirteenth Annual Report,* 253–256.

13. Reutter, *Making Steel,* 50–54.

14. State of Maryland, *Third Annual Report of the State Industrial Accident Commission of Maryland for the Year November 1, 1916, to October 31, 1917 Inclusive* (Baltimore: Baltimore City Printing and Binding, 1917), 31 (quote), 34, table 5, "Parts of Bodies Injured."

15. Reutter, *Making Steel,* 52.

16. Terry Rowden, *The Songs of Blind Folk: African American Musicians and the Culture of Blindness* (Ann Arbor: University of Michigan Press, 2009), 36, 78–79. Estes quoted in Joseph Witek, "Blindness as a Rhetorical Trope in Blues Discourse," *Black Music Research Journal* 8, no. 2 (1988): 178. Gary Davis, "Lord, I Wish I Could See," Matrix 17895-1, American Recording Corporation (unissued), recorded in New York City, July 26, 1935, included on *Preachin' the Gospel: Holy Blues,* Columbia Roots and Blues Series 46799, Sony Entertainment Inc., 1991, compact disc.

17. See Rowden, *Songs of Blind Folk,* 6. Rowden discusses the distinctions between congenital and adventitious blindness.

7. The Biddle Alley District

1. The first confirmed address for Strother and his family in Baltimore is 514 Walnut Street. Garrett Power, "Apartheid Baltimore Style: The Residential Segregation Ordinances of 1910–1913," *Maryland Law Review* 42 (1983): 289–328.

2. For an overview of Black Baltimore in the antebellum period, see Christopher Phillips, *Freedom's Port: The African American Community of Baltimore, 1790–1860* (Urbana: University of Illinois Press, 1997).

3. Entry on Baltimore by Prudence D. Cumberbatch in *The Great Black Migration: A Historical Encyclopedia of the American Mosaic,* ed. Steven A. Reich (Westport, CT: Greenwood Press, 2014), 17–22.

4. Dennis Patrick Halpin, *A Brotherhood of Liberty: Black Reconstruction and Its Legacies in Baltimore, 1865–1920* (Philadelphia: University of Pennsylvania Press, 2019), 68–69.

5. "Strike of Whites Against Blacks," *Baltimore Sun,* April 30, 1905, 11.

6. "The Reminiscences of Thurgood Marshall, Columbia Oral History Research Office, 1977," in *Thurgood Marshall: His Speeches, Writings, Arguments, Opinions, and Reminisces,* ed. Mark V. Tushnet, The Library of Black America (Chicago: Lawrence Hill Books, 2001), 313–14.

7. "Feared Negro Influx," *Baltimore Sun*, Nov. 1, 1909; Antero Pietila, *Not in My Neighborhood: How Bigotry Shaped a Great American City* (Chicago: Ivan R. Dee, 2010), 54–57.

8. Pietila, *Not in My Neighborhood*. Halpin, *Brotherhood of Liberty*, 146–48.

9. Kemp defined the Biddle Alley District as 215 houses in the interior of the block bounded by Biddle and Preston Streets and Druid Hill and Pennsylvania Avenues. Association for the Improvement of the Conditions for the Poor and the Charity Organization Society, *Housing Conditions in Baltimore: Report of a Special Committee* (Baltimore: Federated Charities, 1907), 16–18.

10. *Housing Conditions in Baltimore*, 19; Power, "Apartheid Baltimore Style," 293.

11. Cab Calloway and Bryant Rollins, *Of Minnie the Moocher and Me* (New York: Crowell, 1976), 15. Jo Ann E. Argersinger, *Toward a New Deal in Baltimore: People and Government in the Great Depression* (Chapel Hill: University of North Carolina Press, 1988). Samuel Kelton Roberts Jr., *Infectious Fear: Politics, Disease, and the Health Effects of Segregation*, Studies in Social Medicine Series (Chapel Hill: University of North Carolina Press, 2009).

12. *Housing Conditions in Baltimore*, 17, 33.

13. *Housing Conditions in Baltimore*, 16, 71. Katie M. Hemphill, *Bawdy City: Commercial Sex and Regulation in Baltimore, 1790–1915* (Cambridge: Cambridge University Press, 2020).

14. *Housing Conditions in Baltimore*, 18.

15. *Housing Conditions in Baltimore*, 20. On Black marriage in the nineteenth century, see Tera W. Hunter, *Bound in Wedlock: Slave and Free Black Marriage in the Nineteenth Century* (Cambridge, MA: Belknap Press, 2017). On the Black family in this period, see S. Philip Morgan, Antonio McDaniel, Andrew T. Miller, and Samuel H. Preston, "Racial Differences in Household and Family Structure at the Turn of the Century," *American Journal of Sociology* 98, no. 4 (1993): 799–828, and Steve Ruggles, "The Origins of African-American Family Structure," *American Sociological Review* 59, no. 1 (1994): 136–51.

16. William Taylor, 594 W. Preston Street, Baltimore, Maryland, to Governor James Price, Richmond, Virginia, July 19, 1938, and Aug. 20, 1939, James Lee Strother pardon file.

17. Hemphill, *Bawdy City*. James H. N. Waring is listed at 1230 Druid Hill Avenue in 1903 and at 509 Mosher Street in 1905 and 1909. Baltimore City Directories, 1903, 1905, 1909. Biography of Waring in *The Crisis*, May 1917, 33. He would later head an orphanage on Long Island, New York, practice medicine in Massachusetts, and became superintendent of the Downington Industrial and Agricultural School in Chester, Pennsylvania.

18. James H. N. Waring, *Work of the Colored Law and Order League, Baltimore, Maryland* (Cheyney, PA: 1908), 10.

19. Waring, *Work of the Colored Law and Order League*, 9. *Housing Conditions in Baltimore*, 18. Susan Sweik also notes the hardening attitude of Black elites toward beggary and poverty as well as their attempts to explain it in *The Ugly Laws: Disability in Public* (New York: New York University Press, 2009), 296.

20. Waring, *Work of the Colored Law and Order League*, 11–12.
21. Waring, *Work of the Colored Law and Order League*, 24–25; *Baltimore Sun*, April 9, 1908, 12.
22. Quoted in Waring, *Work of the Colored Law and Order League*, 28.
23. Waring, *Work of the Colored Law and Order League*, 9.
24. *Housing Conditions in Baltimore*, 16.

8. Rock Steady, Children

1. John A. Lomax, *Adventures of a Ballad Hunter* (New York: Macmillan, 1947), 153–55. Nolan Porterfield, *Last Cavalier: The Life and Times of John A. Lomax* (Urbana: University of Illinois Press, 1996), 340–41.
2. "Defends His Guitar Playing," *Baltimore Sun*, July 9, 1902.
3. Roberta Freund Schwartz, "How Blue Can You Get? 'It's Tight Like That' and the Hokum Blues," *American Music* 36, no. 3 (2018): 382.
4. Howard W. Odum and Guy B. Johnson, *The Negro and His Songs: A Study of Typical Negro Songs in the South* (Chapel Hill: University of North Carolina Press, 1925), 166.
5. For early Victorian eroticism, see David S. Reynolds, *Beneath the American Renaissance: The Subversive Imagination in the Age of Emerson and Melville* (Oxford: Oxford University Press, 1989). For bawdy cylinder recordings, see the CD set *Actionable Offenses: Indecent Phonograph Recordings from the 1890s*, Archephone Records, 2007, compact disc. On the Allen Brothers, see Tony Russell, *Country Music Originals: The Legends and the Lost* (New York: Oxford University Press, 2007), 72–74.
6. Interview with Dom Flemons, May 12, 2021, video recording in the author's possession. Stephen Wade, liner notes to *Black Appalachia: String Bands, Songsters, and Hoedowns*, Rounder Records, 1999.
7. Strother, "Poontang Little, Poontang Small," AFS 750-B, is the longer, unissued version.
8. G. Legman, "Poontang," *American Speech* 25, no. 3 (1950): 234–35.
9. The term appears in Tennessee Williams, "Cat on a Hot Tin Roof," act 2, part 1, and in Thomas Wolfe, *Look Homeward, Angel: A Story of the Buried Life* (New York: Random House, 1929), 166, 174, and 343.
10. Bruce Jackson, *Get Your Ass in the Water and Swim Like Me: African American Narrative Poetry from Oral Tradition* (New York: Routledge, 2017), 157–60, entry 48B. Clara Smith, "Oh! Mister Mitchell," Columbia 14536-D, recorded in New York, Dec. 9, 1929.
11. Cecelia Conway, "Black Banjo Songsters in Appalachia," *Black Music Research Journal* 23, no. 1/2 (2003): 149–66, quote on 156–57. Stephen Wade conjectured that the tune represented a widespread "transition of the music from banjo song to proto-blues." The strophic, eight-bar tune uses a straightforward I-IV-I-V-I blues chord progression, but the picking patterns and syncopation suggest a ragtime feel. Wade, liner notes to *Black Appalachia*.

12. Some transcribers have rendered the concluding line as "Oh my babe, took my salty thing."

13. Lucille Bogan, billed as "Bessie Jackson," recorded two versions of "Shave 'Em Dry" on March 5, 1935, for the American Recording Corporation (ARC). The decidedly tamer version appeared in July on ARC's Banner label and subsequently on its other dime-store lines: Melotone Records (M 13342), Oriole Records (8487), Romeo Records (5487), and Perfect Records (0332). The unexpurgated version sat unreleased until 1991, appearing on the compilation album *Raunchy Business: Hot Nuts & Lollypops,* Columbia/Legacy CK-46783, compact disc. Keith Briggs speculates that this take reflects the rowdy atmosphere in more lowdown venues and clubs; see liner notes to *Lucille Bogan (Bessie Jackson) Complete Recordings, Vol. 3, 1934–1935,* Document Records BDCD-6038, 1993, compact disc. Armenter Chatmon, known musically as Bo Carter, recorded with the Black string band Mississippi Sheiks and as a solo blues artist. A good overview of his music is *Banana in Your Fruit Basket: Bo Carter, Red Hot Blues, 1931–1936,* Yazoo Records, YAZCD 1064, 1991.

14. Katie M. Hemphill, *Bawdy City: Commercial Sex and Regulation in Baltimore, 1790–1915* (Cambridge: Cambridge University Press, 2020), 217–24.

15. Yvonne P. Chireau, *Black Magic: Religion and the African American Conjuring Tradition* (Berkeley: University of California Press, 2006). Roland L. Freeman, *The Arabbers of Baltimore* (Centerville, MD: Tidewater Publishers, 1989), 19. "Herb Doctor Said to Have Hit Patient," *Danville Bee,* Aug. 20, 1933.

16. Schwartz, "How Blue Can You Get?," 367–93, quoting Ralph Ellison. Albert Murray, *Trading Twelves: The Selected Letters of Ralph Ellison and Albert Murray* (New York: Modern Library, 2000), 29. James H. Cone, *The Spirituals and the Blues: An Interpretation* (New York: Seabury Press, 1972), 132.

17. Interview with Flemons.

18. James H. N. Waring, *Work of the Colored Law and Order League, Baltimore, Maryland* (Cheyney, PA, 1908), 11.

19. Kerr quoted in David K. Hildebrand and Elizabeth M. Schaaf, *Musical Maryland: A History of Song and Performance from the Colonial Period to the Age of Radio* (Baltimore: Johns Hopkins University Press, 2017), 134.

20. Bruce Bastin, "From the Medicine Show to the Stage: Some Influences upon the Development of a Blues Tradition in the Southeastern United States," *American Music* 2, no. 1 (1984): 29–42. Helen Jackson Lee, *Nigger in the Window* (Garden City, NY: Doubleday, 1978), 26.

21. Lee, *Nigger in the Window,* 29.

22. Adam Gussow, "Langston Hughes and the Scandal of Early Blues Poetry," in *Whose Blues? Facing Up to Race and the Future of the Music* (Chapel Hill: University of North Carolina Press, 2000), 142–43.

23. Cone, *Spirituals and the Blues,* 42.

24. I am indebted to Nancy-Elizabeth Fitch for first alerting me to the possible connection between "Big Boy" and Calvin Davis many years ago. Charles H. Rowell, "'Let Me Be with Ole Jazzbo': An Interview with Sterling A. Brown,"

Callaloo 14, no. 4 (1991): 795–815; Robert B. Stepto, "'When de Saint Go Ma'chin' Home': Sterling Brown's Blueprint for a New Negro Poetry," *Kunapipi* 4, no. 1 (1982). According to Stepto, "When de Saints Go Ma'chin' Home" first appeared in *Opportunity: A Journal of Negro Life* 5 (July 1927): 48 and won the journal's award for poetry in 1928. "Odyssey of Big Boy" first appeared in *Caroling Dusk,* ed. Countee Cullen (New York: Harper and Brothers, 1927); "Long Gone" in *The Book of American Negro Poetry,* ed. James Weldon Johnson (New York: Harcourt, Brace, 1931). All three "Big Boy" poems were collected in Brown's *Southern Road* (New York: Harcourt, Brace, 1932).

25. Bruce Bastin, *Red River Blues: The Blues Tradition in the Southeast,* Music in American Life (Urbana: University of Illinois Press, 1986), 306. Brown said the "Odyssey of Big Boy" was a "picture of an itinerant guitar player and ex-coal miner," and "he also taught me a great deal about railroad lore, he was a great railroad man." Sterling Brown reading his poems, July 9, 1973, Archive of Recorded Poetry and Literature, Library of Congress, Washington, DC.

26. Sterling A. Brown, "When de Saints Go Ma'ching Home," in *Southern Road,* 12.

27. Ma Rainey, "Lost Wandering Blues," Paramount 12098, recorded in Chicago, IL, ca. Feb. 25–March 1, 1924. Blind Lemon Jefferson, "Matchbox Blues," OKeh 8455, recorded in Atlanta, GA, March 14–15, 1927. Willie Walker, "Dupree Blues," Columbia 14578-D, recorded in Atlanta, GA, Dec. 16, 1930. Booker T. Washington "Bukka" White, "Panama Limited," Victor 23295, recorded in Memphis, TN, May 26, 1930. Blind Willie McTell as "Blind Sammie," "Travelin' Blues," Columbia 14484, recorded in Atlanta, GA, Oct. 30, 1929.

28. Harry Carrington Bolton, *The Counting-Out Rhymes of Children: Their Antiquity, Origin and Wide Distribution; A Study in Folk-Lore* (London: Elliot Stock, 1888), 102. I think the earliest US mention is in Jonathan Ware, *A New Introduction to the English Grammar* (Windsor, VT: Jesse Cochran, 1814).

29. James Mellon, *Bullwhip Days: The Slaves Remember* (New York: Weidenfeld & Nicolson, 1988), 119–20.

30. J. Ralph Jones and Tom Landess, "Portraits of Georgia Slaves," *Georgia Review* 22, no. 1 (1968): 125–27.

31. E. C. Perrow, "Songs and Rhymes from the South, II: Songs in Which Animals Figure," *Journal of American Folklore* 26, no. 100 (1913): 123–73. Arthur Kyle Davis Jr., *Folk-Songs of Virginia: A Descriptive Index and Classification of Material Collected Under the Auspices of the Virginia Folklore Society* (Durham, NC: Duke University Press, 1949), 222. Entry for Bruce W. Stringfellow, 1930 US census, Town of Culpeper, Culpeper County, VA, enumeration district 24–1, sheet 15A.

9. The Medicine Show

1. Michael Torbenson and Jonathon Erlen, "A Quantitative Profile of the Patent Medicine Industry in Baltimore from 1863 to 1930," *Pharmacy in History* 49, no. 1 (2007): 15–27.

2. Liner notes to Benjamin A. Botkin, ed., *Negro Religious Songs and Services,* AFS L10, Library of Congress, 1943.

3. Marshall Wyatt, *Good for What Ails You: Music of the Medicine Shows, 1926–1937,* Old Hat Records, Old Hat CD 1005, 2005.

4. Wyatt, *Good for What Ails You.*

5. The *Emmitsburg Chronicle* quoted in the *Catoctin Clarion,* Jan. 23, 1908. *Democratic Messenger* (Snow Hill, MD), Nov. 19, 1904.

6. "Cumberland, Maryland Through the Eyes of Herman J. Miller," unpublished typescript based on oral history collected by Dr. Harry Stegmaier, p. 124, Western Maryland Historic Library at Western Maryland Regional Library.

7. On the music of the medicine and traveling shows, see Paul Oliver, *Songsters and Saints: Vocal Traditions on Race Records* (Cambridge: Cambridge University Press, 1984), 78–108. On Tom Ashley's medicine-show experiences, see Ambrose N. Manning and Minnie M. Miller, "Tom Ashley," in *Tom Ashley, Sam McGee, Bukka White: Tennessee Traditional Singers,* ed. Thomas G. Burton (Knoxville: University of Tennessee Press, 1981), 26–30. For Pink Anderson, see his entry in Benjamin Franklin V, *An Encyclopedia of South Carolina Jazz & Blues Musicians* (Columbia: University of South Carolina Press, 2016). On Hubie Blake, see David K. Hildebrand and Elizabeth M. Schaaf, *Musical Maryland: A History of Song and Performance from the Colonial Period to the Age of Radio* (Baltimore: Johns Hopkins University Press, 2017), 128. For an overview of the medicine show, see Ann Anderson, *Snake Oil, Hustlers and Hambones: The American Medicine Show* (Jefferson, NC: McFarland, 2000).

8. Ralph Matthews, "Wandering Reporter Finds Many Changes Taking Place," *Baltimore Afro-American,* March 26, 1927.

9. "Police Not Part of Show," *Baltimore Sun,* Nov. 30, 1903.

10. *Baltimore Daily Record,* Sept. 1, 1905. William T. Brantly, *Reports of Cases Argued and Adjudged in the Court of Appeals of Maryland,* vol. 103 (Frederick, MD: Charles H. Baughman, 1907), 112–19.

11. *Baltimore County Union* (Towsontown, MD), July 19, 1902; *Frederick City Citizen,* March 3, 1899; *Highland Recorder* (Monterey, VA), Aug. 3, 1917.

12. Kip Lornell's liner notes to the original Blue Ridge Institute release correctly place this song in the minstrel and tent show idiom.

13. Strother's banjo approach here stands in contrast to both the stroke style of "Thought I Heard My Banjo Say" and to "Blood-Stained Banders," where Strother maintains a march-like rhythm with downstrokes to produce a direct, straight pulse supporting his singing. Strother's ability to change his approach based on his material is reminiscent of Gus Cannon. See Tony Thomas, "The Colored Champion Banjo Pugilist of the World and the Big World of the Banjo," in *Banjo Roots and Branches,* ed. Robert B. Winans, Music in American Life (Urbana: University of Illinois Press, 2018), 272–88.

14. Some dictionaries of slang have cast doubt on the railroading origins of the expression, even positing that the 1913 song discussed below gave rise to the usage by railroad men. I found three examples of the railroad usage that are roughly

contemporary in time to the first musical usage (1913), and all three suggest that the expression was already in wide use. See J. P. Power, "Railroad Slang," *The Editor: The Journal of Information for Literary Workers* 44, no. 9 (1916): 359; *Railroad Telegrapher* 35, no. 9 (1918): 1162; and *Railroad Trainman* 45 (1928): 27.

15. Eileen Southern, *The Music of Black Americans: A History* (New York: W. W. Norton, 1971), 352–53. Oliver, *Songsters and Saints,* 51–53. Lynn Abbott and Doug Seroff, *Ragged but Right: Black Traveling Shows, Coon Songs, and the Dark Pathway to Blues and Jazz,* American Made Music Series (Jackson: University Press of Mississippi, 2007), 171, 191–92, 197, 273.

16. The *Dictionary of American Regional English* gives all of the above meanings. See Frederic G. Cassidy, *Dictionary of American Regional English,* vol. 2, *D–H* (Cambridge, MA: Harvard University Press, 1991), 140. The expression also entered children's play songs and dance by the 1930s. See Kyra D. Gaunt, *Games Black Girls Play: Learning the Ropes from Double-Dutch to Hip-Hop* (New York: New York University Press, 2006), 199–202. Lead Belly, "Eagle Rock Rag," in *The History of Jazz, Vol. 1: The "Solid" South,* Capitol Records, set C-16, 1945, track B.

17. Bessie Smith, "Baby Doll," issued on Columbia 14147-D, recorded in New York, May 4, 1926.

18. *Indianapolis Freeman,* Feb. 22, 1913; May 2, 1914.

19. *Kentucky Folklore Record* 10 (Bowling Green: Kentucky Folklore Society, 1964), 7. Robert Pounds, "Anybody Here Want to Buy a Little Dog," AFC 1941/001; AFS 05394 A03, recorded in Farmington, AR, in Feb. 1942, Vance Randolph Collection, American Folklife Center, Library of Congress, Washington, DC. David Griffiths, *Hot Jazz: From Harlem to Storyville* (Lanham, MD: Scarecrow Press, 1998), mentions promoter Billy Mitchell, whose theme song was "Anybody Here Want to Buy a Little Dog" and who ran a show through Philadelphia and Atlantic City in 1926. Unfortunately, I haven't been able to find any further documentation of this song.

20. Adam Gussow, "W. C. Handy and the 'Birth' of the Blues," *Southern Cultures* 24, no. 4 (2018): 54.

21. *The Negro Motorist Green-Book* (New York: Victor H. Green, 1940).

22. Early transcriptions of the song performed by white informants include E. C. Perrow, "Songs and Rhymes from the South, VI: Songs Connected with Drinking and Gambling," *Journal of American Folklore* 28, no. 108 (1915): 180–81 (collected in South Carolina); *English Folk Songs from the Southern Appalachians Collected by Cecil J. Sharp . . . Including Thirty-Nine Tunes Contributed by Olive Dame Campbell,* ed. Maud Karpeles, vol. 2 (London: Oxford University Press, 1932), 358 (collected in Kentucky). Early commercial recordings by white artists from the 1920s include the Hill Billies and the like.

23. James W. Loewen, *Sundown Towns: A Hidden Dimension of American Racism* (New York: New Press, 2005), 245.

24. Terry Zwigoff, "Louie Bluie: The Life and Music of William Howard Armstrong (Part 2)," *78 Quarterly* 1, no. 6 (n.d.): 47–48.

25. "Mob Overpowers Jailors and Hang Negro to Tree," *Richmond Times-Dispatch*, Nov. 30, 1918.

26. James H. Cone, *The Spirituals and the Blues: An Interpretation* (New York: Seabury Press, 1972), 80–81.

10. The Street

1. "Old Goucher Neighborhood: Strengthening a Community Identity Through an Exploration of the Past," report conducted by the University of Maryland School of Architecture, Planning and Preservation, Graduate Program of Historic Preservation, Fall 2013, p. 15, https://static1.squarespace.com/static/5a4ed553e45a7c26de75126d/t/5a5d67fc4192027395ef24e5/1516070948247/OldGoucher_Part1-UM_Historic_Preservation.pdf.

2. For details on the Baltimore residences of Strother and his extended family, see *Sanborn Fire Insurance Map of Baltimore*, Baltimore County, MD, 1914, vol. 2, sheet 168 (514 Walnut Street, three story, brick), vol. 7, sheet 702 (204 Ware Street and Hudson Place), vol. 7, sheet 689 (2025 Oak Street, three story, brick with basement), vol. 7, sheet 703 (2409 and 2411 Mace Street, two story, brick), Library of Congress Geography and Map Division, Washington, DC. On Waller, see Rev. J. J. Pipkin, *The Negro in Revelation, in History, and in Citizenship* (St. Louis, MO: N. D. Thompson, 1902), 110–13, and "Baltimore's Leading Divine," *The Colored American* (Washington, DC), May 25, 1901. Reflecting the reordering of Baltimore's neighborhoods, Trinity purchased St. Paul's English Evangelical Lutheran Church on Druid Hill Avenue in 1920. The congregation still worships there today.

3. Strother sang in a baritone range that spanned at least two octaves. His opening notes on "Do Lord, Remember Me" takes him down to G2 (the second G below middle C) as he sings the melody in the key of C an octave below Joe Lynn Lee. It definitely sounds near the bottom of his voice. The choice of key on this song may have been dictated by several factors—the ubiquity of C as a standard guitar key as well as finding a range suitable to both vocalists. Strother ranges upward to almost reach A4 (the first A above middle C) on "Thought I Heard My Banjo Say." Strother's recordings tend to be pitched slightly sharp of standard A440—not surprising for a solo folk performer.

4. Ian Zach, *Say No to the Devil: The Life and Musical Genius of Rev. Gary Davis* (Chicago: University of Chicago Press, 2015), 38. Bruce Bastin, *Red River Blues: The Blues Tradition in the Southeast,* Music in American Life (Urbana: University of Illinois Press, 1986), 230–31.

5. Susan M. Schweik, *The Ugly Laws: Disability in Public* (New York: New York University Press, 2009), 200. "A Street Musician's Income," *Washington Post*, Jan. 18, 1896, 11.

6. Identification of "Consul Seagrave" from *Civil Service Register* (Indianapolis) 2, no. 10 (1893): 92. "Itinerant Musicians," *Musical News* (London) 1, no. 26 (1891): 521–23.

7. Marion Grubb, "Little Brothers of Business," *The Commonweal: A Weekly Review of Literature, the Arts, and Public Affairs* 12, no. 10 (1930): 278–79.

8. David K. Hildebrand and Elizabeth M. Schaaf, *Musical Maryland: A History of Song and Performance from the Colonial Period to the Age of Radio* (Baltimore: Johns Hopkins University Press, 2017), 134. Roland L. Freeman, *The Arabbers of Baltimore* (Centerville, MD: Tidewater Publishers, 1989).

9. Grubb, "Little Brothers of Business," 278–79.

10. Some of the studies of world blind musicians that influenced my work include Hugh de Ferranti, *The Last Biwa Singer: A Blind Musician in History, Imagination, and Performance* (Ithaca: Cornell East Asia Series, 2009); Natalie O. Kononenko, *Ukrainian Minstrels: And the Blind Shall Sing*, Folklores and Folk Cultures of Eastern Europe Series (Armonk, NY: M. E. Sharpe, 1998).

11. Madeline Sutherland-Meier, "Toward a History of the Blind in Spain," *Disability Studies Quarterly* 35, no. 4 (2015).

12. Ferranti, *Last Biwa Singer*, 265–70.

13. John E. Zucchi, *The Little Slaves of the Harp: Italian Child Street Musicians in Nineteenth-Century Paris, London, and New York* (Montreal and Kingston: McGill-Queen's University Press, 1992), preface.

14. "Itinerant Musicians," 521–23.

15. "Itinerant Musicians."

16. "Itinerant Musicians."

17. John H. Gwathmey, *Justice John: Tales from the Courtroom of the Virginia Judge* (Richmond: Press of the Dietz Printing Co., 1934).

18. "Melody at the Southern," *Baltimore Evening Sun*, Aug. 5, 1910.

19. "Blind Player Dismissed," *Richmond Times Dispatch*, July 5, 1910. "Temple of Justice," *Norfolk Virginian-Pilot*, Dec. 20, 1899.

20. Bastin, *Red River Blues*, 216.

21. Baltimore City Police Department, Criminal Docket, Central District, 27 April through 20 June 1915, Maryland State Archives, Annapolis, MD.

22. Dennis Patrick Halpin, *A Brotherhood of Liberty: Black Reconstruction and Its Legacies in Baltimore, 1865–1920* (Philadelphia: University of Pennsylvania Press, 2019), 92–113.

11. The Politics of Race and Disability

1. "Plea for Blind Negro: Collector Writes Indignant Letter to Mayor Preston," *Baltimore Sun*, Jan. 27, 1915. "Mr. Stone Flays Charity Methods: The Collector Bitterly Arraigns J. W. Magruder," *Baltimore American*, Jan. 27, 1915.

2. *Baltimore Sun*, Jan. 27, 1915.

3. Frank Richardson Kent, *The Story of Maryland Politics* (Baltimore: Thomas and Evans, 1911), 210–12, quote on 210.

4. *The Race Standard*, Jan. 2, 1897; *The Commonwealth*, July 24, 1915. Dennis Halpin, *A Brotherhood of Liberty: Black Reconstruction and Its Legacies in Baltimore, 1865–1920* (Philadelphia: University of Pennsylvania Press, 2019), 114–43.

5. *Baltimore Afro-American Ledger,* Nov. 15, 1913; March 14, 1914. Halpin, *Brotherhood of Liberty,* 114–43.

6. "Plea for Blind Negro." "Mr. Stone Flays Charity Methods."

7. Biographical profile of Magruder in the *Baltimore Sun,* Sept. 7, 1907, and in *Charities and the Commons* 18, no. 7 (1907): 220–21.

8. Magruder quoted in the *Baltimore Sun,* Oct. 31, 1910.

9. Kerry Segrave, *Begging in America, 1850–1940: The Needy, the Frauds, the Charities and the Law* (Jefferson, NC: MacFarland, 2011), 168–69. "Stopping Mendicancy in Baltimore City," *The Survey: A Journal of Constructive Philanthropy* 29, no. 4 (1912): 89–90. It is worth noting that Baltimore's police department was (and still is) a Maryland state agency as of this writing. The state took over control in 1860 after the brief reign of the Know-Nothings in city politics. In fact, it wasn't until 1978 that the mayor was given the power to appoint the police commissioner.

10. Segrave, *Begging in America,* 168–69. "Stopping Mendicancy in Baltimore City," 89–90. J. W. Magruder, secretary of the Federated Charities of Baltimore, quoted in the *Baltimore American,* Jan. 27, 1915. John and Alan Lomax, *Our Singing Country: A Second Volume of American Ballads and Folk Songs,* ed. Ruth Crawford Seeger (New York: Macmillan, 1941). James Strother #33927, State Farm, Virginia, to Governor James H. Price, Richmond, Aug. 24, 1939, RG 13, Secretary of the Commonwealth, Executive Papers, 1939 Sept. 12–20, accession 24938, box 1113, Library of Virginia, Richmond.

11. Joseph Witek, "Blindness as a Rhetorical Trope in Blues Discourse," *Black Music Research Journal* 8, no. 2 (1988): 177–93. J. and A. Lomax, *Our Singing Country.*

12. Strother to Price, Aug. 24, 1939.

13. Sami Schalk, "Reevaluating the Supercrip," *Journal of Literary & Cultural Disability Studies* 10, no. 1 (2016): 71–86.

14. Susan M. Schweik, *The Ugly Laws: Disability in Public* (New York: New York University Press, 2009), 199–200. Also see Luigi Monge, "The Language of Blind Lemon Jefferson: The Covert Theme of Blindness," *Black Music Research Journal* 20, no. 1 (2000): 35–81.

15. Elijah Wald, *Josh White: Society Blues* (London: Routledge, 2002), 11–25.

16. Thomas C. Leonard, *Illiberal Reformers: Race, Eugenics, and American Economics in the Progressive Era* (Princeton, NJ: Princeton University Press, 2016), xi (quote).

17. Leonard, *Illiberal Reformers.* Daniel T. Rodgers, "The Promise of American History: Progress and Prospects," *Reviews in American History* 10, no. 4 (1982): 113–32. Lawrence B. Glickman, "Still in Search of Progressivism?," *Reviews in American History* 26, no. 4 (1998): 731–36.

18. Bruce Bastin, *Red River Blues: The Blues Tradition in the Southeast,* Music in American Life (Urbana: University of Illinois Press, 1986), 244.

19. "Colored Workers for Charity," *Baltimore Afro-American Ledger,* Nov. 7, 1915.

20. Helen Jackson Lee, *Nigger in the Window* (Garden City, NY: Doubleday, 1978), 25.

21. For more on Thurman, see Peter Eisenstadt, *Against the Hounds of Hell: A Life of Howard Thurman* (Charlottesville: University of Virginia Press, 2021). The biblical story is found, with some variations, in Mark 10:46–52, Luke 18:35–43, and Matthew 20:29–34.

22. Howard Thurman, *Deep River and the Negro Spiritual Speaks of Life and Death* (Richmond, IN: Friends United Press, 1975), 37–43.

12. Blanche Greene

1. The 1900, 1910, and 1920 censuses all indicate that he owned his property free and clear. For acreage and value, see Land Tax Book, 1919, Clerk's Office, Culpeper County Courthouse, Culpeper, Virginia; Samuel T. Bitting, *Rural Land Ownership Among the Negroes of Virginia* (Charlottesville: Publications of the University of Virginia Phelps-Stokes Fellowship Papers, 1915), 17–18. For the average value of acreage on Virginia's farms, see Department of Agriculture and Immigration of Virginia, *Bulletin*, no. 169 (Oct. 1921): 2. Robert Lee Greene is identified as "Lee" in the land tax books, on the marriage certificate of Blanche Greene and Jim Strother, and in other records.

2. Will of Noah Greene, Culpeper County Will Book Y, p. 598, Sept. 18, 1893. Noah Green's deed, 1886 (ten acres). Both Lee and Noah bought land from the same person, J. Ambler Brooke, administrator of John Cooke Green's estate.

3. Deed, Noah Greene's Heirs, July 17, 1906, Culpeper County Courthouse, Culpeper, Virginia.

4. "Poll Book, 2nd District, Madison County, State of Virginia, Colored," 1867, LVA.

5. T. O. Madden Jr. with Ann L. Miller, *We Were Always Free: The Maddens of Culpeper County, Virginia, a 200-Year Family History* (Charlottesville: University of Virginia Press, 2005); Culpeper petitions quoted on 89–90.

6. Madden, *We Were Always Free*. Philip J. Schwarz, *Migrants Against Slavery: Virginians and the Nation* (Charlottesville: University of Virginia Press, 2001), 152–56; Daniel E. Sutherland, *Seasons of War: The Ordeal of a Confederate Community, 1861–1865* (New York: Free Press, 1995), chap. 1. Eugene M. Scheel, *Culpeper: A Virginia County's History Through 1920* (Culpeper, VA: Culpeper Historical Society, 1982), 242.

7. According to the 1910 census, all five children were attending school in 1909. National Register of Historic Places Nomination for Eckington School, Culpeper County, Virginia, 2000, Virginia Department of Historic Resources File Number 23-5041, section 8, pp. 3–4, https://www.dhr.virginia.gov/VLR_to_transfer/PDFNoms/023-5041_Eckington_School_2001_Final_Nomination.pdf.

8. *Culpeper Exponent,* Dec. 15, 1921. "Afro-American News," *Culpeper News,* Aug. 20, 1909.

9. *Culpeper Exponent,* Dec. 15, 1921; June 7, 1912.

10. *Culpeper Exponent,* Nov. 8, 1912.

11. Interviews with James C. and Shirley Greene, Culpeper County, Virginia, Oct. 6–7, 2020.

12. Luke Jordan, "Cocaine Blues," Victor 21076, recorded Aug. 16, 1927, Charlotte, North Carolina, 78-rpm record.

13. Paul Oliver, *Conversation with the Blues,* 2nd ed. (Cambridge: Cambridge University Press, 1997), 53.

14. Alexandria city directories, 1919, 1923. Entry for Harrison household, 1920 US census, Alexandria City, VA, enumeration district 5, sheet 3A.

15. Blanche is listed with her parents and eight-month-old James in the 1920 US census. Also see "I married a woman who had had two children out of wedlock before I married her," James Strother #33927, State Farm, Virginia, to Governor James H. Price, Richmond, May 1, 1939, James Lee Strother pardon file. Third Baptist Church, Rev. Ross: https://www.thirdbaptistalexva.org/content.cfm?id=306. Blanche and Jim Strother's unnamed child lived a half day, according to the certificate, indicating a live birth, not a miscarriage. Teacher Registers, 1928–1932, Culpeper County, Virginia, private collection, copies in the possession of the author.

16. "Police Hunting Lewis Ellis for Fatal Shooting," *Virginia Star* (Culpeper), June 11, 1925.

17. Barry Lee Pearson, *Sounds So Good to Me: The Bluesman's Story* (Philadelphia: University of Pennsylvania Press, 1984), 70.

18. Barry Lee Pearson, *Virginia Piedmont Blues: The Lives and Art of Two Virginia Bluesmen,* Publications of the American Folklore Society (Philadelphia: University of Pennsylvania Press, 1990), 159–66.

19. *Culpeper Exponent,* Aug. 30, 1907; Aug. 14, 1908.

20. Scheel, *Culpeper,* 219, 293–94, 300. "Bootleggers in the Toils of the Law: Rumors of Bootlegging Going on in Culpeper Proved to Be True," *Culpeper Exponent,* Sept. 9, 1910.

21. Clutchie Mack, "Jeff Scott," *Living Blues* 43, no. 5 (2012): 26–31.

22. Records indicate that William B. Lacy was born in 1864 and his wife around 1867, so both would have been in their early twenties when the Greens left Locust Dale. Noah Greene and family, 1880 US census, Locust Dale Magisterial District, Madison County, VA, population schedules, enumeration district 109, p. 27. Lacy Family in the 1900 US census, Locust Dale District, Madison County, VA, population schedule, enumeration district 85, sheet 19. Nannie Lacy and her children in the 1930 US census, Town of Culpeper, Catalpa District, Culpeper County, VA, population schedule, enumeration district 24–1, sheet 17A; 1940 federal census, Town of Culpeper, VA, population schedule, enumeration district 24–1, sheet 16A. Lacy lived at 414 North East Street in 1940.

23. Charles E. Bowmar, "A Story of James C. Greene," typescript in the possession of the Greene family, copy in the possession of the author.

13. Murder on Barbour Alley

1. The earliest accounts of the murder are "Negro Woman Shot by Mate," *Culpeper Exponent,* April 4, 1935, and "Colored Man Shoots Wife," *Virginia Star* (Culpeper), April 4, 1935. Also see "Colored Woman Dies in Hospital," *Virginia Star,* April 11, 1935; "Blind Negro, Indicted for Murder, 'Aimed at Her Feet,'" *Virginia Star,* April 18, 1935; and "Jim Strother Sentenced to 20 Years for Killing Wife," *Virginia Star,* April 25, 1935. The Strothers' residence is listed on an "unnamed street" between entries for Tin Cup Alley and Cameron Street.
2. "Negro Woman Shot By Mate."
3. "Blind, He Shoots Wife," *Sunday Star* (Washington, DC), April 7, 1935; "Colored Man Shoots Wife."
4. "Negro Woman Shot by Mate." "Jim Strother Sentenced to 20 Years."
5. "Colored Woman Dies in Hospital."
6. Strother's court appearances are documented in Law Order Book No. 19, Circuit Court of the County of Culpeper, Culpeper County Courthouse, Culpeper, VA, pp. 33, 36, and 39,
7. Identification of the jurymen based on entries in the 1900, 1910, 1920, and 1930 US census.
8. "Blind Negro, Indicted for Murder."
9. Law Order Book No. 19, p. 36.
10. "The Commonwealth of Virginia v. James A. and Philip J. Strother. (Culpeper Circuit Court)," *Virginia Law Register* 12, no. 12 (April 1907): 947–77. Eugene M. Scheel, *Culpeper: A Virginia County's History Through 1920* (Culpeper, VA: Culpeper Historical Society, 1982), 230, 290, 293, and 307.
11. Obituary of Judge Burnett Miller Jr., *Richmond Times-Dispatch,* Aug. 22, 1954. Scheel, *Culpeper,* 364, gives Burnett Miller Jr.'s service dates in the legislature.
12. Law Order Book No. 19, p. 39.
13. *Evening Star* (Washington, DC), July 14, 1935.
14. James Strother #33927, State Farm, Virginia, to Governor James H. Price, Richmond, March 27, 1938, and Oct. 10, 1938, James Lee Strother pardon file.
15. Strother to Price, March 27, 1938.
16. R. A. Bickers, Commonwealth's Attorney for Culpeper County, to Miss Laura H. Allen, Secretary to the Governor, Richmond, Virginia, June 21, 1939, RG 13, Secretary of the Commonwealth, Executive Papers, 1939 Sept. 12–20, accession 24938, box 1113, LVA.
17. "Jim Strother Sentenced to 20 Years."
18. Bickers to Allen, June 21, 1939.
19. The stories and quotes here and in the following paragraphs are from Charles E. Bowmar, "A Story of James C. Greene," typescript in the possession of the Greene family, copy in the possession of the author.

14. The Virginia State Prison Farm

1. *The Prison Problem in Virginia: A Survey,* vol. 81 (Washington, DC: Prison Industries Reorganization Administration, 1939), 22. Superintendent R. R. Penn to State Prison Board, Nov. 30, 1936, reports: "Our motion picture machine and sound equipment are very badly in need of repairs and we would like to get the permission of the Prison Board to expend $184.25 for the necessary repairs." Records of the Virginia State Penitentiary, Series IV, Office of the Superintendent, 1869–1991, box 451, accession 41558, State Records Collection, LVA.

2. Prisoner photographs of James Strother, inmate number 33297. Records of the Virginia State Penitentiary, Series II, Prisoner Records, 1865–1990; Subseries B, Photographs and Negatives, 1906–1961, 1965–1966, accession 41558, State Records Collection, LVA.

3. Unnumbered Prison Register 3, Prisoner Receipt Book, vol. 57, Records of the Virginia Penitentiary, Series II, Prisoner Records, 1865–1990, accession 41558, State Records Collection, LVA. *Prisoners in State and Federal Prisons and Reformatories 1935* (Washington, DC: US Department of Commerce, Bureau of the Census, 1937), tables 3 and 27; *Fifteenth Census of the United States: 1930. Population, Vol. II* (Washington, DC: US Government Printing Office, 1933), p. 43, table 17.

4. See Matthew J. Mancini, *One Dies, Get Another: Convict Leasing in the American South, 1866–1928* (Columbia: University of South Carolina Press, 1996).

5. Scott Reynolds Nelson, *Steel Drivin' Man: John Henry, the Untold Story of an American Legend* (Oxford: Oxford University Press, 2006). J. Owens, "John Henry" (AFS 730A), recorded at the Virginia State Penitentiary, Richmond, Virginia, in May 1936, American Folklife Center, Library of Congress, Washington, DC.

6. Mancini, *One Dies, Get Another,* 5–9. Also see Dale M. Brumfield, *The Virginia State Penitentiary: A Notorious History* (Charleston, SC: History Press, 2017).

7. "Crop Acreage at the Virginia State Farm, Goochland County, 1934" and "State Farm—Stock Report, August 18, 1934" in Records of the Virginia State Penitentiary, Series IV, Office of the Superintendent, 1869–1991, box 452, accession 41558, State Records Collection, LVA.

8. R. R. Penn to State Prison Board, June 7, 1937, Records of the Virginia Penitentiary, Series IV, Office of the Superintendent, 1869–1991, box 451, accession 41558, State Records Collection, LVA.

9. *Prison Problem in Virginia,* 22.

10. The superintendent of the farm reported a population of 204 convicts on July 1, 1935, and 329 on June 30, 1936. *Annual Report of the Board of Directors of the Penitentiary with Accompanying Documents for the Fiscal Year Ending June 30, 1936* (Richmond, VA: Division of Purchase and Printing, 1936), 51–52.

11. "Prison Farm Criticized in Report After Probe," *Richmond Times-Dispatch,* Sept. 9, 1919.

12. *Norfolk Post,* Sept. 20, 1922; *Roanoke World-News,* Sept. 5, 1922. Sources on

Penn include the 1880, 1900, 1920, and 1940 censuses and a death certificate dated April 23, 1945.

13. William R. McCraw, Secretary, State Prison Board, to Dr. I. C. Riggin, Commissioner, Virginia Department of Health, Jan. 31, 1935, Records of the Virginia State Penitentiary, Series IV, Office of the Superintendent, 1869–1991, box 451, accession 41558, State Records Collection, LVA.

14. Superintendent R. R. Penn to State Prison Board, Feb. 23, 1937, Records of the Virginia State Penitentiary, Series IV, Office of the Superintendent, 1869–1991, box 451, accession 41558, State Records Collection, LVA.

15. Barry Lee Pearson, "Rappahannock Blues: John Jackson," *Smithsonian Folkways Magazine,* June 2010. John Jackson, "Knife Blues," track 20 on *Don't Let Your Deal Go Down,* Arhoolie 378, 1992, compact disc.

16. Newman I. White, *American Negro Folk Songs* (Cambridge, MA: Harvard University Press, 1928), 261–62. Dorothy Scarborough, *On the Trail of Negro Folk-Songs* (Cambridge, MA: Harvard University Press, 1925), 218–21.

17. Kevin Kehrberg and Jeffrey A. Keith, "Somebody Died, Babe: A Musical Coverup of Racism, Violence and Greed," *Bitter Southerner,* Aug. 4, 2020 (digital publication).

18. Clifton Wright and Prisoners, "Take This Hammer," AFS 00726 B01, recorded at the Virginia State Penitentiary, May 31, 1936, American Folklife Center, Library of Congress, Washington, DC.

19. Al Hopkins and His Buckle Busters, "Nine Pound Hammer," Brunswick 177, recorded in New York City, May 13, 1927. Other recorded versions include Frank Blevins and His Tar Heel Rattlers, Columbia 15280-D, Atlanta, GA, April 17, 1928; Grayson and Whitter, Victor V-40105, New York City, July 31, 1928; John Hurt, "Spike Driver Blues," OKeh 8692, New York City, Dec. 28, 1928; Blue Ridge Mountain Entertainers (ARC unissued), New York City, Dec. 2, 1931; and Ernest and Eddie Stoneman, Vocalion 02655, New York City, Jan. 8, 1934, all 78-rpm records. See Norm Cohen, *Long Steel Rail: The Railroad in American Folksong* (Urbana: University of Illinois Press, 2000), 571–82. Archie Green, *Only a Miner: Studies in Recorded Coal-Mining Songs,* Music in American Life (Urbana: University of Illinois Press, 1972).

20. Monroe Brothers, "Nine Pound Hammer," Bluebird B-6422, recorded Feb. 17, 1936, in Charlotte, NC, 78-rpm record.

15. Recording the Folk

1. John A. Lomax, *Adventures of a Ballad Hunter* (New York: Macmillan, 1947), 157–58. Spivacke would become the Acting Chief of the Division of Music in 1937.

2. J. Lomax, *Adventures.* Also see Nolan Porterfield, *Last Cavalier: The Life and Times of John A. Lomax* (Urbana: University of Illinois Press, 1996), 392–93. Oral history interview with Harold Spivacke, 1968, Carnegie Corporation Project, Part 1, Oral History Archive, Columbia University, New York.

3. J. Lomax, *Adventures*, 157.

4. Carlton Sprague Smith, "Harold Spivacke (1904–1977)," *Musical Quarterly* 63, no. 3 (1977): 425–27. Oral history interview with Harold Spivacke, 1968, p. 9.

5. For example, see Patrick B. Mullen, "The Dilemma of Representation in Folklore Studies: The Case of Henry Truvillion and John Lomax," in "Issues in Collaboration and Representation," special issue, *Journal of Folklore Research* 37, no. 2/3 (2000): 155–74, accessed March 18, 2020, https://www.jstor.org /stable/3814631.

6. See John W. Work, Lewis Wade Jones, and Samuel C. Adams Jr., *Lost Delta Found: Rediscovering the Fisk University–Library of Congress Coahoma County Study, 1941–1942,* ed. Robert Gordon and Bruce Nemerov (Nashville: Vanderbilt University Press, 2005).

7. John A. Lomax to Ruby Terrill Lomax, June 18, 1936, referenced in Porterfield, *Last Cavalier,* 537.

8. Erich Nunn, "Country Music and the Souls of White Folk," *Criticism* 51, no. 4 (2009): 626–27.

9. Erich Nunn, *Sounding the Color Line: Music and Race in the Southern Imagination* (Athens: University of Georgia Press, 2015), 38.

10. Benjamin Filene, "'Our Singing Country': John and Alan Lomax, Leadbelly, and the Construction of an American Past," *American Quarterly* 43, no. 4 (1991): 618–19. "'Sinful' Songs of the Southern Negro: Experiences Collecting Secular Folk-Music," *Southwest Review* 19, no. 2 (1934): 128–29.

11. Robert B. Winans, "Black Instrumental Music Traditions in the Ex-Slave Narratives," *Black Music Research Journal* 10, no. 1 (1990): 44. His father was John Dabney, a favorite caterer of the Virginia elite. See Philip J. Schwarz, "John Dabney (ca. 1824–1900)," in *Encyclopedia Virginia,* Virginia Humanities, accessed Jan. 10, 2021, https://encyclopediavirginia.org/entries/dabney-john -ca-1824-1900/. Lynn Abbott and Doug Seroff, *Out of Sight: The Rise of African American Popular Music, 1889–1895* (Jackson: University Press of Mississippi, 2003), 251–55. Eileen Southern, *The Music of Black Americans: A History* (New York: W. W. Norton, 1971), 308. Tony Thomas, "Why African Americans Put the Banjo Down," in *Hidden in the Mix: The African American Presence in Country Music,* ed. Diane Pecknold (Durham, NC: Duke University Press, 2013), 143–69.

12. Culpeper's proximity to Washington, DC, and Alexandria surely facilitated the presence of guitars. W. G. Collins, "the great banjo instructor and performer," advertised in the Culpeper newspapers in the 1880s, offering banjo sheet music ("Rickett's Jig" as well as jigs by Horace Weston and Converse) and strings at his Washington, DC, location. For example, see the *Culpeper Exponent,* March 17, 1882.

13. Strother uses the usual E-A-B7 chord shapes favored in almost all traditional renditions of the song, but he is tuned a half-step high or using a capo, placing the song in the key of F. For comparative versions of eight-bar blues from the region, see John Jackson, "Red River Blues," track 19 on *Don't Let Your*

Deal Go Down, Arhoolie Records, CD 378, 1992, compact disc; John Tinsley, "Red River Blues," track 14 on *Virginia Traditions: Western Piedmont Blues*, Blue Ridge Institute, BRI 003, 1995, compact disc; Brownie McGhee, "Key to the Highway," Alert 400, 1946, 78-rpm record.

14. John and Alan Lomax, *Our Singing Country: A Second Volume of American Ballads and Folk Songs*, ed. Ruth Crawford Seeger (New York: Macmillan, 1941), 370.

15. Dick Justice, "Old Black Dog," Brunswick 395, recorded in Chicago, IL, May 20, 1929. Both the Justice recording and the Bayless Rose version incorporate aspects of the lyrics and melody of a complex of tunes associated with "The Deal," also known as "Don't Let Your Deal Go Down."

16. Robert M. W. Dixon and John Godrich, *Blues and Gospel Records 1902–1942* (London: Storyville, 1969). Tony Russell, *Country Music Records: A Discography, 1921–1942* (Oxford: Oxford University Press, 2004).

17. Christopher C. King, "Bayless? Bailey? A Rose by Another Name," *78 Quarterly* 12 (n.d.): 59–68. Roberta J. Estes, Jack H. Goins, Penny Ferguson, and Janet Lewis Crain, "Melungeons, a Multi-Ethnic Population," *Journal of Genetic Genealogy*, April 2012.

18. Bayless Rose, "Black Dog Blues," Gennett 7250, recorded in Richmond, IN, 1930.

19. Robert Winslow Gordon, *Folk Songs of America* (New York: National Service Bureau, 1938), 78–80. Another version collected by a folklorist can be found in *The Frank C. Brown Collection of North Carolina Folklore*, vol. 3, *Folk Songs from North Carolina*, ed. Henry M. Belden and Arthur Palmer Hudson (Durham, NC: Duke University Press, 1952), contributed in 1923 by Lucille Cheek of Chatham County, North Carolina.

16. The Pardon

1. James Strother #33927, State Farm, Virginia, to Governor James H. Price, Richmond, March 27, 1938, and Governor Price's secretary to James Strother, June 11, 1938, RG 13, Secretary of the Commonwealth, Executive Papers, 1939 Sept. 12–20, accession 24938, box 1113, LVA.

2. James Strother #33927, State Farm, Virginia, to Governor James H. Price, Richmond, June 12, 1939, RG 13, Secretary of the Commonwealth, Executive Papers, 1939 Sept. 12–20, accession 24938, box 1113, LVA.

3. William Taylor, 594 W. Preston Street, Baltimore, Maryland, to Governor James Price, Richmond, Virginia, July 19, 1938, and Aug. 20, 1939, Strother pardon file. Strother and family, 1910 US census, 17th Ward, Baltimore City, Maryland, population schedule, enumeration district 287, sheet 9B.

4. William Taylor, 1029 Rice Street, Baltimore, Maryland, to Governor James Price, Richmond, Virginia, Strother pardon file.

5. Listings for James Strother in the 1909 (7 East Ware Street), 1915 and 1916 (2411 Mace Street), and 1917 (2025 Oak Street) Baltimore city directories.

Hannah Johnson, William Taylor, Lillie Truman, and others in the 1910 census (204 Ware Street); Sarah Truman, Walter Truman, and Hannah Johnson in the 1920 census (2409 Mace Street).

6. World War I draft card for Gillis Eli Johnson, Baltimore, Maryland, Sept. 12, 1918. The 1910 census doesn't list him as blind, but he has no occupation. In the 1900 census he is a farmhand. Gillis Johnson listed as employee in *Third Report of the Maryland Workshop for the Blind, for the Two Years Ending Sept. 30th, 1913* (Baltimore: Published by the Corporation, 1913), 21.

7. Thomas P. MacCarthy, Acting Executive Secretary, Maryland Division of Parole and Probation, Baltimore, Maryland, to R. L. Jackson, Governor's Office, Richmond, Virginia, Aug. 17, 1939, RG 13, Secretary of the Commonwealth, Executive Papers, 1939 Sept. 12–20, accession 24938, box 1113, LVA.

8. Dan Tulli, "James H. Price (1878–1943)," *Encyclopedia Virginia,* Virginia Humanities, accessed Sept. 4, 2020, https://encyclopediavirginia.org/entries/price-james-h-1878-1943/.

9. *The Prison Problem in Virginia: A Survey,* vol. 81 (Washington, DC: Prison Industries Reorganization Administration, 1939), statistics from 81, table 22; quote on 82.

10. Report of John H. McFaul Jr. to the Parole Commissioner of Maryland, Aug. 25, 1939, RG 13, Secretary of the Commonwealth, Executive Papers, 1939 Sept. 12–20, accession 24938, box 1113, LVA.

11. R. A. Bickers, Commonwealth's Attorney for Culpeper County, to Miss Laura H. Allen, Secretary to the Governor, Richmond, Virginia, June 21, 1939, RG 13, Secretary of the Commonwealth, Executive Papers, 1939 Sept. 12–20, accession 24938, box 1113, LVA.

12. "Register of Prisoners Pardoned, Paroled, Discharged, Died or Escaped," vol. 122, Records of the Virginia Penitentiary, Series II, Prisoner Records, 1865–1990, accession 41558, State Records Collection, LVA. 1940 US census, 17th Ward, Baltimore City, Maryland, population schedule, enumeration district 287, sheet 9B. Sarah Truman is listed as living at 1314 ½ on the parole document in 1939 and as a "cousin by marriage." William Taylor's World War II draft card lists his employer as the Enterprise Coal Company, 1514 Maryland Avenue, Baltimore.

17. Do Lord, Remember Me

1. The newspaper editor's quip is in the *Virginia Star* (Culpeper), April 25, 1935. For Strother's enduring relevance, see *Deep River of Song: Black Appalachia, String Bands, Songsters and Hoedowns,* Rounder Records 1823, 1999; *A Treasury of Library of Congress Field Recordings,* selected and annotated by Stephen Wade, Rounder Records 1500, 1997; *Field Recordings, Vol. 1: Virginia 1936–1941,* Document Records DOCD-5575. Jefferson Airplane, "Good Shepherd," side 1, track 2, on *Volunteers,* RCA Victor LSP-4238, 1969. Peter and Charles

Seeger, "If You Want to Go to Freedom," *Broadside* 33 (Oct. 12, 1963). Mike Seeger, *Solo: Oldtime Country Music,* Rounder Records 0278, 1991.

2. John and Alan Lomax, *Our Singing Country: A Second Volume of American Ballads and Folk Songs,* ed. Ruth Crawford Seeger (New York: Macmillan, 1941).

3. Typescript letter, Alan Lomax, Assistant in Charge, Archive of American Folk Song, to Jimmy Strothers [*sic*], State Farm, March 18, 1942, Jimmie Strother Correspondence File, Archive of Folk Culture, American Folklife Center, Library of Congress.

4. John Szwed, *Alan Lomax: The Man Who Recorded the World* (New York: Viking, 2010).

5. Benjamin Botkin to Susan Taylor, July 21, 1943, and Benjamin Botkin to Blanche Greene, July 21, 1943, Jimmie Strother Correspondence File, Archive of Folk Culture, American Folklife Center, Library of Congress.

6. Charles T. Harrell, "The Library of Congress Radio Research Project," *ALA Bulletin* 35, no. 7 (1941): 448–49, 452.

7. *The Ballad Hunter, Part 7, Spirituals: Religion Through Songs of the Southern Negroes,* Library of Congress, five sixteen-inch transcription discs, 33 1/3 speed, of ten fifteen-minute radio programs. The transcriptions can be heard online from the NYPR Archive Collections, WNYC, New York, https://www.wnyc.org/story/pt-7-spirituals-religion-through-songs-of-the-southern-negroes. The set was reissued on vinyl in 1958 as *The Ballad Hunter,* Library of Congress, Music Division Recording Laboratory, AAFS L49–53 (LC 1977–86), 1958, five slipcases, 33 1/3 rpm microgroove, https://lccn.loc.gov/r59000033.

8. Advertising brochure for *The Ballad Hunter,* John A. Lomax and Alan Lomax Papers (AFC 1933/001), Archive of Folk Culture, American Folklife Center, Library of Congress.

9. *Service Bulletin of the FREC* (Washington, DC) 3, no. 3 (1941): 3. Advertising brochure for *The Ballad Hunter.*

10. Advertising brochure for *The Ballad Hunter.*

11. Liner notes to Benjamin A. Botkin, ed., *Negro Religious Songs and Services,* AFS L10, Library of Congress, 1943.

12. William Francis Allen, Charles Pickard Ware, and Lucy McKim Garrison, eds., *Slave Songs of the United States* (New York: A. Simpson, 1867), 12.

13. Early examples of the song from commercial recordings include Ernest Phipps and His Holiness Quartet, "Do, Lord, Remember Me," Victor 20927, recorded in Bristol, TN, July 26, 1927; Deacon Leon Davis, "Do My Lord Remember Me," OKeh 8495, recorded in New York, Feb. 22, 1927, reissued on *Preachers and Congregations, Vol. 2 (1926–1941),* Document Records DOCD-5529, 2005, track 16. Garner Brothers, "Do Lord Do Remember Me," Jubilee Gospel Singers 20089, recorded in Richmond, IN, Jan. 9, 1925.

14. John W. Work, *American Negro Songs and Spirituals* (New York: Crown Publishers, 1940), 82.

15. Work, *American Negro Songs and Spirituals,* 26.

16. Charles L. Perdue, Thomas E. Barden, and Robert K. Phillips, eds., *Weevils in the Wheat: Interviews with Virginia Ex-Slaves* (Charlottesville: University of Virginia Press, 1976).

17. Liner notes to Botkin, *Negro Religious Songs and Services*.

18. Linda C. Burman-Hall, "Southern American Folk Fiddle Styles," *Ethnomusicology* 19, no. 1 (1975): 49. John Minton, "West African Fiddles in Deep East Texas," in *Juneteenth Texas: Essays in African-American Folklore*, ed. Francis Edward Abernethy et al., Publications of the Texas Folklore Society 54 (Denton, TX: University of North Texas Press, 1996), 302.

19. W. C. Handy quoted in Eileen Southern, *The Music of Black Americans: A History* (New York: W.W. Norton, 1971), 168.

20. Ira W. Ford, *Traditional Music of America* (New York: E. P. Dutton, 1940; reprint, Hatboro, PA: Folklore Associates, 1965), 129–30. Reaves White County Ramblers, "Ten Cent Piece," Vocalion 5218, and "Drunkard's Hiccoughs," Vocalion 5247, recorded in Chicago, IL, April 27, 1928. Accounts of the practice that span the American South include Gerald Milnes, *Play of a Fiddle: Traditional Music, Dance, and Folklore in West Virginia* (Lexington: University Press of Kentucky, 1999), 11–13; Bob Buckingham, "J. P. Fraley: The Fiddler's Fiddler," in *Fiddler Magazine's Favorites* (Pacific, MO: Mel Bay Publications, 1999), 32; Wayne W. Daniel, *Pickin' on Peachtree: A History of Country Music in Atlanta, Georgia* (Urbana: University of Illinois Press, 2001), 34–35; Gregory Hansen, *A Florida Fiddler: The Life and Times of Richard Seaman* (Tuscaloosa: University of Alabama Press, 2007), 48–49; and *Great Big Yam Potatoes: Anglo-American Fiddle Music from Mississippi*, Mississippi Department of Archives and History AH002, 1985.

21. Joe Lynn Lee, "Rise, Run Along, Mourner," AFS 835 B2, recorded at the Virginia State Prison Farm, Goochland County, VA, June 14, 1936, American Folklife Center, Library of Congress, Washington, DC.

22. Tracking down an inmate with as common a name as "Joe Lee" took some digging. The best clue was the inscription on the back of the well-known photograph of Lee and Strother, which lists his name as Joe Lynn Lee. I think that a bad transcription of this inscription has also perpetuated the incorrect locating of the Virginia State Prison Farm as being in "Lynn, Virginia." There is no such place in Goochland County. Typically, letters were simply addressed "State Farm, Virginia." 1880, 1900, 1910, 1920, and 1930 census. Unnumbered Prison Registers, Vol. 3, Records of the Virginia Penitentiary, Series II, Prisoner Records, 1865–1990, accession 41558, State Records Collection, LVA. "Herb Doctor Said to Have Hit Patient," *Danville Bee*, Aug. 20, 1933. On the relationship of Christianity and magic, see Yvonne Chireau, "Conjure and Christianity in the Nineteenth Century: Religious Elements in African American Magic," *Religion and American Culture: A Journal of Interpretation* 7, no. 2 (1997): 225–46.

23. John A. Lomax to Ruby R. Terrill Lomax, June 18, 1936, John Avery Lomax Family Papers, Dolph Briscoe Center for American History, University of Texas at Austin.

18. The Folk Process

1. Jefferson Airplane, "Good Shepherd," side 1, track 2 on *Volunteers*, RCA Victor LSP-4238, 1969, LP album. "Historic Rock Landmarks in Santa Clara County," *San Jose Mercury News*, June 29, 2008.
2. Jorma Kaukonen, "Bend, Oregon . . . Roger Perkins and Things That Might Have Been," Feb. 10, 2013, entry on his website Cracks in the Finish, accessed and screen captured June 17, 2021, https://jormakaukonen.com/cracksinthe finish/?p=2350.
3. Video performance of "Good Shepherd" by Larry Hanks in the author's possession. Jorma Kaukonen, *Been So Long: My Life and Music* (New York: St. Martin's Griffin, 2018), 132.
4. John A. Lomax, *The Ballad Hunter*, New York, National Broadcasting Company Radio Recording Division. ("Lectures by John A. Lomax, introduced by Philip H. Cohen. Reissued by the Library of Congress under a special grant from the Carnegie Corporation of New York" from sixteen-inch transcriptions.)
5. Katherine Skinner persuasively argues that Smith's 1952 release has been retrospectively canonized by later writers and scholars. She recognizes its influence on the major folk revival figures mentioned above, but she also points out its relative scarcity in the marketplace and its poor sales. See "'Must Be Born Again': Resurrecting the 'Anthology of American Folk Music,'" *Popular Music* 25, no. 1 (2006): 57–75. Several labels appeared in the 1960s that reissued rare early recordings on LP and issued new recordings of older traditional artists, such as Origin Jazz Library (1960), Arhoolie (1960) and its Old Timey Records subsidiary, County Records (1965), and Heritage Records in London (1959). Some of the major labels also began to recognize that a market existed for reissues; a good example is Columbia's 1961 Robert Johnson reissue.
6. A dedicated group of small record companies supported the 1950s movement by issuing recordings by contemporary singers. These included Elektra Records, Folkcraft Records, Folk Dancer Records, Folkways Records, Israel Music Foundation, Kismet Record Company, New England Music Center, Riverside Records, Sing Out!, Stinson Records, Tradition Records, and World Wide Games.
7. "Newc" (Sarah Newcomb) to Joe Hickerson, Aug. 24, [1957], Series 3: The Folksmiths, Joe Hickerson Papers, Oberlin College Archives, Oberlin, Ohio.
8. Ricky Sherover, "The Folksmiths: Eight Students Who Had Some Singing to Do," *SING OUT!* 8, no. 1 (1968): 17–21. The Folksmiths, *We've Got Some Singing to Do: Folksongs with the Folksmiths*, Folkways FA 2407, 1958. Ruth Crawford Seeger recast the song as "Don't You Hear the Lambs A-Crying" in *American Folk Songs for Christmas* (New York: Doubleday, 1953). Her children and grandchildren reprised her arrangement on Mike Seeger, Peggy Seeger, and Penny Seeger, *American Folk Songs for Christmas*, Rounder Records—Rounder CD 0268/0269, 1989. *Fly Down Little Bird*, recorded at the home of Mike Seeger and Alexia Smith in Lexington, VA, Aug. 2008, released Aug. 30, 2017.

9. Eileen Southern, "Hymnals of the Black Church," *Black Perspective in Music* 17, no. 1/2 (1989): 158.

10. Marshall W. Taylor, *A Collection of Revival Hymns and Plantation Melodies* (Cincinnati: Marshall W. Taylor and W. C. Echols, 1882), 145–46.

11. Taylor, *Collection of Revival Hymns*, 245–46.

12. Taylor, *Collection of Revival Hymns*, 7. For background on Taylor and his songbook, see Irene V. Jackson-Brown, "Afro-American Song in the Nineteenth Century: A Neglected Source," *Black Perspective in Music* 4, no. 1 (1976): 22–38.

13. F. S. Hoyt, introduction to Taylor, *Collection of Revival Hymns*, i–ii.

14. Taylor, *Collection of Revival Hymns*, 5.

15. A forty-year-old America Bell resided in Xenia, near Wilberforce University, in 1870. Given her son's age and birth in Ohio, they probably migrated across the Ohio River before the Civil War. I could not find another trace of her in public records. America Welsh in the 1870 and 1880 censuses, Danville, KY, and 1900 census, Cincinnati, OH. America Bell Welch in 1900 census, Cincinnati City, Hamilton County, OH, population schedule, enumeration district 137, p. 358. The first reference to her in Cincinnati is the 1890 city directory. Her maiden name was established by the death certificates of her daughters.

19. Songs of Protest

1. Golden Gate Quartet, "The Blood Stained Bandits," Thesaurus 1131, NBC, recorded ca. June–Aug. 1943. For background on the Hampton Roads quartet tradition, see Vaughan Webb, "Why Don't You Rock My Soul: The African-American Quartet Tradition in Hampton Roads," *Virginia Cavalcade* 51, no. 3 (2002): 100–111.

2. Golden Gate Quartet, "No Restricted Signs (Up in Heaven)," Columbia 37832 (*Golden Gate Spirituals*, Set C-145), 1947.

3. Peter and Charles Seeger, "If You Want to Go to Freedom," *Broadside* 33 (1963).

4. Robert E. Weir, *Beyond Labor's Veil: The Culture of the Knights of Labor* (University Park: Pennsylvania State University Press, 1996), 103–43. Augusta V. Jackson, "A New Deal for Tobacco Workers," *Crisis* 45 (1938): 322–24.

5. Howard W. Odum, "Folk-Song and Folk-Poetry as Found in the Secular Songs of the Southern Negroes," *Journal of American Folk-Lore* 24, no. 93 (1911): 267.

6. "[F]ew songsters would have performed them to a white or mixed Southern audience, except under the cover of a heavy screen of other associations." In Paul Oliver, *Songsters and Saints: Vocal Traditions on Race Records* (Cambridge: Cambridge University Press, 1984), 102. Bruce M. Conforth, *African American Folksong and American Cultural Politics: The Lawrence Gellert Story*, American Folk Music and Musicians Series (Lanham, MD: Scarecrow Press, 2013). Steven Garabedian, "Reds, Whites, and the Blues: Lawrence Gellert, 'Negro Songs of Protest,' and the Left-Wing Folk-Song Revival of the 1930s and 1940s," *American Quarterly* 57, no. 1 (2005), 179–206.

7. For Gellert's life, his collecting, and his involvement with Left politics, see Con-

forth, *African American Folksong.* Garabedian, "Reds, Whites, and the Blues." John A. Lomax, "Self-Pity in Negro Folk-Songs," *Nation* 105 (1917): 141–45. Thomas W. Talley, *Negro Folk Rhymes,* ed. Charles K. Wolfe (Knoxville: University of Tennessee Press, 1991).

20. The Songster Tradition

1. Phil Wiggins and Frank Matheis, *Sweet Bitter Blues: Washington, DC's Homemade Blues,* American Made Music Series (Jackson: University Press of Mississippi, 2020). Information on "Boo" Hanks from Music Maker Foundation website, accessed April 4, 2023, https://musicmaker.org/artist/boo-hanks/. Information on Michael Wells from Contemporary Acoustic Roots and Country Blues website, https://www.thecountryblues.com/artist-reviews/lightning-wells/.
2. Craig Morrison, "Folk Revival Roots Still Evident in 1990s Recordings of San Francisco Psychedelic Veterans," *Journal of American Folklore* 114, no. 454 (2001): 478–88. Jeff Tamarkin, *Got a Revolution! The Turbulent Flight of Jefferson Airplane* (New York: Simon & Schuster, 2003), 199. *Volunteers (Original Masters)* (media notes), Jefferson Airplane, BMG Heritage.
3. Interview with Dom Flemons, May 12, 2021, video recording in the author's possession.
4. Interview with Flemons.
5. As noted above, "Fighting On" appears in the 1891 expanded version of Thomas P. Fenner, *Cabin and Plantation Songs as Sung by the Hampton Students* (New York: G. P. Putnam's Sons, 1891), 93. It also appears, as "Fighting On! Hallelujah!," in *Jubilee and Plantation Songs: As Sung by the Hampton Students, Jubilee Singers, Fisk Students, and Other Concert Companies* (Boston: Oliver Ditson, 1887), 53.
6. Dom Flemons, "We Are Almost Down to the Shore," track 6 on *Traveling Wildfire,* Smithsonian Folkways, SFW40237, 2023, compact disc.

21. Mount Auburn

1. Report of R. R. Penn, Superintendent, Virginia State Prison Farm, to R. M. Youell, Superintendent, Virginia State Penitentiary, regarding James Strother, n.d., RG 13, Secretary of the Commonwealth, Executive Papers, 1939 Sept. 12–20, accession 24938, box 1113, LVA.
2. *Opportunity: Journal of Negro Life* 7, no. 12 (1929): 367–68. Landmark Designation Report, Samuel Coleridge-Taylor Elementary School #122, 1999, https://chap.baltimorecity.gov/sites/default/files/Samuel%20Coleridge%20Elem.%20Landmark%20Designation%20Report.pdf.
3. Lynn Abbott and Doug Seroff, *Ragged but Right: Black Traveling Shows, Coon Songs, and the Dark Pathway to Blues and Jazz,* American Made Music Series (Jackson: University Press of Mississippi, 2007).

4. Peter La Chapelle, *I'd Fight the World: A Political History of Old Time, Hillbilly, and Country Music* (Chicago: University of Chicago Press, 2019), 106–7. Marshall Wyatt, *Good for What Ails You: Music of the Medicine Shows, 1926–1937,* Old Hat Records, Old Hat CD 1005, 2005, liner notes, pp. 15–16; Pamela Grundy, "'We Always Tried to Be Good People': Respectability, Crazy Water Crystals, and Hillbilly Music on the Air, 1933–1935," *Journal of American History* 81, no. 4 (1995): 1591–620. *Annual Report of the State Board of Health of Maryland for the Year Ending December 31, 1936* (n.p.: King Brothers, 1936), 150.

5. James Strother #33927, State Farm, Virginia, to Governor James H. Price, Richmond, June 12, 1939, Strother pardon file.

6. For an excellent overview of Richmond's cemeteries and current preservation efforts, see Ryan K. Smith, *Death and Rebirth in a Southern City: Richmond's Historic Cemeteries* (Baltimore: Johns Hopkins University Press, 2020).

7. Justin Fenton, "Baltimore's Oldest Black Cemetery Finally Restored, With Help of Inmates," *Baltimore Sun,* May 14, 2012.

INDEX

www.ingramcontent.com/pod-product-compliance
Lightning Source LLC
Chambersburg PA
CBHW031936160125
20482CB00006B/532

* 9 7 8 0 8 1 3 9 5 2 3 1 4 *